Always Virginia

by

Virginia Fritscher

Virginia Day Fritscher, 16th Birthday, July 12, 1935

Always Virginia

A Memoir and Diary of a Girl's Life in
Kampsville and Jacksonville, Illinois,
and Routt High School
in the 1920s and 1930s

by
Virginia Day Fritscher

Edited by Jack Fritscher

Palm Drive Publishing
Sebastopol CA

©2020 Jack Fritscher

In this book, the opinions and statements expressed are solely those of the persons quoted, and not necessarily those of the editor.

Except for brief passages, no part of this book may be reproduced, stored in or introduced into a retrieval system, or transmitted in any form without the prior written permission of the copyright owner.

Cover photograph: Virginia Day, age 16, July 12, 1935
Cover and book art design: Mark Hemry

Published by Palm Drive Publishing, Sebastopol CA
Email: Mark@PalmDrivePublishing.com

Library of Congress Control Number: 2019951272

Fritscher, Virginia 1919-2004
Fritscher, Jack 1939-

p.cm
ISBN 978-1-890834-24-1 print
        978-1-890834-43-2 ebook

1. Autobiography 2. Memoir 3. Women's Studies 4. Illinois History 5. Irish History—Southern Illinois 6. Jacksonville Illinois 7. Peoria Illinois 8. Routt High School 9. Calhoun County—Illinois 10. O'Dea Clan 11. Day Family Genealogy 12. Center for American Archeology—Kampsville Illinois

First Printing 2020
10 9 8 7 6 5 4 3 2
Palm Drive Publishing, Sebastopol CA
www.PalmDrivePublishing.com

Dedication

For my mother, Virginia,
my grandmother, Mary Pearl,
and my namesake uncle, John B. Day
who all gave voice to this memoir

— Jack Fritscher, editor

With gratitude
to Mark Hemry
who made this book possible

Virginia Day Fritscher, 1951

Contents

Foreword	ix
Day Family Origin Story 1819-2019	1
My Life in Kampsville	21
Diary	49
The Wedding	151
Obituary	157
Mary Pearl Lawler Day	165
Father John B. Day	191
Newsclips	197
The Wag: November 1935	203
The Geography of Women	248

Mother and Son, Virginia Day Fritscher and Jack Fritscher, off to Ireland, 1993. Photo by Mark Hemry

FOREWORD

ALWAYS VIRGINIA

A GIRL'S LIFE: KAMPSVILLE, JACKSONVILLE, AND ROUTT HIGH SCHOOL IN THE 1920s AND 1930s

by Jack Fritscher

100th Birthday Edition
1919-2019

In 1919, my mother Virginia Day was born into 9,000 years of continuous local civilization in Kampsville near the Koster archeological site in Calhoun County. Her slice-of-life diary is itself an anthropological artifact from the 1920s and 1930s. As a girl in the town of 300 folks, she collected arrowheads, hunted mushrooms and ginseng, teased teachers, bought candy at Benninger's and clothes at Draper's Dry Goods, delivered mail, and at age 14 paid a pilot 75-cents to fly her over Kampsville and Jacksonville. She was best friends with the Kamp twins, Edna and Edwina, at the Kamp Store owned by their father, Joseph Kamp, son of the founder of Kampsville who opened the store in 1902. In 1991, the Kamp store became the Visitor's Center and Museum of the Center for American Archeology, and the old post office where her cousin was postmistress and her father postman became an archeological laboratory. Her granduncle John Day was a Calhoun County judge.

Her parents met in summer 1910 when her Irish mother, Mary Lawler, born in St. Louis in 1888, took a riverboat 70 miles north to Hamburg to visit her cousins in Kampsville where, in one version of their meeting, she spied a redheaded man crossing a field and said, "That's the man I'm going to marry." In an amusing 1972 interview included in this family memoir of two female generations, she adds her voice to her daughter's about courting Hamburg local

Bartholomew Day, a school teacher who later took a second job as a postman beloved on rural routes around Kampsville—where they started their family in 1911 before moving their five children to Jacksonville in 1930 to attend Routt High School where Virginia was literary editor of the school paper, *The Wag*.

On her 14th birthday in 1933, despite the Depression, she began her optimistic "Daily Diary" about her high-spirited teen life in Jacksonville with friends, school, jobs, dances, movies, and ice-cream-social events with students at the Illinois School for the Deaf. At Routt, she met varsity scholarship letterman George Fritscher in 1935. (She signed her graduation photo to him, "Always, Virginia.") Her brother John B. Day, the priest who in World War II became a famous Army Chaplain, married them at Our Saviour's Church in July 1938. They welcomed their first son at Our Saviour's Hospital in June 1939 before moving to Peoria in 1941 to find work at Caterpillar.

> When I was small, we used to drive uphill to Hamburg to visit my Grandma Day and uncles and aunts and cousins. We'd push with our hands and feet on the back of the front seat as Daddy went up the hills, because cars were new to everybody and we thought pushing on the seat was helping the old Model T to climb.

She left her heart in Kampsville and Jacksonville. On her last visit to Kampsville in 1980, she was as delighted to meet the young archeologists as they were to trade stories with her who donated to them the arrowheads, pottery shards, and river pearls she had collected seventy years before the world heard of Koster.

This charming diary of a girl and her family is not a history of big world events. It's a playful American story of Southern Illinois nostalgia told in the eager voice of the teenage author happily involved in family, courtship, and the popular culture of two small heartland towns. Included are photos and news clippings about the family. Oh, what a lovely major motion picture it will one day make!

16th Birthday,
July 12, 1935

April 1, 1938

Virginia Day Fritscher, Christmas 1994

Baby Bart Day between father, Bartholomew Day, and mother, Mary Lynch Day, with brothers Tom, Joe, John, and Jim, and sister Margaret (Mag), 1891

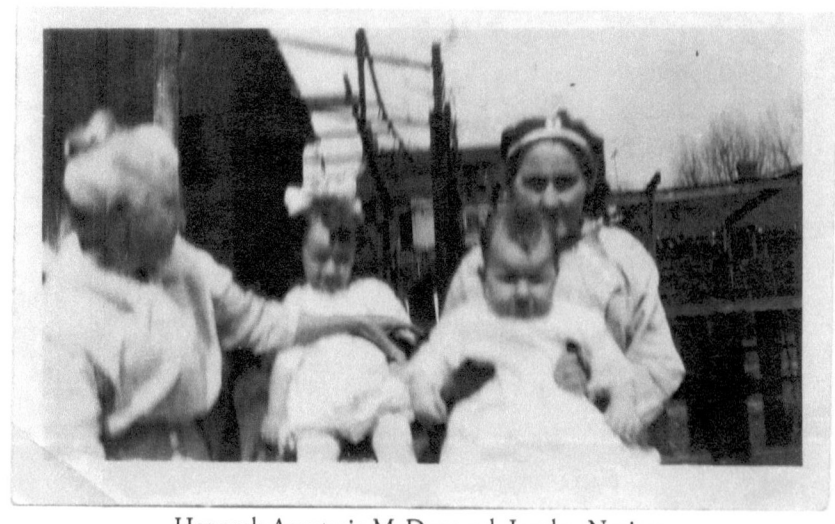

Honorah Anastasia McDonough Lawler, Norine, Mary Pearl Lawler Day, and baby Virginia, 1920

DAY FAMILY ORIGIN STORY
1819-2019

by John Joseph (Jack) Fritscher, PhD.,
a Seanachie of Clan Ó Deághaidh,
at the 1920s desk of his grandfather
Bartholomew Day, III (1887-1954)
who gave it in 1948 to his mother
Virginia Day Fritscher (1919-2004)
who gave it to him in 2001

Farmers, Judges, Teachers, Wives,
Authors, Priests, Veterans, and Postmasters
The past is prologue and context is everything.

John Tyrrell Day, son of Bartholomew Day (aka Dey aka O'Dea aka Ó'Deághaidh) and Margaret Tyrrell (aka Terrell), was born near the town of Fethard in Tipperary in 1819 exactly one hundred years before the birth of his grandniece, Virginia Claire Day Fritscher, in Kampsville in 1919. He left the hard times of the Potato Famine in Ireland in 1849 to join the California Gold Rush announced in January 1848. He bought a ticket to sail across the Atlantic on one of the coffin ships, on which by average one in five passengers died, taking three weeks to reach New Orleans where many Irish entered America. Before heading west, he traveled by steamboat from New Orleans to St. Louis, paying five dollars for the six-day trip up the Mississippi following Irish immigration patterns to look for business opportunities. After wintering in St. Louis and Hamburg, Illinois, where parcels of land were for sale, he joined a wagon train that took nearly six months to make the 3000-mile trek across the plains to San Francisco and the gold fields of California.

The immigrant from a small island nation occupied by the British braved becoming a pioneer of a large continent discovering itself. He endured the California Trail that opened a rugged route to wagon trains during the 1840s, heading to San Francisco whose population of 200 in 1846 had boomed to 36,000 by his arrival in 1850. Striking it rich enough as a prospector, he returned east sailing out of San Francisco and around Cape Horn to New Orleans. It was a voyage of four to five months, but he was not about to repeat the cross-country hardship of a wagon train. He had little choice. At that time, stagecoach travel, one-way, at 24-hours a day for 28 days, would not begin until 1861, and transcontinental railroads until 1869. In the early 1850s when the population of a thousand English settlers in Calhoun County boomed to 3200 with the arrival of German and Irish immigrants, his success allowed him to buy several large tracts of land near Hamburg in Irish Hollow with strategic access to transportation on the Mississippi which became an even more vital highway during the Civil War. In Calhoun County in 1850, farmland in Hamburg cost around five dollars an acre increasing to ten dollars in 1860, to nineteen in 1870 when he married, and to twenty-seven when he died in 1888.

He settled in as a farmer and orchardist who put down his roots and sold his produce north to Peoria, locally to Jacksonville, and down river to St. Louis where thousands out of a population of 160,000 were dying in a cholera pandemic that lasted from 1852 to 1860 at the same time St. Louis, populated by Catholic Irish and German immigrants, was divided on the issues of slavery and abolition, but remained in the Union. He had arrived seasoned by the mass death of the Famine and the politics of the Famine Rebellion against British landowners that took place near his home in Tipperary in 1848 when revolution swept Europe. During the Famine from 1845-1849, a million Irish were starved to death, and another million Irish, including him, left the island. His mother's family, the Catholic Tyrrells of Westmeath, had been fighting the Protestant British occupiers since the time of the first Queen Elizabeth.

Because Tipperary is only 130 miles from Ireland's sacred burial cairn Newgrange that at 5000-years-old predates Stonehenge and the Pyramids, the new colonist may have appreciated the ancient burial mounds on the land he bought in the fertile delta between the Mississippi and the Illinois rivers known as the "Nile of North America." Calhoun County as a peninsula becomes virtually an island like Ireland when frequent flooding closes the bridges and ferries isolating the residents. The first known white men to contact the indigenous people were the explorers Father Marquette and Louis Joliet who recorded landing in 1673 near what would become Kampsville. They were followed in 1680 by the French fur-trader and explorer Lasalle. Because trappers, mountain men, and arrowhead collectors had been trafficking ever since around this ancient Indian Territory, he may have learned from the cracker-barrel tales of local migratory history and myth that his was just the most recent generation to be living on the site of the oldest civilization in North America—settled consistently for over 9,000 years by native peoples whose prehistoric aboriginal culture and burial mounds would in the 1970s rise to fame worldwide as the largest archeological dig in North America.

Settling into a forested Indian hunting ground of wilderness and underbrush teeming with wolves and rattlesnakes and wild turkey and deer, he would have learned from local lore that the first white settler, an Acadian French trapper known only as O'Neal, lived there from 1801 to his death in 1842. He would have known that the peaceful local Illinois tribe was decimated by the Iroquois around the time of the Louisiana Purchase in 1803, just as the explorers Lewis and Clark barged by on their keelboat in 1804. After the aggrieved tribe signed a piece of paper in 1816 giving their land to the United States government, they were overcome when the State of Illinois—founded in 1818 and named after their tribe—renamed their homeland "Calhoun County" in 1825, causing them to retreat west to reservations managed by the Bureau of Indian Affairs founded by the War Department in 1824, making the formerly sovereign native peoples wards of the government.

In 1819, five families of pioneer whites immigrated into the area, settling near the only structure, an Indian trading post. The first apple trees were planted and the first ferry was launched. The last few visible Indians were exiled westward by 1835, fifteen years before John T. Day, the colonist immigrant from an occupied country, found himself caught up, perhaps with a certain judge-like empathy, occupying a county whose ancient civilization could not survive his. In the sweep of history's ironies and erasures, as cultures rise and fall, he could not have predicted that a century later the very Kampsville postoffice where his nephew, Bartholomew (Bart/Batty) Day III, would be a rural carrier, and his grandniece, Cecelia Day Stelbrink, would be postmaster for thirty-six years, would become, fate's full circle, a world-famous laboratory for the international Center for American Archeology founded to study and preserve the grace and refinements of Calhoun County's local Native American culture.

As a new citizen in Calhoun County, John T. Day, Senior, was a Democrat who served on election and other boards in the county named—long before he arrived as the first of four generations of impartial Day family judges—for the family of the ill-famed Democrat John Calhoun who as a Southern nationalist won the Electoral College vote to be the seventh Vice-President of the United States in 1825 and then resigned as a defender of slavery and states rights in 1832.

At a Lincolnesque six-feet-two, Judge John T. Day, Senior, was a slender, dignified, handsomely moustached man who, unmarried at the start of the Civil War in 1861 when he was 41, was drafted for service in the Union Army, but was exempted, after his travels as a fit young man, because of a leg crippled, likely by the Irish heritage of arthritis, or perhaps by a farming injury. That infirmity and his farming success eventually impelled him to bring his unmarried younger brother, Bartholomew, Junior, from Tipperary sailing on May 15 from Queenstown, Ireland, on the immigrant ship, *S. S. Helvetia*, to New York in 1868. It is yet to be discovered why the devoted brothers waited almost twenty years after John's arrival for Bartholomew, Junior, to immigrate and become business partners.

In the *S. S. Helvetia* manifest, Bartholomew, Junior, was listed as "Barth Day, Passenger 905, age 24 [he was actually 39], laborer." Because the Day family in Ireland was large, John T. Day, Senior, the American patriarch, who was regarded as the family's founding Calhoun County chieftain of the Clan Ó Deághaidh, also assisted the immigration to Hamburg of other Irish in-law families already married to Day women in Ireland by the name of Kelly, Hughes, O'Connell, and Corbett. He brought two of his own several sisters over, and one, named Margaret, married Edmund Hughes, and the other married a Corbett.

In fact, "Passenger 906" on the *S. S. Helvetia* was the cousin of John T, Senior and Bartholomew, Junior, "Barth Corbett, 31, laborer," who left his father Edmund and his mother Mary Day Corbett, the sister of John T., Senior, and Bartholomew, Junior, behind in Tipperary. Another sister staying in Ireland married a Kelly. With less than a dollar between them, they traveled from New York to New Orleans by train and then by boat to Calhoun County. The best existing example of how these immigrants lived is the restored primitive village of Lincoln's New Salem only one hundred miles away. Batty Corbett's story typifies the mid-nineteenth-century pioneer history of the Day brothers and cousins.

The 1891 book, *A Portrait and Biographical Album of Pike and Calhoun Counties* profiled Bartholomew "Batty" Corbett, who married Catherine Hughes of St. Louis, as it could have profiled in parallel John T. Day, Senior, and Bartholomew Day, Junior, who became a citizen on June 17, 1873. In its workaday details the *Album* entry resembles the 1920s-1930s homespun details in Virginia Day Fritscher's memoir of her Day family life in this book.

For a time after his arrival young [Bartholomew] Corbitt [sic] worked as a farm hand, cut cord wood [sold to steamboats] and did various odd jobs such as he could find to do, carefully hoarding his resources preparatory to securing for himself a home. He finally bought one hundred and sixty acres of the land he now occupies, which was covered with timber and in the wild condition in which it had been left by the aborigines. He was obliged to do the pioneer work of clearing the place, and for several years after he settled thereon he occupied a little shanty, 10x12 feet, made of logs with a clapboard roof. He lived in this dwelling until he was able to build a better house. He added to his estate as his affairs prospered and now owns two hundred and eighty-five acres which he has brought to a firm condition as regards its tillage and improvement. Mr. Corbitt [sic] has served as School Director with credit to himself and his constituents. In politics he is a Democrat and in religion a Catholic. He has acquired a leading place among the Irish-American citizens of Hamburg Precinct, having gained the confidence of the business community by his honesty and industry, and the respect of all who admire sturdy enterprise, thrift and a law abiding spirit.

Not long after Bartholomew, Junior's arrival, the bachelor brothers decided that in the hard-work prosperity of their middle-age, having built their "better houses," they should each marry "a nice Irish girl" as a helpmate. According to the 1860 census, 87,563 Irish immigrated to Illinois where they were five percent of the population and where there were 92,000 more men than women. Bartholomew, age 39 or 40, traveled to the Kerry Patch neighborhood in St. Louis, just north of the present Convention Center, where he was introduced to Mary Lynch, age 20, who was born thirty miles from Fethard in Waterford, and whose father, John (Jack) Lynch, was a sailor who drowned in Lake Erie, leaving her with a maiden aunt. The name "Lynch," from Clan

O'Loinsigh, comes—coincidentally or not—from the word "loinseach" meaning "sailor" or "mariner." Years later, because of this family tragedy, her youngest son, Bartholomew III (1887-1954), would constantly warn his own five children about the dangers of living along the flooding river at Kampsville, saying: "Drowning runs in our family."

His daughter Virginia Day Fritscher wrote: "Back in Ireland, the Day family knew the Lynch family. My grandmother Mary Lynch was a twin with black hair and blue eyes. Her twin had red hair and blue eyes and stayed in Ireland when Mary was sent to meet my grandfather, Bartholomew, who was twenty years older. Her father died and she never saw her family again. My daddy [Bartholomew III] had reddish hair that somehow turned brown when his prospective wife, who became my mother, said she could not marry anyone with red hair. So in the summer of 1910, he went west for about three months, thinking about marriage while visiting his brother Tom in Portland, Oregon, and when he returned his hair was brown."

As to Virginia's interest in multiple births in the Day family, her son George Robert, married to Sharon Lee O'Farrell, had "Irish Triplets" when their twin daughters, Dianna and Laura were born in 1964, a quick ten months after their first son, Scott, was born in 1963. Judge John W. Day on May 5, 1993, answered Virginia's letter about her upcoming June trip to Ireland: "Nice to hear from you. Regarding your question, the only Days I know of [in Ireland] lived near Fethard about twenty-five years ago and were located by our cousin Loretta Corbett Booth of St. Louis....[She said] the head of the family was Tom Day and he had triplet daughters who were about age nine then. Tom Day is probably dead as he was in his fifties or so when they were born, according to Loretta. I doubt there were any other triplets in the area and you ought to be able to find them." On August 22, 1993, he wrote: "Dear Virginia, We hope you enjoyed your trip to Ireland and arrived home safely. Enclosed is a copy of the Day Family history I promised to send."

Bartholomew, Junior's older brother, John T., Senior, attended the Lynch-Day wedding (c. 1870) with the thought of traveling on to New Orleans, or, according to one story, Tipperary, if need be, in search of a bride. Instead, age 51, he danced with that never-married aunt of Mary Lynch, Catherine Dorsey (1816-1909), who was born in Youghal in Cork, was three years older than he, and was so independent in spirit that in his later years, he was inclined to say out of her presence, according to Judge John W. Day, that "It was a sad day for me when I met 'Irish Kate.'" Their senior marriage of convenience that became inconvenient produced no children. As a result, his dutiful brother Bartholomew, Junior, gratefully named his first son, John Tyrrell Day, Junior, thus turning "John T. Day" into "John T. Day, Senior," in the local newspapers and history books like *The History of the Illinois River Valley*.

This essay preserves the "Senior" and "Junior" labels to match that exact usage in historical documents, and then switches to the more common use of Roman numerals for the third generation. So Bartholomew staying in Tipperary is "Senior"; his son, Bartholomew, the immigrant, is "Junior"; and Junior's son, Bartholomew (Bart/Batty), born in Michael, Illinois, is "III."

In 1952, when Virginia Day Fritscher's son John/Jack, age thirteen, asked his grandfather, Bartholomew III, why he had no middle name, he joked, "We were too poor to afford one." In the 1930 census, and seemingly only in the 1930 census, there is a "Valentine Day" listed, without the "Bartholomew," whose life-details as "head of household" match Bartholomew III; but this name "Valentine," appearing nowhere else in the Day short-list of names, seems to be a mistake, or a census-satirizing subversive joke made to the serious census taker by Bart who was known for his kidding sense of humor. Who, besides Stage Irish vaudeville comedians, engaged in the stereotypes of Paddywhackery, would saddle their child with the name "Valentine Day"? In that same census, Mary Pearl Day is listed off-kilter as "Pearl M. Day." Twenty-four years later in 1954, Bartholomew died on February 13, the Eve of St. Valentine's Day.

Always Virginia

In researching "Bartholomew Day," the singular difficulty is that search engines confuse that name a million times over with the "St. Bartholomew Day Massacre" of French Protestants by French Catholics in 1572.

When John T. Day, Senior, died April 17, 1888, the farmland went to Catherine Dorsey Day as a life estate, and then to Bartholomew, Junior, and Mary Lynch Day. In short, Bartholomew Day, Junior, from Tipperary (May 20, 1829-September 6, 1903) married (c. 1870) Mary Lynch from County Waterford (1848-1925), and they became the parents of five sons and two daughters including their first-born Mary Katharine Day who died a few days after birth. Their surviving children were:

1. Judge John T. Day, Junior (1872-1942), their second-born, who married schoolteacher Addie Fowler in 1904, and had four children: Mary Day Roth, Loretta Day Ritter, Catherine Felice Day Hagen (who was a look-alike for Virginia Day Fritscher), and Judge John William Day;

2. James Day (1875-1951), the licensed engineer and steamboat captain who, taking after his (drowned) sailor grandfather, successfully took a flat-bottomed steamboat ballasted for ocean travel down the Mississippi through the Gulf of Mexico to Portland, Oregon, and, in a marriage cut short by his wife's death, was the father of one child, Howard Day, a Middleweight Boxing Champion of the Navy in the 1920s; James Day was, according to Mary Pearl Lawler Day, a look-alike for her grandson John (Jack) Fritscher;

3. Margaret (Mag) Day (1878-1938), named for her Tyrrell grandmother, who married Casper Joseph Stelbrink in 1900 and had two children: Joseph and the never-married postmaster Cecelia;

4. Thomas Day (1880-1945) who moved west as a broncobuster around 1900 and settled in Portland where he married and worked in the shipyards, and was buried in Riverview Cemetery in Oregon next to his wife Anna Etta Mackey, daughter of John Mackey and Pluma St. Ores, with whom he had one child: Margaret

who, according to Judge John W. Day, "was almost an identical look-alike for Helen Day, the daughter of Joe and Ella Day";

5. Joseph Day (1883-1960) who was a postmaster in Hamburg and married Addie Fowler's sister, schoolteacher Ella Fowler (who was also a Hamburg postmaster) in 1911, and had two children: Helen and Joseph, Junior;

6. and the youngest, Bartholomew (Bart/Batty) Day III (1887-1954), who married Mary Pearl Lawler from her paternal Clan Ó Leathlobhair and from her maternal Clan MacDonnchadha in 1911, and was the father of their five children—of whom the males died young in their fifties: including: the Catholic priest and Army Chaplain John Bartholomew (John B. Day, 1912-1967), James T. (1914-1968), Margaret Norine Day Chumley (1917-1996), Virginia Claire Day Fritscher (1919-2004), and Harold Joseph (1922-1977).

In 1932, while many eyewitness fact-checkers of this generation of the Day family were still alive, John Leonard Conger and William Edgar Hull confirmed, as sorted above, the line of descent from Virginia's grandfather, Bartholomew Day, Junior, in *The History of the Illinois River Valley*:

> Bartholomew Day [Junior] served on the school and village boards, as well as on many grand and petit juries. He devoted his attention to farming, and was a Catholic in his religious faith. To him and his wife were born five sons and two daughters, namely: John T., Junior; James, who is an engineer on the Mississippi River Improvement Service; Mrs. Margaret Day Stelbrink, of Kampsville; Thomas, who is employed in shipyards in Portland, Oregon; Joseph, who is engaged in fruit raising; Bartholomew, who is a rural mail carrier out of Kampsville, and Katherine [named after Catherine Dorsey], who died in infancy.

Calhoun County Judge John W. Day (1919-2013), the son of Judge John T. Day, Junior, wrote to his cousin Virginia Day Fritscher on August 8, 1993, that the two oldest brothers, John and

Joe—who was also over six feet tall—had a special regard looking after their youngest sibling, Bartholomew, III, who was sickly as a boy and shorter at five-feet-ten. Bartholomew III's, wife, the stylish St, Louis beauty with Gibson Girl hair, Mary Pearl Lawler Day, recalled how in the early years of their marriage, Bart nearly died from one incidence of what may have been hemorrhagic purpura.

She said the attending physician told her, "You'll be a widow by morning." She recalled in an interview recorded by her grandson Jack Fritscher on May 8, 1972, and included in this book: "Daddy [Bartholomew III] used to say we were descended from Irish kings, because he one time had that blood disease only royalty gets...where the blood just comes out of your pores. Daddy was in the hospital for six weeks and they cured him by giving him horse serum and he was never sick again."

She always referred to her husband as "Daddy" and he called her "Mom." She never liked his nickname "Batty" which his birth family called him to distinguish yet one more "Bartholomew" from his grandfather, father, and cousins. Even so, she named her own firstborn, John Bartholomew. She herself preferred to be called "Mary" or "Mrs. Day," even though some old-timers, and her son-in-law Jim Chumley, sometimes called her "Pearl," a name she disliked, while her grandchildren always called her "Nanny."

In self-fashioning their family clan, Mr. and Mrs. Bartholomew Day, Junior, gave pride of place to their firstborn, John Tyrrell Day, Junior, Virginia Day Fritscher's uncle, who was profiled by Conger and Hull:

> One of Calhoun County's most distinguished citizens is John T. Day, Junior, who has been officially connected with the county for twenty-four years, eight years as county clerk and sixteen years as judge of the county court. He is also one of the county's leading orchardists and farmers and has been very successful in all of his affairs. He was born on the 2nd of November, 1872, on a farm formerly owned by his uncle, but now owned by himself, and

located near Hamburg.... He attended the public schools and Whipple Academy, which is the academic department of Illinois College, at Jacksonville. Later he was a student in a private Normal School at Bushnell, Illinois, and also took a course in bookkeeping at that place. He received a first-grade certificate, permitting him to teach for eight years, and he served seven years of that period in the home school at Hamburg, of which he had charge. He then entered politics, and was elected clerk of Calhoun County, in which position, by successive reelections, he served for eight years, after which he was elected to the bench of the county court. As a judge he has shown himself a man of calm and dispassionate judgment, sincere and conscientious in everything he does, and has honored the position which he has filled for so many years.

In 1904 Judge John T. Day, Junior, was united in marriage to Addie M. Fowler, a daughter of Rev. W. P. Fowler [a Methodist preacher at the Oasis Church in Hardin and in Batchtown], who taught school for twelve years at Hamburg, Indian Creek, and Gilead....Judge Day is a strong supporter of the Democratic party and has attended many county, district and state conventions, as well as the national convention at Kansas City in 1900. For many years he was either chairman or secretary of the county central committee. He is president of the Hamburg Chamber of Commerce and is a member of the Woodmen, the State Horticultural Society and the County Farm Bureau, of which he was formerly secretary. During the late war he served as chairman of the exemption board, belonged to the Four-Minute Speakers and the legal advisory board. [The Four-Minute Speakers were commissioned by President Wilson to promote American involvement in the first World War by standing up to give quick pop-up patriotic speeches in town meetings, movie theaters, and restaurants.] No worthy cause has appealed in vain for the Judge's support and he is numbered among Calhoun County's most progressive and public-spirited citizens.

John T. Day, Junior's children, the cousins and playmates of Virginia Day Fritscher were, as noted: Mary Eleanor Day (Leo) Roth; the doomed bride Loretta who married the dentist, Dr. Phil A. Ritter, and died from pneumonia two months prior to childbirth at 22; Catherine Felice Day (Renard) Hagen; and Judge John William Day whose son, with Wannie Bell Day, John Patrick Day, C.P., was ordained a Catholic priest in 1972.

After Judge John T. Day, Junior, married Addie Fowler, his brother, Joe Day, married Addie's sister, Ella. Joe was an accountant and bookkeeper who could play a dozen instruments from the violin to the slide trombone and in his teens traveled across the country with various bands before settling down for several years as a working-partner farming with his favorite brother, John T, Junior, who was also musical. Joe and Ella ran a farm in Gresham Hollow just a couple miles south of Hamburg.

Virginia Day Fritscher wrote in 1980: "Two of my daddy's brothers married sisters and their children always let us know they were double-cousins more related to each other than to us. They always called their parents 'The Folks' and when they'd come over unexpectedly some Sunday afternoon, they'd tell us kids the 'The Folks' were planning on staying for supper so we'd tell mom and she'd have us go down to the store and get some choice cold cuts, etc. as we had our big dinner of roast or chicken at noon, and needless to say after feeding seven, there wasn't enough for four more.... They both, uncle John and uncle Joe [the two oldest brothers] ran huge apple orchards."

Virginia added in 1982: "My uncle John's son, John W., my cousin who married Wannie Bell, is now a judge in Granite City. I'm also very proud that my brother Jimmy's son [James W. Day] is now a judge continuing our family heritage of three judges in three generations. He is in Carrollton where my brother, his father, owned the famous Day's Café on the town square in the 1950s."

For many years, James W. Day was a resident and presiding circuit judge of the Seventh Circuit Court in Illinois. He was admitted to the bar in 1963, retiring from his post as circuit judge on December 6, 2020. His son with Greene County historical preservationist Dotty Allen Day, James Allen Day, became the fourth-generation judge in the Day family when he received a lifetime appointment as a United States Administrative Law Judge in 2016. In 2013, Dotty Day saved the 130-year-old Fry Octagonal Barn in Carrollton. She collected its history, and, with the engineering help of the Day cousins at J. J. Chumley Builders of Whitehall, moved it three hundred feet out of the path of incoming new homes to preserve it on their Day family farm where they began living in 1970.

Virginia Day Fritscher's father, Bartholomew Day III, was the youngest son of Bartholomew, Junior, and Mary Lynch Day, and married Mary Pearl Lawler Day in a private ceremony conducted by the Reverend J. J. Furlong at St. Columbkille's Church in St. Louis on July 12, 1911. Their marriage banns were not announced from the pulpit and they were wed in secret to avoid threats from Francis Devine, the fiancé Mary Pearl had dropped upon meeting Bart/Batty that previous summer when she had taken the steamboat to visit her cousins in Hamburg—and in one version of their meeting—saw Bart crossing a field, and said, "That's the man I'm going to marry."

Her Lawler family, according to Judge John W. Day, "were people of some means." In her 1972 recorded interview, she recalled her parents. Her father, John (Jack) Patrick Lawler, born of immigrant parents in St. Louis c. 1859, died there in 1920. Her mother, Honorah Anastasia McDonough (1862-1925), was born in St. Louis of parents whose four parents were immigrants from Ireland. She once mentioned that one of her grandmothers was named Mary Higgins. After her husband Jack Lawler's death, Honorah lived with her only daughter's family in Kampsville where she retreated to an upstairs room and died in April 1925.

Bart and Mary Pearl Day began their family of five children in Hamburg with their firstborn son, the handsome and athletic John Bartholomew Day, a young newspaper reporter for five years for the Jacksonville *Journal-Courier*, who was ordained a Catholic priest in 1938 and was a chaplain serving with the rank of Major in the Battle of the Bulge. During the blizzard snowstorms of that bloody and confusing turmoil over Christmas 1944 and New Year's 1945, the U. S. Secretary of War sent Western Union Telegrams that both he and his brother-in-law, Jim Chumley, were each reported, separately, as "missing in action" in the Ardennes Forest. Weeks later, they were reported safe. At that time, families dreaded seeing the uniformed Western Union boy park his bicycle and ring the doorbell to deliver a telegram on yellow paper pasted with tickertape text that read like this: "Washington D. C. Date. Address: Parent or Spouse. The Secretary of War desires me to express his deep regret that your son (Name and Rank) has been reported missing in action since (sample) seventeen December in Belgium. If further details or information are received you will be promptly notified. —James Alexander Ulio, The ADJ General." On March 22, 1945, a news photo of Major John B. Day, chaplain, was printed on the front pages of newspapers across the country, and in *Time* magazine, April 2, 1945, showing him standing in mud in a huge field of open graves and thousands of crosses, saying Last Rites while burying unidentified American soldiers in the largest Allied military cemetery in Europe at Henri Chapelle, Belgium.

Father John B. Day, as he signed himself, then served as a parish priest in Collinsville, Quincy, Granite City, and Springfield. When his father retired from thirty years with the postoffice in 1948, he invited his parents to leave their apartment on Delmar Boulevard in St. Louis, and live with him in his St. Cabrini parish house in Springfield where they became "Father John's gardener and housekeeper." Insofar as Father John became the Day family patriarch upon his father's death in 1954, his mother became the revered Day matriarch in the 1950s and 1960s. As a widow, she was highly respected in the parish as "Mrs. Day" because she was, as Catholics said then, "the greatest thing a Catholic woman can be: the Mother of a Priest." Her popular son was active in civil rights in the 1960s, and managed the design and construction of the new church and new school buildings for his growing parish where in the rectory bathroom, early on the morning of May 9, 1967, while shaving to say Mass, he called out in distress, and died of a heart attack on the floor in his mother's arms. He was an Irish baritone who sang a beautiful High Mass. His favorite song was "Stardust." One of his sermons and his biography appear later in this book.

Their second son, James T., married schoolteacher Mildred Horn, the daughter of William Horn (German born) and Nettie Caroline Vahle Horn, and lived as a restaurateur in Carrollton where they had three children: Judge James; restaurateur Carolyn, and Cynthia.

Bart and Mary Pearl's youngest three children were Margaret Norine, Virginia Claire, and Harold Joseph.

Norine married James Thomas Chumley, the engineer son of Jacksonville Alderman and building contractor Thomas C. and Myrtle Cannon Chumley, who helped build Eero Saarinen's Gateway Arch, memorializing explorers and immigrant pioneers like the Day family, in St. Louis where they had five children: Ted, Patrick, Michael (Mickey), Rosemary, and Tim.

Virginia, the first of their children to wed, married Routt High School varsity athlete George Fritscher, son of Austrian immigrant farmers Joseph and Amelia Fritscher of Heron Lake, Minnesota, and had three children: writer and university professor John Joseph (Jack), Ph.D,, the first grandchild of Bart and Mary Pearl, born June 20, 1939, in Jacksonville; Vietnam veteran George Robert (Bob) who died of military-related illnesses, and psychologist Mary Claire, both born in Peoria.

Harold married Rosemary Walsh, the daughter of Maurice and

Alma Walsh of Murrayville, and lived in Palmyra, Hannibal, and St. Louis with their three children: lawman and military veteran John Terrence (Terry), Mary Janice Day Campbell, and Martha Elizabeth Day Stuckenberg.

"Irish and Catholic, thank God," said Mary Pearl Lawler Day.

"We've always been Catholic," said her daughter Virginia Day Fritscher.

"Except before Saint Patrick when we were all pagan Druids," said their grandson and son, Jack.

To which the eighty-four-year-old Mary Pearl Day replied: "'Bless us and save us,' said Mrs. O'Davis."

During a trip to Ireland in 2019, John Terrence (Terry) Day and his wife, Kathy Pflueger Day, visited and dined with the large and genial O'Dea family of Tipperary who, they were given to understand, were still living on the same farm where John T., Senior, and Bartholomew, Junior, had lived with their parents and brother, Thomas, whose descendants they are.

In this book of Irish stories about this certain Day family in Illinois, Virginia Day Fritscher's eyewitness diary recalls with loving heart and nostalgic voice the colorful comedy, the geneological drama, and the moving parts of the first 150 years of several generations of a lively Irish immigrant family putting down new roots in Hamburg, Kampsville, and Jacksonville. The ancient history of the Days can be found at https://odeaclan.org/clan-history.

—Jack Fritscher, PhD, born 1939, a Seanachie of Clan Ó Deághaidh, San Francisco, 2019

Author's Note. With respect to the past, and to the future, every effort has been made in the present by this direct descendent of his great-great-grandparents, Bartholomew Day, Senior, and Margaret Tyrrell Day, who stayed in Ireland, to write this report with accuracy, including information from available public sources as well as from stories the author began collecting in the 1950s from his grandfather Bartholmew Day III, including his 1972 recording of his grandmother Mary Pearl Lawler Day and the writings and diary of his mother Virginia Day Fritscher; from the letters written in 1993 by his first cousin once removed, Judge John W. Day; and from research on the ground in Ireland and Calhoun County by his first cousin John Terrence "Terry" Day, retired Senior Chief Warrant 4 United States Army, and Terry's grandson, Tyler Day.

Two invaluable books are: *A Portrait and Biographical Album of Pike and Calhoun Counties*, Biographical Publishing Company, Chicago: 1891, found at https://www.loc.gov/item/rc01002078//; and *The History of the Illinois River Valley*, Biographical Volume II, by John Leonard Conger and William Edgar Hull, Chicago, S. J. Clarke Publishing Company, 1932 which was digitized by the Internet Archive in 2012 with funding from University of Illinois Urbana-Champaign http://archive.org/details/historyofillinoi02cong pp. 298-300. Research also included *Population of the United States 1860 Census Statistics*: https://www2.census.gov/library/publications/decennial/1860/population/1860a-02.pdf

Please send corrections and additions to the author.

John (Jack) Patrick Lawler, Father of Mary Pearl Lawler Day, Grandfather of Virginia Day Fritscher

Judge John T. Day, Jr., Granduncle of Virginia Day Fritscher

Dysert O'Dea Castle, Corofin, County Clare Ireland

(monis birth) OCTOBER 2

1933 Went to school as usual. In the evening I went down to Gloria's house and studied and played cards. The ladies surprised mamma
19

1935 I went to see "Top Hat." next eve — Came down again. Bob Thomas. — Said that boarders said M. Dawn & I were the best looking girls in R. south. came down
1936 ran a nail in his foot. Went to doctor in aft. went riding. Stayed home in eve.

19

OCTOBER 3

1933 Went to school. Went over to Poochie's after school. In the evening I bought some marshmallows and we roasted them. Sold a pr. of hose.
19

In eve. I had a date with C.P. Joy M.C. Worsham, H. Schumm, F. Widdicomb
1935 came down again.
We took the dog walking.
Did'nt [crossed out] went
[crossed out] ...
1936 Mother & I went up town. Geo. stayed here. In nite. we saw "Bengal Tiger." Swell
Went to newsreel. I stayed home
19 Geo. I went down to Cecil's.

September 1980

My Life in Kampsville

I was born in this little town of about 200 population — named Kampsville, in Calhoun Co. — the only Co. in the U.S. without a railroad. Most everything came in by boat & therefore things were very expensive. In order to get out of the Co. you had to cross the Ill. river by ferry boat or go to Hamburg, Ill. — where my father was born & my parents lived the first few years of their married life, & cross by ferry boat over the Mississippi. In later yrs. they did build a bridge on Hardin, Ill. about 9 mi. So. of Kampsville where one could cross the Ill. river & which many times ev. & other could use as sometimes there was a long wait to get on the ferry boat as Kampsville also was a summer resort and with a lovely beach, cottages & dance pavilion which was frequented in the summer by people from St. Louis, & surrounding larger cities. (Same as Charleston)

One of my first recollections of living in this little town was the back porch on the house we lived (in the So. end of town called Staringtown) or where my Mom would lift us up (no steps to porch) really a side porch & give us fresh, hot cold roly-poly made out of pie-crust sprinkled with cinnamon & sugar. I also had a rabbit (a white pet — my

MY LIFE IN KAMPSVILLE
1919 to 1930
by Virginia Day Fritscher
hand-written September 1980, age 61

I was born July 12, 1919, on my Mom and Daddy's eighth wedding anniversary, in this little town of about 200 population, named Kampsville, in Calhoun County, Illinois, the only county in the United States without a railroad. Most everything came in by boat and things were very expensive. In order to get out of the county, you had to cross the Illinois River by ferryboat or go to Hamburg, Illinois, where my Daddy was born and my parents lived the first few years of their married life, or cross by ferryboat over the Mississippi.

My mother was Mary Pearl Lawler Day, born in St. Louis, October 2, 1888–December 6, 1972. My father Bartholomew was born in Michael, Illinois, October 17, 1887–February 13, 1954. Because my mother's former fiancee, Francis Devine, threatened he would kill her on her wedding day, my parents married in a secret ceremony in St. Louis in 1911 on July 12 which date in 1919 also became my birthday, and in 1938 my wedding anniversary.

In later years the State did build a bridge at Hardin, Illinois, about nine miles south of Kampsville, where one could cross the Illinois River, and which many times we and others would use as sometimes there was a little wait to get on the ferryboat because Kampsville was also a summer resort, with a lovely beach, cottages, and dance pavilion which was jammed in the summers I was a girl by people dancing the Charleston, come up from St. Louis and surrounding other little towns.

One of my first recollections of living in this little town was the back porch on the house we lived in (in the south end of town called Stringtown) on which my Mom would lift us up (no steps to porch), really a side porch and give us fresh, hot-baked roly-polies made out of pie-crust rolled up and sprinkled with cinnamon and sugar. Bake til golden brown. That's the whole recipe. I also had a rabbit (a white pet—my very own) which I really do not remember, but my parents always told me about it as it would only come to me when called, but some mean older boys up the street killed it by throwing it by its legs in the air and letting it fall to the ground dead.

My next recollection was when I was three years old and we moved into our new home which my parents purchased—a big 8-room concrete block home—fenced-in yard—upstairs porch and front porch. It was the second house on the right from the main street. None of the streets had names. I remember trying to open the gate the day we purchased it and we all went up to look at it. I don't remember the actual moving-in day but we spent many a happy day there until we moved when I was eleven to Jacksonville.

I had three brothers, John, Jimmie, and Harold, and one sister, Norine. My two older brothers, John and Jimmie, used to come into our room at night and run their hands up and down the wallpaper and make my sister and me think it was a bat, as once a bat did get in and we were a little apprehensive about being in that room, because my maternal grandmother [Honorah Anastasia McDonough-Lawler] died in that room when I was five years old. I always remember Grandma Lawler always had big round mints in her room with the Triple "XXX" on them and would give them to us. She took to her room when she was sixty years old, and never came down except to rock for three years until she died at age sixty-three.

Living in such a small town, I liked the woods which were only about two or three blocks away on what was called the Illinois River bluffs, and we always went there in the spring and picked wild flowers or just to hike. My brothers, John and Jimmie, went mushrooming, ginseng hunting (used to sell it to the local doctor), walnut gathering, and trapping possums. One morning when they went to check their traps before school, they had caught a skunk. Needless to say the smell did not get off their shoes before school and one of the nuns said to John, "John, you smell like skunk." And he said, "You'll get used to it, Sister." John was my brother who became a priest. My Daddy and brothers always went coon, opossum, and etc. hunting at night and had a very good hunting dog. My brother Jimmie always made cornbread with bacon strips in it for the hunting dog. Jimmie who was the second oldest after John, see, turned out to be the owner and cook at Day's Café, his famous little restaurant in Carrollton.

Daddy and John and Jimmie would put the skins of their animals on boards and dry them in the two big rooms we had upstairs that weren't used for living quarters where we used to store a few bushels of good Calhoun apples and Christmas toys (which my brothers used to sneak in and play with before Christmas). They sold the animal skins. Daddy did have a fur made for my Mom and older sister, Norine, then and many years later one matching fox fur each for me, my Mom, and sister, and sisters-in-law, Mildred and Rosemary, but he didn't hunt these latter foxes which he bought.

They also went squirrel hunting all the time (in season) and Daddy took me one day and we got five squirrels. You had to be very quiet in the woods so you wouldn't scare them away. So Daddy had me stay back and he went a few yards further, but I was right behind him and he asked me "why" and I said, "Daddy, there's a snake up there." We had lots of snakes in Calhoun County and many times they were in our yard, because they'd come in on a wagon with the farmers. My Daddy, being a strict Irish Catholic, got a piece of some kind of tree limb, burned it, and with the ash part made a cross on our arm every St. Patrick's Day to keep us from getting snake-bitten—an old Irish custom, based on St. Patrick driving all the snakes out of Ireland. My family besides being Catholic has always been Democrats.

I liked to work in the yard, and would surprise my Daddy and pull all the weeds or when he'd come home from his U.S. Rural

Mail route, I'd proudly show him and be rewarded with a quarter, which was lots of money in those days [mid 1920s]. We used to get 15 cents every Saturday if we were good and get to go to the movie in Kampsville, which cost 10 cents, and spend the other nickel on goodies. My favorite movie stars were Bob Steele and Clara Bow, the "It Girl" of the 20s.

When I was smaller and the rest of the family, or rather part of the family, would go to the show, I'd stay home and be happy if they brought me a "load" of gum. That's what I called a package as it was stacked like the loads of wood we would get many times a winter to burn in our Heatrola in the living room and cook stove in the kitchen. The boys had to keep the wood chopped and we girls would carry it in and put it in the woodbox behind the kitchen stove.

One day when my brother John, who was twelve or thirteen years old, was chopping wood, it was almost dusk and very cold. I was out watching him sitting in my swing and he kept telling me [age four or five] to go in as it was too cold, and I'd say "I'm rough and I'm tough, and I'm hard to bluff!" This would make him very angry, as he didn't think it was too ladylike to begin with and was afraid it was, really, too cold.

On winter evenings we'd sit and watch the fire burn in the Heatrola and make out different images it projected on the little windows of the door. On Saturday night a tub of hot water was brought in and set to warm up by the Heatrola and there we'd take our baths. Saturday everyone shined shoes for church in the A.M. (I can still smell the shoe polish.)

One morning when I was five, my Mom and Daddy were getting ready to go to Church. I was in the kitchen and I cut off one of my curls. I disliked my curls as it hurt to have them twisted around a hot curling iron. And I threw the curl under the icebox, but Norine ratted on me. Mom couldn't tell my curl was missing as I had so many, but I was reprimanded. Speaking of curls, I was never so glad or so proud to have them cut off by "Casey Jones," our local barber. I was taken by my Daddy, and on the way home stopped by my Aunt Mag's [Margaret Day-Stelbrink, my Daddy Bart's only sister] to show her and my paternal grandmother [Mary Lynch-Day] who lived with her. They both cried as did my maternal grandmother [Honorah Anastasia McDonough-Lawler] when I got home and showed her. My, I was proud of my new "wind-blown bob," and no more tangles.

My maternal grandmother, Grandma Lawler [Honorah], after whom Norine was named, died of a stroke at our home in April, 1924, when I was five years old and in first grade. I remember the neighbor coming over to our little school, which was just across the street, to get us. She remained unconscious for three days at our home because there was no hospital in this little town. I can always remember the death rattle for that period of time. My paternal grandmother, Grandma Mary Lynch Day died the next year in June, 1925, at age 80 years and 4 days. My maternal grandmother, Grandma Honorah McDonough Lawler, was 63. I believe my paternal grandmother had a stroke also. Grandma Lawler was buried in St. Louis and Grandma Day in Michael, Illinois, a town of about 25 where she was married and all her children baptized.

We used to go often to visit her grave and the grave of my grandfather, Bartholomew Day, born in Ireland, about 1824, who I never saw because he died in 1903 when my Daddy was a boy of sixteen. My Daddy's father was much older than his mother, my grandma, Mary Lynch Day. My grandfather Bartholomew came from Ireland in 1868. When he was about forty years old and ready to marry around 1870, he traveled from Hamburg to St. Louis where he was introduced to Mary Lynch who was born at the start of the Potato Famine in 1844. She was from Waterford, was twenty years younger, and had a twin sister who, I think, stayed in Ireland.

Our only relative remaining in Kampsville was my Aunt Mag. Her husband, Uncle "Cap" (Casper Stelbrink), was twenty years older and very crabby, and they were quite wealthy. When I was twelve, Aunt Mag took care of us five when my Mom had to have gall-bladder surgery and went to the hospital in Jacksonville, Illinois, where she almost died. Daddy kept us at night. We had our school picnic while my Mom was in hospital. Usually we never ate often at my Aunt's as we were five children in our family and they only had two—a boy and a girl, Joe and Cecilia, older than my oldest brother, John.

The Stelbrink boy was my cousin Joe, and on one occasion when our school visited Springfield, Illinois, to see Lincoln's tomb and home, Joe was one of the drivers of the car I was riding in. Just for the excitement of it, I gave him a quarter to pass a car on the way home and he took it. That made my Daddy angry. Daddy made Joe give the quarter back to me the next day. Joe mellowed in his older years and married and had three or four children, but his sister Cecilia, never married.

We had to call Cecilia's friends "Miss Josephine," "Miss Mildred," and "Miss Helen." Those three were "the Kamps," the oldest girls in the Kamp family, and sisters of my best friends who were the younger Kamp twins named Edna and Edwina Kamp, for whose grandfather our town was named. The Kamp girls' father owned a grocery store in Kampsville and outside on one of the metal posts supporting the roof, one could get a small electric shock by holding onto it and twirling around. The Kamp twins and I did everything together—so much so that Sister Salvatore, one of the German nuns teaching at St. Anselm's school, tied us together with rope one A.M.

Once, Sister Salvatore, who used to hit us with her pointer, said to me when I spilled ink all over my dress, "Oh, Virginia Day, you look like you fell in a sauerkraut barrel." And Mom told me, "Virginia Day, you tell Sister Salvatore that only Germans fall in the sauerkraut." Also at Christmastime, Santa visited at our Christmas program, and he gave me a stick. He must have been maybe a German nun dressed up like a German Santa, because that's a German custom of giving coal and a stick to bad children. I cried, as, not being German, I was afraid my Irish Mom and

Daddy would think I'd been bad in school as they were very strict, though kind and loving.

If we were sick, Daddy would come up to our room after supper and visit with us an hour or so. He was a US mail carrier and we always wanted to go with him on his rural route, but couldn't unless he paid postage on us. That's what he always said. On our birthday we girls, Norine and I, got to go once. The boys, my older brothers, John and Jimmie, were Daddy's subs as was my cousin Joe, so they were allowed to go with him. It wasn't a very long mail route, but in those days in bad weather, Daddy'd have to go by horse and buggy. We had two horses, Snip and Topsy.

There were many creeks that would swell when it rained and one day my Daddy and cousin Joe almost drowned when they were swept away in a red Model T Ford in one of the smaller creeks. I can remember Mom lighting candles at home and praying for Daddy as maybe it'd be 6 P.M. in bad weather when Daddy would get home. That night he got home much later, because it took awhile for his Model T to float into the trees and get caught so he and cousin Joe could climb out and save themselves. Sometimes he'd get home at 8 or 9 and would always leave before 7 A.M., go to post office, put up his mail, and leave. On good days he'd leave at 7 and maybe be home at noon. One day he had an unexpected piece of mail with him: my black bloomers. Mom and Norine and I searched the house for them before I went to school, and much to our surprise Daddy said he picked them up with some of his things. Norine said my bloomers got to go on the postal route before I did.

At Christmastime Daddy would come home like Santa Claus loaded down by his mail patrons with goodies like fresh country sausage and all good farm things like that. We had so much we shared them with the priest and sisters who lived in the St. Anselm rectory and convent across the street from us.

Speaking of the priest, he had a housekeeper who had a daughter my age named Elizabeth. One day I was engrossed playing ball out in front of my house and Elizabeth kept calling me. I told her

I wasn't coming over, but she kept begging me. So I picked up a rock, went over to the gate—I was about four, I believe—and said, "Come here, Eliz," and hit her in the head with the rock. Needless to say, my Mom soon heard of it and I was punished. The worst punishment though was when I walked into Church the next day. Father Faller shook his finger at me. I thought, "Oh, he knows." I was embarrassed. I never again hit a priest's housekeeper's daughter in the head with a rock.

I used to get into a few interesting wrestling matches and fights. One fight was with Kermit Suhling. "Kermie" did something I didn't like, so I beat him up. My Mom kept saying at the door, "Shame on you, a little girl fighting a boy." Well, Kermie gave me no trouble from then on. He lived in a beautiful home in the park, as I recall, where there were three homes owned by wealthy families. We were allowed to go to the park every night if we had behaved and we used to ride the "Ocean Wave" like a "Merry-Go-Round" that rocked. Our Daddy saw us and said, "Don't ride the 'Ocean Wave' any more." He was afraid we'd get hurt as big kids used to push it and get it going so fast. Well, about six weeks later we figured it was OK, but he saw us. He came over and got us and gave us a spanking then and there. We did not ride the "Ocean Wave" anymore.

One evening, Norine and I [six and three] decided to build a little fire under the front porch, because the boy next door (who wasn't exactly normal) dared us to, but Daddy caught us and spanked us. We used to kid him in later years and say, "Daddy, we got punished just for trying to start a fire under the front porch." There wasn't a fire department in Kampsville.

We had a big swing on that front porch and used to enjoy many a happy hour there. I would swing my puppy and then he'd get sick. We had two dogs, one Jimmie's hunting dog and one our pet and they both had pups at the same time and we had about sixteen dogs all at once. We kept the sassiest pup and named him "Teddy" and how he loved the woods. When I was eleven in 1930 and we moved from Kampsville to Jacksonville, we, of course, brought Teddy; but in Jacksonville we thought Teddy was dying of homesickness, so we gave him to people in the country, but he was back in our yard the next day. We never gave him away again. He liked us better than he liked the country. We liked that dog and his name. My sister Norine named her first child "Ted."

My brother, Harold, the youngest of all five of us, got his big toe stuck in our high porch swing one afternoon. Mom tried and tried to get it out, but to no avail. When Daddy came home, he managed to free Harold's toe. Harold also got scarlet fever and we were quarantined. Harold was named after one of Mom's favorite writers she read and liked, Harold Bell Wright, who wrote *The Shepherd of the Hills* and *The Winning of Barbara Worth*. While Harold had scarlet fever, they boarded my brother Jimmie out across the street, but he got the flu, most likely homesickness, just like Teddy, and I can remember Daddy and the man across the street carrying him home. During the scarlet fever, we were in Harold's room playing games every day, and none of the rest of us got scarlet fever though we all had every other childhood disease, I believe, at different times of course. Harold died at age fifty-five of a stroke while taking a shower. Rosemary said she heard him call out: "Oh, dear God, take me to heaven or get this pain out of my head." (All three of my brothers died when they were 53, 54, and 55.)

In those days they quarantined you for everything. John was already away at school going to the seminary, so he didn't come home during the quarantine period. He was studying to be a priest and my Mom said she heard three knocks on her bed one night and a voice saying, "I want John." It scared her so she had Daddy call the school to see if he was OK and he was fine. Mom always believed that if your son had a calling for the priesthood, God would let you know and she always believed that the priesthood was John's calling.

John made a wonderful priest til the day he died of a massive heart attack stepping into the shower to bathe before saying early

Mass on April 9, 1967. Mom lived with him there in his rectory at St. Cabrini's parish house in Springfield, and she held him in her arms on the bathroom floor. He was fifty-four; she was seventy-eight. [This incident is fictionalized in the short story, "Silent Mothers, Silent Sons," in the book, *Sweet Embraceable You: 8 Coffee-House Stories*, by Jack Fritscher, published in May, 2000.]

John used to hitchhike home most every weekend as it was very safe then to do so. He'd write a letter home and draw a cup with the handle off with the caption, "Norine broke the last one." And he'd draw a donut as a big hint so Mom would have fresh raised donuts when he came home. I don't think I ever tasted any as good since.

My Mom was very ambitious for a girl who was raised in a house with an adoring father and four brothers named Jim, Ed, Jack, and Will who was a sleepwalker who once climbed a ladder up the outside of the house with a lighted coal lantern. Her mother, Honorah, made Mom do all the work. Mom said she herself used to stand on a little stool to make the bread, while her Daddy "carried her mother around in his hands," as they used to say, because she always had headaches, and whenever there was an argument brewing, he'd put on his hat and go for a walk until the storm front had cleared.

I can always recall those long, hazy days of summer when she'd be canning twelve jars of everything for our family of seven and making lots of jelly. (I used to run around saying, "Seven Days! We're a 'week' family!") Daddy had two big lots where we grew a big garden as we raised most of our food. Oh, those strawberries! People would flock from St. Louis for a weekend in the country to enjoy Aunt Pearl's delicious strawberry pie, Uncle Bart's delicious sweet corn, potatoes, and cabbage, and to attend the dance at the beach. Just the way years later people flocked up from St. Louis to eat at my brother Jimmie's famous Day's Café in Carrollton.

My Mom used to have her wash on the line by 7 A.M., doing it on a washboard, have a big dinner cooked, and when we came home from school, she'd have something baked and be sitting at the window reading her *Good Housekeeping* magazine. Every evening she and Daddy would sit in the dining room and read, and we'd study in the kitchen, or when I was smaller, I'd lie on the floor and be intrigued with the rockers my Mom and Daddy were rocking on, and I'd get my hands closer and closer until I managed to get my fingers under the rocker. No wonder my fingers are crooked. My Grandma Lawler used to always sit in there too. The living room was reserved for guests and special occasions, though we had our piano in there and I took lessons and so did my sister from the banker's wife. I did not like to practice and hated being called in from play to do so. The songs I played most were "The Fairy Queen Gavotte," "The Fairy Queen Waltz," and "The Bumble Bee."

The piano was big, and I was little—like my mom, small for my age, until in high school I grew taller than my mom and sister—and there were little levers to raise the bench. One day as I was getting ready to practice, I just raised one lever and the bench tipped over. That did it. Mom thought I tipped over the bench on purpose, and she said she got the message, so I didn't have to take piano lessons anymore. Anyhow I wanted to play the saxophone. Daddy said, "You're so little, you couldn't lift one." I idealized the Foiles girls in town. One played the piano and one the saxophone, and I thought my sister and I could be like them. One of the Foiles girls was my 2nd and 3rd grade teacher, "Miss Grace." I went to Catholic school in 1st grade, but 2nd, 3rd, and 4th to public as our town was so small we couldn't get Sisters every year. I went to Catholic school, though, my 5th and 6th years. We always put on little school plays and I loved them.

I remember when we got electricity in the house. I recall the man saying it cost three cents everytime you turned the light on and off. Then we got our first electric radio, a Crosley named "Buddy Boy Crosley" that we used for many years, so we no longer used the battery set we had before that with headphones.

Kampsville, where tourists came for weekends, had many

beautiful sights like the "locks" and the "flat rocks." We would go out wading in the water very shallow, clear and cool, running over the flat rocks. When the river rose, part of the town was under water and the men would put up boardwalks. The water never came up as far as our house, but I can remember the spooky feeling walking on the boardwalks over the flood waters trying to get to Overjohn's grocery or to Draper's who had a dry goods store with a little restaurant where I'd order up a little ice cream cone which I always bought whenever my parents made ice-cream as I didn't care for the home-made kind, because at Drapers, they would fill the cone with ice cream and then dip it in candy stars–which they didn't do at home. What a treat!

There also was a store named Benninger's. We would stop there on our way back to school and buy a penny's worth of blackies, whities, brownies, or banana chews. We always had a few cents, because we would write Daddy a note at school and give it to him at noon, asking for a penny for the afternoon. All that candy led to some visits to the dentist who came up from St. Louis two or three times a week. He was Dr. Sweeney, and he made the amazing discovery that I had two sets of permanent teeth come in (just in front). I found out much later my teeth were just like my cousins Cecilia and Loretta Day who also had two sets of teeth come in just in front. I always claimed Dr. Sweeney pulled the wrong set, but he was far better than the old dentist we had there in Kampsville, because that old dentist, Dr. Holner, was alcoholic. We used to go visit Dr. Holner or rather the Tillisons, the people he boarded with, and I'd rock Dr. Holner's dog to sleep while Mom and Daddy played cards with the Tillisons or just visited. I always loved dogs and was always bringing a stray home.

Mom belonged to the Women's Club, a national organization, and when they'd meet at our house we kids would always laugh to hear them sing their opening song, "Illinois." Very funny hearing them singing, "By the river gently flowing, Illinois." The ladies played bridge and I knew from watching how to play bridge since I was seven years old, the way I learned pinochle from Daddy having his cronies in to play pinochle, and we'd be upstairs in our room, listening, and when they'd rap their knuckles down on the table while playing out a card, I always thought that's why they called it "P. Knuckle."

We also had good friends across the street by the name of Ruyles. Orland was my brother John's age. Eustacia was my age. Their mother and father always called them "brother" and "sister." So Orland and Eustacia called each other "brother" and "sister." Like my Daddy, Mr. Ruyle was a Star Route mail carrier who had to move to Carrollton, Illinois, but they would come over lots of weekends to visit us. All of seven miles. One night when they were there my whole mouth and face was so swollen so Daddy took me to old Doc Woltman whose office looked like Doc's in *Gunsmoke*, and he pounded on my teeth with a big nail and said, "It's her teeth." Next day Mom took me to the dentist and it was a boil inside my upper lip. The twins, Edna and Edwina Kamp, came over to see me next day and brought me a cupcake, but I wouldn't let them see me, because I thought I looked like a monkey.

A Protestant church was right across the street from us, and we used to cut across there to go to the store and one day a hen with little chicks chased me and I've been scared of chickens ever since, but not Protestants. They called us "cat lickers" and we called them "pot lickers." People don't do that now.

Another thing we did in May, on May Day, May 1, was to make May baskets and bring them to the porches of people we liked. People who we disliked would get a string tied to their May basket, and then when they opened the door to pick it up, one of the older boys would pull the string. They used to do this a lot to a Mrs. Skeel, another doctor's wife. Dr. Skeel was a good doctor, but was never sober, so no one went to him much.

We went fishing a lot, so we made our own poles. One day John and Jimmie were fishing and the town bully, Milo Pontero, began throwing rocks in the calm water. He wouldn't stop so Jimmie, who was about twelve, got up to stretch, and Milo thought Jimmie was coming after him, so he threw a rock at him, and hit him in the head and Doctor Woltman said if it'd been a quarter inch closer to his brain it would have killed him. Jimmie won a bike selling the paper, *The State Register*, and I can always remember trying to get on it and ride it, but I was too small. I was so small, and a year ahead of myself in school, and I made my First Communion at St. Anselm's when I was only five, because my brother John, who became a priest, took me to the pastor and told him I knew everything the six-year-olds knew. As a result, I graduated from high school when I was sixteen.

Another game we used to play in the yard was Mumbly Peg.

On midnight Christmas eve, we'd all be awakened and taken to Midnight Mass, but we couldn't look at our toys before we went or when we came back. We had to wait until morning. One Christmas eve I remember my sister, Norine, saying she wanted a manicure set and it was there the next morning. We thought Santa had gone by the window when she said it. One year we got "Bye-Lo-Babies" made by Grace Story Putnam who copied off her own three-day-old baby. There's a "Bye-Lo-Baby" in the museum at Springfield now. There weren't too many made. Ours got broken. We should have ordered new heads for them.

We used to play movie stars a lot. We cut out pictures of them and then made them up to pretend they were going to parties. As I mentioned, there was one movie theater in Kampsville and the first movies I saw were silent. The first sound movie I saw was *The Bridge of San Luis Rey*, after my brother John came back from Jacksonville when I was nine or ten and told us at Jacksonville they had talking movies and you could hear them breathe. Some years later, I got some horse hair from the tail of Tom Mix's movie-star horse when he was at the fair in Jacksonville. I just walked in and asked if I could clip some souvenir hair and they let me.

From my money I earned when I was fourteen selling hosiery, I also spent 75 cents and took a ride by myself with a pilot in a little plane called "Big Ben." My brothers told me not to go because it might crash. It wasn't much of a thrill, and I was so disappointed, but it was nice to be the first one we knew to take off in Jacksonville and fly twenty miles to circle the view down all over Kampsville, Carrollton, and Eldred to see where I came from.

Before a storm, I can remember we used to always run like crazy around the house. Mom burned palm from Palm Sunday to make the storm stop. She'd stand outside the door on the porch lighting the braided palm and sticking her arm out into the rain, shaking off the ash, which made us all feel better. The yard seemed so big then, and decorated beautifully with Daddy's big, blooming, red cannas, but when I went back in 1968, the yard seemed so small.

On occasion I would go over and spend the day with my Aunt Mag and help her churn butter.

* * * *

This is amusing to say, as I just had the chance to visit my old home September 6 and 7, 1980. It's now on the map. Really! There is an article from the *Wall Street Journal* this very week reporting all the archaeological digging that started in Kampsville a few years back. I noticed in our Peoria paper a Kampsville trip sponsored by Lakeview Museum in conjunction with the museum's exhibitions, "The Rise of Life at Koster." Until recently, Koster was a cornfield I once played in, and now it's the oldest site of civilization in America, dating back centuries before Christ to 9500 B.C. The trip included a tour of the Ansell Site, which was on my Daddy's old rural mail route. The archeology laboratories are located in the old post office that my Daddy worked out of and in which my cousin, Cecilia Stelbrink, worked as postmistress, I think, for thirty-six years.

I went down Friday at 5:45, September 6, with a group from Lakeview. We crossed the Illinois River by ferry that Friday night, and crossed over to Kampsville from Greene County. Many on the tour had never ridden a ferry before. Now it's operated free, but when I lived there in the 1920s, it cost 50 cents each way and took so long. For the ten minutes it now takes we all got out of the vans and stood in the ferry. There was a huge barge coming down the river, the longest one I ever saw. We were standing so close to the gate of the ferry that water splashed up on us. I left the tour and stayed all night with my cousin, Cecilia. We sat up and talked until 2 A.M. We got up at 6 so we could eat breakfast and go visit the new Catholic Church which was built in 1978. The Church I had attended was 100 years old that year. They have a history book of the Church and the town.

We walked all around town, past my old house, which still looks lovely, although the current owners have knocked out the ceiling of the two rooms, the living room and bedroom, and made a cathedral ceiling and a huge fireplace. Cecilia said an "Arkie" lives there. I asked her who were the "Arkies." I thought maybe the word she was saying meant they were people from Arkansas, but the archaeologists are known as the "Arkies." We went by Cecilia's old house, and Kamp's old grocery store which is now a closed-down clothing store. Kampsville has only one grocery store now and used to have four at least. We walked by my Daddy's old garden lots. The house built on them by my doomed cousin, Loretta Day, and her dentist-husband, Phil Ritter, is still there, and the new bank and new post office are next to them.

That early morning was quite foggy. I didn't remember all that fog when I was little, but guess I was used to it. Our tour started at 8:30, so Cecilia brought me to the Kampsville Inn, where I met the rest of the tour who had stayed overnight at the Inn or dorms the Arkies own and operate. Cecilia and I met for lunch and several from the tour ate with us. All this is being done by Northwestern University, and Kampsville is the oldest spot in the United States where they are digging for these artifacts of the Havana Hopewell Indians in six mounds where they've found 150 skeletons and pearls from the Illinois River, and figurines of men and women and ravens with pearl eyes, and pipes, and arrowheads like we used to find just accidentally walking around.

Also, I remember from the 1920s up as late as the 1940s and 1950s, people used to open Indian mounds as a roadside attraction where for five cents you could go in for the educational experience of seeing broken pottery and skeletons of whole families lying on display in the dust where they found them. People can't do that anymore either. All this archeology started because some man—I think named Gregory Perino—came by Pearl, Illinois, where Perrin Ledge is, and he saw all these old Indian mounds and burial grounds and decided to start digging in Kampsville and thereabouts in Eldred. There is a legend that a man named Gerald Perrin jumped from that ledge, and so this rock got its name. There's a big blue house and the ledge is behind it, and why Gerald Perrin jumped, my Daddy joked, nobody could ask him.

On Saturday morning, we all went to the lab site where the Arkies showed slides about how they found and packaged everything they found and sifted. They explained how they dug everything up. We were also supposed to go to the Audrey Site back across the river, but it was too wet. They had the site we went to all covered with tarps as they'd had heavy rains the night before we arrived, as well as the morning of the day we arrived.

After lunch we went back to the labs, to other rooms, where we were shown a flint-napping demonstration. The Arkie showed us how the Indians made their arrowheads. We used to find them in the woods when I was a little girl and sell them to the local doctor. The Arkie demonstrated how to make an arrowhead and he gave it to me and let me keep it. Everyone on the tour thought it was so neat that I was born there and lived there the first eleven years of my life, and I'm the same person now I was then, though not eleven, and more progressive than some in Kampsville were back then when boys (not my brothers) would throw rocks at any blacks—who worked on the boats delivering goods—if they tried to get off the boats and come into town. Awful.

All of us on the tour later went to what they had turned into a museum, but to me was still the old local butcher shop where I remember always being given a weiner by the butcher, Polly Rice. I remember going down there on afternoons in the summer and getting cold Nehi soda, especially grape, orange, and strawberry. The lady who was in charge of the museum was named Marguerite Becker. Her maiden name was Schumann, and she and her family had lived on my Daddy's mail route. She said how much respect they all had for our family and for Daddy as a mail carrier and for Mom who was so sweet.

One of the archaeologists who was with us most of the time was Lisanne Traxler, and she said if I ever write a book about Kampsville, she wants a copy of it. The Arkies have forty-two sites in the Kampsville area where they are digging. Students from different schools come in and help them in the summer.

The last place we visited was behind the museums which was the backyard of the old doctor's house. The Arkies had built many little primitive huts like the people built in that era before we all came along. In fact, the Arkies were demonstrating building one of the huts out of cattails and mud.

At the end, we all walked back to Kampsville Inn and got in our cars, crossed the ferry, and headed back to Peoria. We stopped at Jacksonville to get gas, almost 45 miles from Kampsville. In Jacksonville, I spent my next 10 years, from eleven to twenty-one (April 1941), and was married there and gave birth to Jack at Our Saviour's Hospital in 1939. Then we stopped in Virginia to eat dinner—a marvelous restaurant for a small town—that attracted people from all around, the way my brother Jimmie's "Day's Café" in Carrollton attracted people from all over in the 1950s. While we were in the restaurant, a terrible rain storm, with wind that turned into the usual tornado came up. The lights went out three times and rain was gushing down the plate-glass windows. It was like someone was sloshing buckets of water on them. We needed my Mom throwing burning palm out into the storm. By the time we finished eating and went to our van to resume our trip back to Peoria, the storm was all over but for the usual destruction for southern Illinois. We drove past uprooted trees, branches, and debris across the highway. The cornfields leveled. We arrived in Peoria safe and sound after a most interesting and enlightening weekend about 10 P.M.

Going to many of the sites in Kampsville brought back many memories. The new people in Kampsville have fairly much buried most of the old ways the people I knew lived with, like we're one of the old tribes that once lived on the site. They've graded most of the hills now, and filled in the creek, and paved the roads, and named the streets. I remember those hills. When I was small, we used to go uphill to Hamburg to visit my Grandma Day and uncles and aunts and cousins. We'd push with our hands and feet on the back of the front seat as Daddy went up the hills, because cars were new to everybody and we thought pushing on the seat was helping the old Model T to climb.

Our main entertainment was going to visit relatives or them coming to see us. Two of my daddy's brothers married sisters [John Day married Addie and Joseph Day married Ella] and their children always let us know they were a dozen times more related to each other than to us. They never started school till 5th grade, because both their mothers were schoolteachers and taught them at home. They called their parents "The Folks," and when they'd come over unexpectedly some Sunday afternoon, they'd tell us kids that "The Folks" were planning on staying for supper, so we'd tell Mom and she'd have us run down to the store and get some choice cold cuts, etc. as we had eaten our big dinner of roast, or chicken, at noon, and, needless to say, after feeding seven, there wasn't enough left for four more, no matter how many dozen times they were related to each other.

My uncle John Day, who also lived in Hamburg was the judge of Calhoun County. They both, Uncle John and Uncle Joe, ran huge apple orchards. Uncle John's son, John W. Day, is now a judge in Granite City, Illinois. Uncle John's daughter, my cousin, the doomed Loretta Day, used to come and stay a week at a time with us, so that her fiancee Phil, the dentist, could visit her at our house. Loretta had a signal set up with my Mom to call down at a certain time when Loretta wanted Phil to leave at night. Loretta married Phil, but she died of pneumonia when she was seven months pregnant. What's sadder than a dead bride? Later, Raymond Draper accidentally ran Phil over, and Phil had to have a metal plate put in his head.

On occasional weekends we'd also drive over to Carrollton, Illinois, to visit the Ruyles I mentioned earlier, the family with the brother and sister, Orland and Eustacia, who moved from Kampsville to Carrollton, and they'd also come visit us. Eustacia, "Sister," and I when we were quite young decided to mow the lawn. Eustacia was smart enough to push at the handle. Dumb tomboy me pushed at the blades, and a little cut finger taught me a lesson about where to push.

Those weekends we had to drive back to Kampsville by Monday so Daddy got back for his mail route and us kids for school and my Mom for the housework. When Daddy would get home early in nice weather after dinner, which we ate at noon, we'd all go in, all five of us kids, and lie down with him on the floor with all our heads on one pillow, and Mom said it looked like the spokes of a wagon wheel. It was very hot and no such thing as even a fan on those days, and we couldn't go out and play right after noon, so we got to lay around with Daddy, until Daddy would go to the post office about 2 P.M. and put up the mail for the next day.

When I was eleven years old in 1930, my parents decided to move to Jacksonville as my brother John was already going to school there at Routt High School and College, and my brother Jimmie was ready for his senior year. Kampsville had only a three-year high school. My Mom and Daddy thought it'd be cheaper to move there than send all five kids away, because my older sister, Norine, was ready to start high school. Daddy transferred up there to that post office, but his transfer didn't go through right away, so he stayed in Kampsville that whole summer and I stayed with him while the whole rest of the family moved on to Jacksonville.

He and I used an upstairs room in the house we had owned, but just sold. We ate our meals out at my Aunt Mag's—except breakfast. Everyday Daddy gave me Post Toasties for breakfast. To this day I can't eat a Post Toastie. I used to kid him about it when I got older, but he denied giving them to me every morning. We always made quite a joke of it. I loved staying with him. I got to spend time with my friends, the Kamp twins, every day, and got lots of individual attention from my Daddy and Aunt Mag and cousin, Cecilia. That summer I used to help my Aunt Mag churn butter. She loved to have me help her as her arms would get tired, and I felt so big doing it. I always had my little purse full of spending coins that she and Daddy would give me. In afternoons the twins and I would take walks and go to the local drug store and sundries shop and have a Coke.

Daddy and I would drive home to Jacksonville every weekend in his little Model T open-touring Ford truck. We'd bring lots of vegetables and fruit from Daddy's lots with us. In the fall, Daddy's transfer was final, so before I started back to school, at a new school in Jacksonville, he started back to work in the Jacksonville post office.

Halloween is coming up soon now and it makes me think of the Halloweens back in Kampsville. The morning after Halloween, outhouses were all pushed over, some, or at least one, I remember, was put up on a telephone pole on the main street across from the Kamp's store. When my sister and I had to go to the outhouse on Halloween, my brothers would sneak out and bang on the walls and make us think we were going to be tipped over. We were allowed out with our real carved pumpkin jack-o-lanterns that we made and put a candle in, and we would walk up and hold them in people's windows for them to see after we knocked at their door. There was no such thing as trick or treat. Just tricks! And my older brothers weren't allowed out after they outgrew the jack-o-lantern trip, as there was too much vandalism or maybe just devilment, and the local constable, whose name was Bennett, would make a few arrests if he found any culprits, and my Mom and Daddy didn't want our family blamed.

We had another friend we visited frequently in Hamburg. Her name was "Mag Kelly," a very dear old friend of my mother, and we always called her "Aunt Mag" even though she wasn't a relative like our real Aunt Mag who lived in Kampsville, and was the only aunt we had by blood. In this very big interesting house, filled with beautiful antiques, lived Aunt Mag Kelly with her sister, Annie—and Annie's husband, Tom—and her sister "Doty" Kelly who was a little slow, as well as her sister Kate Kelly who lived there occasionally, but worked in Staunton, Illinois, and in later days finally moved in full-time with Aunt Mag Kelly. Kate Kelly always told us Santa Claus lived in Staunton, and we believed her. None of those Kelly sisters had ever married, except for Annie who married Tom.

When we'd go over for supper at Aunt Mag Kelly's on Sunday, she'd send us on a wonderful little errand. We'd cross the road, go up a steep hill, and to the Spring House, which was a big wooden box built over where ice-cold water seeped slowly out of the ground. That's where Aunt Mag Kelly kept her butter, cream, etc. The spring itself and the Spring House were delightful. I don't know what happened to Aunt Mag Kelly's house or furnishings after they all died, but the antiques she had in there would be worth a fortune. I always remember the big picture she had in the living room of horses running in a storm. It always intrigued me. Aunt Mag Kelly lived, I'm sure, until after my older son, Jack, was about three in 1942, when my younger son, Bob, was born. I guess none of them at Aunt Mag Kelly's had a will and she was last to go, and everything just vanished, probably still floating around in flea markets. Nobody I knew seemed to know.

There was also a man and lady we visited named Frank and

Maude Rohl. Frank was also a mail carrier. They had no children, but I always remember they had a lawn swing we'd always swing in when we visited them. They had a beautiful back yard, grape arbor and all. I don't believe the Rohls were related to us. If they were, it was way back, and they could have been, because we had Irish relations, and shirt-tail relations, around St. Louis back since about 1849 when my granduncle [John Day] first arrived from Ireland, which was about the same time when my maternal grandparents' parents—both sets [Lawlers and McDonoughs]—came from Ireland themselves. Cecilia knew about the Rohls, but I lost track.

In Kampsville, the cemetery was up on the hill with a long, winding road going to it and we always went sleigh-riding down the cemetery road every winter, which my little brother, Harold, said was convenient if we insisted on killing ourselves. I remember one winter when it snowed real deep and then sleeted, and our back yard turned to a sheet of ice. That one night while Mom and Daddy were reading in our dining room, we snuck out and played sleigh-ride right on top of the crust of snow. There was a creek right behind us and when it'd freeze over, the boys would ice skate on it. We had little 4-runner skates and we girls would skate on it too.

When it rained, winter or summer, that little creek would rise up in a raging current almost to our back fence and we'd throw our tin cans in and watch them float away. Daddy always warned us away from water of any kind. He said drowning ran in our family, but I don't know of any relative who drowned except his mother's father, Jack Lynch, who was a sailor. So I guess he was trying to scare us into being safe. Actually, Daddy himself nearly drowned when his Model T was swept away full of mail.

On the river at Kampsville, we also had "locks" that raised and lowered the water level for boats. The locks were very beautiful with lovely landscaping around them where there were three or four homes where the locks-keeper and some of the other employees lived. I went down there to a party at one of the homes one Saturday. We'd all often go there for picnics and fishing. Mr.

Nordbusch, who ran the locks, kept his family there. He had two boys and the older one, Norbert Nordbusch, was very, very stuffy. When my oldest brother, John, came home from Routt High School in Jacksonville, that stuffy boy Norbert strutted out to meet him and said, "Well, Johnny, did you 'paaass' in everything." It was always a rather standing joke we made on each other. "Did you 'paaass' in everything?" In the church history book the present priest interviews Mrs. Nordbusch who is now in her 90th year. The Nordbusch's finally moved to Peoria for Mr. Nordbusch to take care of the locks during the War in the 1940s.

I don't want to forget one of the highlights of my first eleven years was shaking hands with Governor Len Small, then the governor of Illinois. We were attending a centennial in Hardin and I walked right up to the Governor and shook his hand. Speaking of Hardin, they had a bad cyclone there when I was about nine, and we went down to view the destruction. A piano was hurled out of a home and hanging on an electric wire. I always seemed to be involved in weather—like dust storms so thick coming home from school that in those years we started washing our hair every day.

We had chatauquas with vaudeville acts and concerts and speeches in Kampsville. One time a ventriloquist came to town and his little dummy kept mentioning names of people in the town, and we couldn't figure out how he knew them all, and made such a joke. The chatauquas were held in a big tent set up in the vacant lots across from my Aunt Mag's [Day-Stelbrink] house.

What is the Kampsville Inn now where some of our party stayed in 1980 (used to be a hotel as I mentioned before), but one side of it was a grocery store owned by people the name of Hartman and their daughter, Theresa, who for some reason was crazy about bridge tally score cards and I'd always sell her all the cards I collected from the tables of ladies after Mom had one of Kampsville's famous continuing bridge parties at our house, or went to one and brought me the cards. Theresa paid me from two to five cents each and I used the money for fun. I assume Theresa could have purchased the tally cards herself somewhere in town. Her parents' grocery store could have carried them, but I was delighted she wanted mine. She was in my class at school, and she always had money and candy from the store.

I also had a classmate named Harold Kamp, cousin to the twins, whose father was killed and he was the only boy, and his mother had quite a time with him, as he used to eat pencil shavings and drink ink to show off at school. I believe Cecilia said he's still living. Must have been permanent ink. Of course, I thought eating pencil shavings and drinking ink would kill him, because my brother John told me he was going to call the undertaker when I told him I swallowed tooth paste while brushing my teeth one night and asked him if it'd hurt me.

I think this pretty much sums up my first eleven years I spent in Kampsville, My cousin, Cecilia did tell me, as I mentioned earlier, that when I was down there this September that she and my cousin Loretta Day had two sets of teeth, as I had. Cecilia said when she was little, she was afraid to go to the dentist and her mother shamed her and said, "Virginia Claire Day went alone." She told her mother then she'd go, but wouldn't let the dentist do anything. So I guess she went through life with two sets of permanent of teeth, whatever that means. We grew up with lots of folklore, like believing if you wore rubber galoshes or boots in the house or school, you'd get sore eyes. I guess they told us that so we'd take them off when we came indoors. Back then people told a lot of stories with lessons attached, like my Daddy's drowning story.

I enjoyed my first eleven years at Kampsville, growing up in a real small, woodsy town.

Cecilia called after I got back and said that "Kermie" who's still alive, said he was sorry he missed seeing me.

Christmas Eve 2000. Virginia bakes her pie for her son Jack.
Photo by Mark Hemry

EAT THIS HISTORY

When Virginia Day married George Fritscher in 1938, she was already making this pudding which was the filling for her famous banana cream and coconut cream pies with four-to-five-inch meringue. Her mother, who baked daily when she had a family, made a lemon pie and a coconut cream pie every Friday. "I learned this recipe from my mom, probably back in the late 1920s," Virginia said at Christmas 2000. "The corn starch pudding is good by itself. With bananas stirred in at the last, or with coconut stirred in, the pudding makes a delicious pie. I've baked a million of these pies, and always baked them for Mom and Daddy and Father John when they came to Peoria, and for all my brothers' and sister's visits, and

George's family, and all our guests. It's the most requested dessert I've ever made. July 12 is my birthday as well as my parents' wedding anniversary, my wedding anniversary, and my son Jack's wedding anniversary. Celebrate with a batch of this sweet every July 12th!"

Virginia's Corn Starch Pudding

5-6 tablespoons of sugar (Can cut back to 3-4 tablespoons.)

1 heaping tablespoon corn starch (Be sure to measure in a tablespoon, and not a dessert spoon.) 1-3 eggs (Choose the number for the richness. One is plenty.) 2 cups of scalded skim or whole milk.

1. In first pan, mix sugar, corn starch, egg yolk(s) into pan large enough to hold four cups. Slowly add in 1/4 cup of cold milk, stirring till creamy so it won't get lumpy. Set aside.

2. In second pan, heat the remaining nearly 2 cups of milk till scalded (not quite to boiling).

3. Pour scalded milk from pan #1 into pan #2's creamy corn starch.

4. Add bananas or coconut (if you want) now.

5. Stir constantly over medium to low heat until mixture coats the spoon. Be careful not to scorch the pudding on the bottom of a pan that is too hot.

6. Fold in egg white(s) which can be whipped or not, and stir.

7. Pour from pan to bowl for pudding, cool, and eat.

8. Or, pour from pan into previously browned pie crust, which can then be topped with meringue peaks and baked in oven till meringue tips are golden.

—Virginia Day Fritscher
Christmas 2000

Top: George Magner, Robert Lonergan (Class President), Charles Magner (Valedictorian), Paul Bergschneider (Sec & Treas), Edward Cox – **Row 2**: Gloria Hanley, Luke Zeller, Margaret Cain, Lillian Mallen, John Lair, Howard Anderson – **Row 3**: Robert Ring, Margaret Ring, Lee McGinnis, Virginia Day, William Monahan, Agnes Mernin, John Kennedy, Raphael Behrens, Angela David – **Row 4**: George Fritscher, Leona Hermes, Jean Hoecker, Arthur Hull, Josephine Johnson, Francis Maloney, Bernadine Eckert, Josephine Sweeney, Rose Steer

George Fritscher and Virginia Day
March 22, 1936
Routt High School Graduation 1936

DIARY
Written by Virginia Claire Day [Fritscher]
July 12, 1933 to December 31, 1936
Age 14 to Age 17.5
Jacksonville, Illinois

This diary, in which a real, dramatic, human narrative unfolds, is a small leather-bound book, with gilt on the exposed edges of its pages, measuring 4 inches wide and 5.5 inches tall by .75 inches thick. The brown-leather cover is imprinted on the front cover with 16 small *fleur de lis* (six red, ten gray) surrounding a gray crest, under which is printed in gray: *Five-Year Diary*. Front and back covers are slightly padded between leather and board to give a soft, rounded, comfortable feel.

The diary is secured with a small leather strap, attached to the front cover, which is missing its end: a bronze metal clasp that fit into the small lock on the back cover. The lock has a tiny key hole and the key is long gone. The locking leather strap was torn and the key lost during the tumultuous time of the writing of this diary when competing boyfriends, who knew of the diary, struggled to read it, and sometimes tore out pages that for the most part were glued back into place.

Written with a refillable fountain pen in indelible ink, the handwriting is neat, legible, and sometimes features shorthand for privacy. Each white page, now creamy yellow with age, is printed with a day's date at the top (January 1 to December 31) and five entries for five years down the left side of each page. Each entry space for each year is three light-blue lines, fifteen to a page, with six red lines, each separating one year's entry from the next.

To read the *Five-Year Diary* chronologically means turning through it front to back five times as each page, like the page for December 25, for instance, has five sections allotted for five Christmases, 1933, 1934, 1935, 1936, 1937—although entries were made only from July 12, 1933 to December 31, 1936. The diary covers Virginia Claire Day's life: 1) immediately before meeting George Fritscher; 2) the meeting of George Fritscher when she was sixteen and he was nineteen; and 3) the first fourteen months of their courtship.

In every instance, the printed text is an exact replica of the handwritten original's abbreviations, spelling, and punctuation.

—Jack Fritscher

Handwritten inside the front cover:

**Age 14, Virginia C. Day, 217 Kentucky St.,
Jacksonville, Ill.
Given to me July 12th on my 14th birthday by
Grace Rogers, 515 S. Church St.,
Jacksonville, Illinois,
my best friend.**

1933
Age 14 This Day

July 12. Grace ate my 14th birthday dinner with me. I got this diary from her, and a birthday card. Went uptown in afternoon. Went down to State [Jacksonville State Hospital and School for the Blind and Deaf] to dance and play golf in evening [with teen patients who taught her American Sign Language and empathy].

July 13. Went to library and dentist in the morning with [younger brother] Harold. Went uptown in afternoon. Sold a pair socks in evening. [Her first job was selling hosiery and socks.] Took a walk with Grace and Paul in evening.

July 14. Dorothy set my hair in morning. Went uptown in afternoon and got all kinds of birthday presents. Sent off my hose order in evening, and Grace and I played with Charles [Ford].

July 15. Played with Charles in morning. Went uptown and got 3 Musketeers [candy bar] in afternoon. Went to Church [Our Saviour's Catholic Church]. Went shopping with Fords in evening. Mrs. Ford got new living room suite.

July 16. Got sick at 4:20 in morning. Sick all day. Grace and Catherine came in afternoon, but I was asleep. Went with Daddy in evening. Got my hose order. Stayed home rest of evening.

July 17. Went uptown with [oldest brother] John in morning, and I also delivered hose. Went to see *Oliver Twist* at Majestic in afternoon. Went with Daddy in evening. Had lots of fun.

July 18. Played with Charles in morning. Went uptown in afternoon with Grace and Charles. Saw Beulah Draper and Gertie and her husband. Went down to State [Hospital] in evening, rode merry-go-round 6 times. Teetered with Jimmie Templeton.

July 19. Went to Grace's in morning to sell hose. She bought a pair. Went to park for dinner. Watched them swim. Had lots of fun. Grace, Catherine, and I got candy and soda pop. Went with Daddy in evening.

July 20. Went uptown in morning. Got letter from Sister Ernestine. Played with Charles in afternoon. Went to Catherine's. She, Charles, and I got an ice cream cone. Made candy at Grace's in evening. Went uptown, got popcorn. Came home to her house. Made lemonade.

July 21. Played with Charles in morning. Went to Mayfield's in afternoon and sold 3 pair of hose. Went uptown and got some candy kisses. Went to Catherine's in evening. Went uptown to get some popcorn, and Pete Biggs and Billie Cannon wanted Grace and I to go riding.

July 22. Grace [who gave her the diary ten days before] is moving to Chicago. We went to Grace's house in the morning because they were moving. Went over there in afternoon and they left on 3:07 train. I got their dog Fluffy to keep till Monday. Came home. Went with Daddy in evening and got some candy.

July 23. Eustacia and Betty came up and Eustacia gave me a bracelet and a pair of anklets for my birthday. We ate dinner, played piano, played ball. Took a walk, and we all went on a picnic at the park. Came home, sat in car to sing.

July 24. Helped wash the car. Went to Catherine's house in afternoon for awhile. Erma Gotch, her husband and three children came from St. Louis. We took a ride, ate supper, went down to State Hospital and watched them skate. [Interaction at the Hospital was part of the social life in Jacksonville as people often went there to play miniature golf with the patients.]

July 25. Played with Charles in morning. Miss McGinnis came

down in afternoon and I got Charles. Took a little nap. Stayed home in evening. Got a letter from Audrey Gotch.

July 26. Went over to Catherine's in morning. Played with Charles. Went up to Mary Frances' house in afternoon and had lemonade and cake. Went over to Catherine's and made fudge in evening.

July 27. Went out and sold 4 pair hose in morning. Took Charles to get an ice-cream cone. Went over to Spreen's and ate supper there. Went down to State in evening and rode merry-go-round 4 times.

July 28. Played with Charles in morning. Catherine and I went uptown in afternoon. Came back and went to her house and her Aunt B set our hair. In the evening I went with Daddy to deliver.

July 29. Went uptown in morning with Catherine and Charles. Went by for Pooch. Charles, her, and I went uptown and got some candy. Gave Fluffy [the dog Grace left behind] away. Went with Dad in evening. Went to Church.

July 30. Went to dinner and Communion. Went with Daddy in afternoon to make city collections. In the evening I took a walk and then stayed home rest of evening. Had company.

July 31. In morning stayed home and read. In the afternoon I went uptown and got a darling new pair of rayon pajamas, also went to see Mrs. Ford. Catherine came over and we went with Daddy.

August 1. Went over to Fords. In afternoon, Stella Ford, Ruth Moore, Charles, and I went down to see Mrs. Ford. We went to Ferrys and got a chocolate fausfate [phosphate]. Went to carnival in evening at our Church.

August 2. Played with Charles in morning. In afternoon, Ruth, Louisa, Stella, and I went swimming at park. Went to stand and got a barbecue. Went with Fords in evening and got an Orange-Crush.

August 3. Played with Charles in morning. Went down to hospital and uptown with Stella and Charles and got some candy. Got a letter from Grace. Went with Daddy in evening.

August 4. Played with Charles and Stella. Went uptown in afternoon and got a soda, and a box of butter popcorn with Stella and Charles. In the evening I went to Fords for awhile. Stayed home rest of evening.

August 5. Went over to Catherine's for awhile in morning. Went uptown in afternoon with Harold. Sold 3 pair of hose. In the evening went to Church and went with Daddy.

August 6. Came down to Eustacia's to spend my vacation. Went to park in afternoon. Went to a party at Janet's house in evening. Played all kinds of games and had lots of fun.

August 7. Down at Eustacia's. Worked in morning. Went down to library and confectionery in afternoon. In evening we went to the show to see Slim Summerville and Zazu Pitts in *Her First Mate*.

August 8. Down at Eustacia's. Went to Kampsville with the mail. Saw twins [the Kamp twins after whose family Kampsville was named] and Aunt Mag [Margaret Day Stelbrink, her father's only sister and her only aunt by blood] and Cecilia [Stelbrink, cousin]. Came home to Eustacia's. Went to farmers' sale. Got some candy and popcorn. In evening took a ride in truck.

August 9. Down at Eustacia's. Came to Kampsville to stay all night with Aunt Mag. Ate dinner there. Played all afternoon with twins. Ate supper at twins. The twins and I took a walk and went up to the park.

August 10. Twins and I played croquet. Cecilia and I went to Mrs. Duksmeyer and the Germans. Ate a chicken dinner at Aunt Mag's. Went back to Carrollton with the mail. Came home in afternoon.

August 11. Worked in morning. Went uptown in afternoon and got some Cutex. Came home and Ruth manicured my fingernails. In the evening I stayed with Mrs. Ford while the Fords went riding.

August 12. Mowed the lawn in the morning. In the afternoon I went to the show to see *Arizona to Broadway* with Blanche. We got some candy. In the evening I went with Fords and got an ice-cream cone.

August 13. Went to Church and Communion in the morning. In the afternoon I went uptown and got some popcorn and ydnac [pig latin for candy]. In the evening I went down to the cottage grocery and got some ydnac.

August 14. In the afternoon I went over to Poochie's [Blanche Gilmore] and rode a bike. She came over and we made chocolate fudge. In the evening I went over to Pooch's in the evening and played on a wagon. [She had a mad crush on Pooch's brother, Gilly Gilmore.]

August 15. Stayed home in morning and afternoon, trying to sew up some play shorts. Pooch called me up and wanted to go down to State in evening. We went down and rode the merry-go-round.

August 16. Pooch and I and Jane Spreen and Pooch's little cousin went uptown and got some candy. Jane stayed all day at our house. In the evening I took her home. I got a Baby Ruth.

August 17. Played with Charles in morning. In the afternoon I went over to Pooch's and played all afternoon. We were going to go to the State, but Pooch couldn't go. Stayed home.

August 18. Played with Charles. Went over to Poochie's. In the afternoon stayed home, and rode Donald's bike all afternoon. In the evening, Marjorie and I rode the bike.

August 19. Played with Charles. In the afternoon, Pooch came over and we rode the bike all afternoon. I got a new orange shirt, too little. Pooch and I took it back. Stayed uptown a long time and got candy. Ate supper at Pooch's and got a Butterfinger.

August 20. Went to Church. Played with Charles. Pooch called me up. Pooch came over and we rode the bike and got some candy. In the evening I took a car ride. I made some fudge.

August 21. Pooch called me up. She came over in the afternoon. We went uptown and I got this fountain-pen [to write the diary] and some candy. We delivered some hose. In the evening we saw a horse buck a man.

August 22. In the morning, Pooch and I sold 7 pairs of hose. Eustacia came up. In the afternoon Eustacia and I went to see Bob Montgomery and Helen Hayes in *Another Language* at the Illinois Theater and got candy and popcorn. In the evening went down to State and got some more candy and rode merry-go-round about 5 times.

August 23. In the morning, Eustacia and I played jacks and went up to Kroger's and got some candy. Eustacia went home around noon. Rode the bike all afternoon and read the funnies. Rode the bike all evening.

August 24. I went over to Pooch's and we sold 3 pairs of hose in the morning. I ate dinner there. In the afternoon, we sold 6 pairs of hose. In the evening, I sent in a hose order and I fell down and cut my leg.

August 25. Pooch came over in the morning. In the afternoon Pooch, Harold [younger brother] and I went to the show. Harold paid my way. I got a new pair of two-toned tan oxfords at K Lines. I paid half. Stayed home in evening.

August 26. In morning Mr. Peters brought my hose order. Pooch and I delivered them in the afternoon. In the evening, I collected some of the money and Norine [older sister] and I went uptown and got some candy.

August 27. Went to Church and Communion. Didn't do much of anything in morning. Worked a little. In the afternoon I got a frozen whip. In the evening I took a walk with Harold and got some popcorn. Went to Spreen's.

August 28. Read Sunday papers in morning. In the afternoon went uptown and put some money in the bank for my hose order. In the evening I took a walk uptown with Catherine.

August 29. Catherine called me up in morning. In the afternoon, I delivered hose and sold one pair. In the evening I went down to the State [Hospital] and rode merry-go-round 2 times.

August 30. Blanche came over to stay all day. We played with Charles and went to the store 3 times. In the afternoon, we went to the girls' ball game at State. Rode Donald's bike and made fudge in evening.

August 31. In the morning Blanche and I sold some hose. We sold 6 pairs. In the afternoon I stayed home and rested. In the evening Harold and I went to the fair and bought all kinds of things. I won a sign.

September 1. Played with Charles in the morning. In the afternoon I went over to Neomi's house and we found Baby Ruth candy wrappers. Went over to State Hospital and rode merry-go-round twice in evening.

September 2. Played with Charles in the morning. In the afternoon I went uptown, and got a compass and some candy. In the evening Daddy, Mamma, Harold, Norine, and I went riding.

September 3. Went to Church and Communion. In the morning I took a walk. In the afternoon I helped Mamma get supper for Father Lawler and Father Ingram [Two priest friends of the family; Father Lawler was a cousin]. In the evening went to Fords.

September 4. In the morning Aunt Mag Kelly [not the same as Aunt Mag Day-Stelbrink; "Aunt Mag Kelly" was a friend of her mother, Mary Pearl] came up to spend a couple of days. In the afternoon I went to Poochie's. Sold Geneva a pair of hose in the evening.

September 5. Started to school. Registered in the morning. In the afternoon went uptown and looked for a dress and got some books. In the evening I stayed home.

September 6. Went to school all day. In the evening after school I got a new blouse and skirt. In the evening stayed home and studied and rode the bike.

September 7. Went to school. Got some candy at noon. Walked home from school until Wilma, Norine, and I went to nurse's graduation in evening at Church.

September 8. Went to school all day. Walked home with Wilma. In the evening Harold and I went down to the State Hospital and rode the merry-go-round with Susie Abbot.

September 9. In the morning I sold some hose. In the afternoon Wilma, Harold, and I went to the show, *Shanghai Madness* and saw "Blackstone the Magician" [live onstage]. Went to Pooch's in evening.

September 10. Went to Church and Communion. In the morning I made a cake. In the afternoon I went to see the air circus with John and Harold. In the evening we took a car ride.

September 11. Went to school as usual. John left for school [oldest brother off to Kenrick Seminary in St. Louis where he studied for the priesthood], Mamma, Harold and Jim Magner went too. In the evening I got some candy and sold hose. In the night I studied and Mary Rite came over and we made candy.

September 12. Went to school as usual. In the evening Mamma and Harold came home from St. Louis. In the evening I studied and went to the store.

September 13. Went to school. In the evening we went with Daddy. When we came home, we went riding in the rain in Willie's Buick. Came home and studied.

September 14. Went to school. Drew a map. In the evening we initiated the "Freshies" [at Routt High School] and how! In the night I studied.

September 15. Went to school. After school I played. In the evening I went over to Poochie's. Tommy Devlin came over and we rode his bike all evening.

September 16. In the morning I got a card from Eustacia. In the afternoon went down to Church. I got an ice-cream cone. In the evening we went with Daddy.

September 17. Went to Church and Communion. In the afternoon Eustacia came up. We went out to the park and all afternoon we watched them play "Rook" and swim. I got some candy.

September 18. Went to school. After school I got some candy and walked home with Eileen. In the evening I played with Doris Jean. After supper I rode Donald's bike and copied over my English.

September 19. Went to school as usual. In the evening I rode Donald's bike. In the night I studied my lessons. Gloria Hanley took me a piece home. [Colloquial for "walked me part way home." Gloria joined convent as nun 12-27-36.]

September 20. Went to school. After school Gloria Hanley and

I went to the show, *Pilgrimage*. In the evening I read the papers and studied my English and got it and my geometry.

September 21. Went to school again as usual. Walked home with Wilma. In the evening I went up to Gloria's and studied. We also went into the Public Library.

September 22. Went to school. Walked home part way with Wilma. After school I read the papers. In the evening I went with Daddy down to Gloria's and I made candy.

September 23. Went to the show in the afternoon. In the afternoon Mamma, Norine, and I went uptown. In the evening I sold a pair of hose.

September 24. Went to Church and Communion. In the afternoon I took a walk with Norine, and Dorothy and M. Clay. In the evening Harold and I went uptown and got some popcorn.

September 25. Went to school as usual. After school I got a big sack of candy and I rode Donald's bike. In the evening Gloria came down and we studied.

September 26. Went to school. After school I walked home with Loretta Longergrin. In the evening I read the funnies and got my lessons. Then I went to bed.

September 27. Went to school as usual. After school we had Glee Club. In the evening Mother, Harold, and I went up to the style show and got some candy.

September 28. Went to school. After school Gloria and I translated our Latin. In the night we went to the football game. Routt [where soon George Fritscher, winning an athletic scholarship, will become a student whom she will meet and marry] vs. Quincy. We won 28-0. We got some candy bars.

September 29. Went to school as usual. Gloria took me a piece home. We had Glee Club. In the evening Gloria came down and we made fudge and played cards.

September 30. Went uptown with Pooch. It rained and I ate supper with Pooch. After supper I delivered some hose and went uptown and got some candy.

October 1. Went down to Kampsville [where she was born] and Hamburg [where her father was born and his relatives lived]. Ate dinner and supper with Aunt Mag Kelly. Saw the twins and Aunt Mag Stelbrink, Celia, and everybody.

October 2. (Mom's 45th birthday) Went to school as usual. In the evening I went down to Gloria's house and studied and played cards. The ladies surprised Mamma.

October 3. Went to school. Went over to Poochie's after school. In the evening I bought some marshmallows and we roasted them. I sold a pair of hose.

October 4. Got a free day on account of Father Formaz's feast day, Gloria, Loretta, Charlie, and I went to the show to see *Doctor Bull* with Will Rogers.

October 5. Went to school. After school I played with Charles. In the evening I got my lessons, and read the papers.

October 6. Went to school. After school we had Glee Club. I got a tea-pot for Mamma's birthday. In the night I read my book, *Her Father's Daughter*.

October 7. Played with Charles. In the afternoon Pooch and I went uptown and got some candy. In the evening Billie Cannon, Wilma, and I went riding in the Austin.

October 8. Went to Church and Communion. In the afternoon, I studied and went to the show, *Penthouse*, with Wilma. In the evening, I went to Church.

October 9. Went to school as usual. After school, we had Glee Club. In the evening, I studied my lesson for Latin exam.

October 10. Had Latin exam at school. I got B-. Gloria took me a piece home after school. I went to Church for 40-Hours Devotion in the evening.

October 11. Went to school as usual. Didn't have any exams. Routt "Sophs" had their weiner roast. Had lots of fun. Came home and studied.

October 12. Went to school. I studied for exams. Had History and Geometry exam. Got 96 in History and 100 in Latin. Studied for English exam in evening. Got my new dress for homecoming game and dance.

October 13. Had English exam. I went to the game and dance with Gloria and Agnes. We won 13-0. Had good time at dance.

October 14. Played with Charles. Made some candy for John in the afternoon. Played with Charles. In the evening Mamma, Harold, and I went uptown and to Church.

October 15. Went to Church and Communion. Went to see John at St. Louis. Ate dinner at Webster Groves. In the afternoon went to Dolphy's and rode all over Carondelet Park in St. Louis. [She was visiting May McNulty whose sister had married into the Dolphy family. The sister's son died suddenly and they received a telegram, "My darling son King was drowned today."]

October 16. Went to school as usual. After school had Glee Club. In the night, Wilma came up and we played cards and had lots of fun.

October 17. (Daddy's 46th birthday.) Went to school. Played with Charles after school. In the evening stayed home and studied, played cards and etc.

October 18. Went to school. After school had Glee Club. Then we went to the park on a weiner roast. Mamma, Harold, Jimmie [older brother, second child] and I went to the show to see *Smilin' Thru*.

October 19. Went to school. After school I got my new sweater at Montgomery & Ward. In the evening I studied and Harold and I played checkers.

October 20. Went to school. Wore my new sweater. After school played with Charles. In the evening we played bridge. Had fun.

October 22. Went to Church and Communion. Wilma, Pooch, and I went out walking in the afternoon. In the nite Spreens came over. We played.

October 23. Went to school. After school had Glee Club. I got a carmeled apple. In the evening I got my lesson and we played bridge.

October 24. Went to school. After school I got a new tam [hat]. After supper Dorothy came over and we got our lessons. Dorothy stayed all nite.

October 25. Went to school. After school had Glee Club. We are going to have an operetta and I was appointed as "Bridget." In the evening I studied and got some candy.

October 26. Went to school. After school played with Charles. After supper I studied my lessons. We had a Latin test this morn.

October 27. Went to school as usual. After school I stayed home. We got out early on account of them moving the seats. Went to football game with Wilma and Catherine. Routt vs. Normal, we won 19-12.

October 28. Sold hose in the morning down at Gloria's. In the afternoon Mamma and I went uptown. In the evening I got some candy. I went down to Wilma's and played cards.

October 29. Went to Church and Communion. In the morning I played ball. In the afternoon Catherine and I went to the show, *Too Much Harmony*. It was swell.

October 30. Went to school as usual. After school we had Glee Club. After Glee Club played with Charles. In the night Roberta, Catherine, and I went Halloweening.

October 31. Went to school. After school I fooled around. After supper went down to "Halloween party" at Routt given by *Wag* staff [the *Wag* was the Routt High School paper]. Carl Rief brought me home.

November 1. Didn't have school. Fooled around home in morning. Went down and saw a little dog in the afternoon and took a walk with Mrs. Ford and Charles.

November 2. Went to school again. After school played with Charles. After supper Gloria and I went to the library and tried to get our English.

November 3. Went to school. After school we hung around school and played. After supper we (Gloria and I) went to the football game. We beat St. Theresa, 19-0.

November 4. After I finished working around, I went down to Gloria's. Went uptown in afternoon. Harold and I got lots of candy. Eustacia and I and the rest went uptown in the night. I saw Carl.

November 5. Went to Church and Communion. After Church I got my lessons. After dinner Catherine called me up to come over and we went walking uptown.

November 6. Went to school as usual. After school we had Glee

Club and practiced Act 1 of our operetta, *Miss Cauther's Return*. After supper Cat [Catherine] and I went down to the store.

November 7. Went to school. After school I played with Charles. After supper I got my lessons. Then I played bridge.

November 8. Went to school. After school we had Glee Club. After supper I got my lessons and fooled around awhile.

November 9. Went to school. After school I played with Charles. After supper I got my lessons and then we played bridge.

November 10. Went to school. After school Gloria and I walked around town. In the evening went down to Gloria's to play bridge with them.

November 11. Went down to school to practice for the play. After that Gloria and I went uptown and down to Church. Sat. eve I went uptown.

November 12. Went to Church and Communion. In the afternoon Catherine and I went walking. Then we made fudge. Gloria came down and we took her a piece in the dust storm with all the lights out and real windy and Daddy lost his hat.

November 13. Went to school. After school we had Glee Club. After supper I studied until about 10: o'clock. Then talked awhile and went to bed.

November 14. Went to school. After school Gloria and I took a walk uptown. I went down there after supper. We studied and made fudge and Gloria wanted me to stay all night.

November 15. Went to school. After school we had Glee Club. After supper I got my lessons and wrote in this and I played bridge with Mary.

November 16. Went to school. After school I played with

Charles. After supper I studied. And by now I forgot what else I did (November 21)

November 17. Went to school. After school we went down to Carrollton to Eustacia's birthday party (supper). After supper we took a walk and also a ride.

November 18. We went down to practice our operetta. Gloria and I went uptown afterwards. After supper stayed home and fooled around.

November 19. In the afternoon Loretta Lonergan, Gloria [Hanley], Jean [Hoecker], and I went walking. Gloria came down after supper and we took her home in Willie's car.

November 20. Went to school as usual. After school I delivered some operetta posters. After supper I got my lessons and read the funnies.

November 21. Went to school. After school played with Harold. After supper I read the papers, wrote in this and last but not least got my lessons.

November 22. Went to school as usual. After supper we practiced for our operetta. After practice we (Gloria, Angela, May) went down to Ferry's and got a Coke.

November 23. Went to school. Had 6-weeks exams in English and Geometry. After supper Catherine came over and we played the piano.

November 24. (No school). Friday morning we practiced for operetta. Ate dinner with Gloria. After dinner went to football game, Routt vs. I.S.D. We beat 18-7. Hurrah!

November 25. Went down to Gloria's to get my costume. Had my shoes fixed. Ate chili supper with Gloria. Stayed all night. Jean, Angela also. Went uptown after supper.

November 26. Gloria, Jean, Angela, and I went to Church. I stayed and ate dinner with Gloria. After dinner she came down. Jessie set my hair.

November 27. Went to school. After school gave our operetta, *Miss Cauther's Return*, for the "Irish." After supper I got my lessons.

November 28. Went to school. After supper we practiced. Bergsneider kid brought me home. After supper I studied my lessons.

November 29. Went to school. After supper we put on our operetta. I had to sing by myself, "New York Is Run by the Irish." Put it on in Routt auditorium.

November 30. (Thanksgiving) Fooled around in morning. In the afternoon Gloria, Angela, and I took a walk. After supper I stayed home and played some bridge.

December 1. In the afternoon Gloria, Angela, and I went to the show to see *Sweetheart of Sigma Chi*. After supper stayed home, played bridge.

December 2. Went down to Gloria's. Harold and I got a "Snow Ball." We went uptown and looked around. After supper I stayed home and made fudge.

December 3. Went to Church and Communion. After dinner Gloria came down. Mrs. H. [Hanley] and us went riding out to Chapin. I ate supper with Gloria.

December 4. Went to school as usual. After school we had Glee Club. After supper Gloria came down and we got our lessons.

December 5. Went to school. After school Gloria and I went uptown. After supper I went down to Gloria's and we studied.

December 6. Went to school. I went up to Gloria's and we went to Angela's.

December 7. Went to school. After school we went down to Wally's station and uptown. Angela, Gloria, and her aunt came down.

December 8. Went to Church. Went uptown. Gloria and I went to library, and uptown. After supper I stayed home and read.

December 9. Fooled around in morning. In the afternoon Gloria and I went uptown. After supper went with Fords.

December 10. Went to Church. Mary P. came down and spent the day. In the afternoon we went out to her house. I stayed at Gloria's all nite.

December 11. Went to school. After supper I stayed home and studied. After school we had Glee Club.

December 12. Went to school. After school I went to Gloria's. After supper I went to the show at the State with Catherine to see *Professional Sweetheart*.

December 13. Went to school as usual. After school we had Glee Club. After supper I went down to Gloria's and studied.

December 14. Went to school. After school Gloria and I went uptown. After supper Gloria and I, and Norine went to the library.

December 15. Went to school as usual. After supper I went down to Gloria's with Harold, and we walked home with Catherine.

December 16. Played with Charles. After dinner I went uptown with Mamma and Norine. After supper I went to basketball game, Routt vs. I.S.D. We beat!

December 17. Went uptown and to Church. After dinner I went down to Gloria's and we studied. After supper I studied and went up to the P.O.

December 18. Went to school. We had our Glee Club party in the night. I had a date with Carl Reif. We also went on a scavenger hunt.

December 19. Went to school. After school I fooled around. After supper Catherine wanted me to go to the show, but I stayed home and studied.

December 20. Went to school. After school I had Glee Club and John came home [from the seminary] for Xmas. After supper Gloria came down and we studied.

December 21. Went to school again as usual. After supper, the Glee Club went out Xmas caroling at the Sisters' house [the convent] and other places.

December 22. Went to school. After supper Gloria and I went to the football game, Routt vs. Quincy. We got beat both games. Too bad!

December 23. Mamma, Norine, and I went uptown and looked for a dress for me. In the evening Harold and I went down to Gloria's.

December 24. Christmas eve. Went to Church. After dinner I went up to Gloria's. We took the car out by ourselves and went riding. Went to bed early.

December 25. Christmas. Got up at 3:15 A.M. and went to 5:00 o'clock Mass at Carrollton. John was sub-deacon [on the altar at the Mass]. I went up to Gloria's and Harold, her, and I went to the show, *Alice in Wonderland*.

December 26. Fooled around in morning. In the afternoon Mother and I went to a party at Gloria's. After supper stayed home and fooled around.

December 27. Stayed home in morning. In the afternoon

Harold and I went to the show, Zasu Pitts and Will Rogers in *Mr. Skitch*. In the evening I played checkers.

December 28. In the afternoon I went down to Gloria's. Gloria and I went to the Yuletide dance at the State Hospital. Gloria stayed all night with me.

December 29. Gloria stayed down for dinner. After dinner we went up to her house and then we went uptown. After supper I stayed home.

December 30. Fooled around with Charlie in morning. After dinner Mother and I went uptown. After supper we fooled around at home.

December 31. Went to Church. After Church I played with Charles. After dinner I went down to Gloria's house. After supper I listened to the radio.

End of "good old '33'" Ha! Ha! Virginia C. Day

1934

Age 14, will turn 15 on 12 July 1934

January 1. Went to Church. Went down to Ruyle's at Carrollton to spend the day. In the afternoon we took a walk. Came home, ate supper and read.

January 2. Fooled around in morning. Had my shoes fixed. Played with Charles in morning and afternoon. After supper I went to the housewarming at W. school.

January 3. Started to school next day. After school we had Glee Club. After supper I stayed home and studied and played cards.

January 4. Went to school next day. After school went over and played with Charles. After supper I got my lessons and went to bed.

January 5. Went to school. After school fooled around. After supper went to basketball game. Routt vs. Spaulding. We lost.

January 6. Went over to Poochie's in afternoon. In morning Poochie came over. John left. He went back to school [the seminary]. Went uptown in evening.

January 7. Went to Church and Communion. After dinner Gloria and Angela came down. We played cards and went to show in night, *Midshipman Jack*.

January 8. Went to school. After school we had Glee Club. Went to see Charles after school. After supper I studied.

January 9. Went to school as usual. After school I went to the show with Margaret Cain and saw *Little Women*. Studied at night.

January 10. Went to school again. After school we had Glee Club. I wanted Gloria to stay all nite but she couldn't. Dorothy came over.

January 11. Went to school. After school I went over at Charlie's. After supper I studied and played a couple games of cards.

January 12. Went to school as usual. After school went to the store. After supper there was a b.b. [basketball] game. Routt vs. Barry. We won. I didn't go. It was raining.

January 13. Went to store and looked around in morning. After dinner went uptown. After supper went to b.b. game (Routt vs. Springfield, we lost) with Gloria and Jean. Carl asked me to go to the dance and party.

January 14. Went to Church. After dinner, went up to Gloria's. Margaret and Jean were down there. I stayed all night. So did Jean. After supper, Carl Reif and Frank Wiedlocker came down.

January 15 Went to school. After school we had Glee Club.

After supper, I stayed home and studied. After I studied, I went to bed.

January 16. Went to school. After school I went to see Charlie. After supper I stayed home and studied, then went to bed.

January 17. Went to school in morning. I stayed home in afternoon. Got a semi-formal and new pair of shoes for dance. Went to dance and party. Had lots of fun.

January 18. Went to school. After school played with Charles. After supper I stayed home and studied. Had geometry test next day.

January 19. Went to school as usual. After school we had Glee Club. Virginia Smith called me up and asked us to go to party. Went to b.b. game, Routt vs. Cath. They won.

January 20. Fooled around in morning. Went up to Gloria's in afternoon. We went uptown. Went to party at Va. Smith's house. "I won booby prize." Gloria, Angela, Dorothy, M. Eliz, Norine, Virginia S, G, & R.

January 21. Went to Church. M. Pat. came down and spent the day. Poochie came over. Norine, M. Eliz, Dorothy, Virginia S. and I went walking and went to Ferry's, played bridge in evening.

January 22. Went to school as usual. After school had a Glee Club business meeting. I didn't go. Went to see Charlie. Studied in evening.

January 23. (Norine's 18th birthday) Went to school again. After school I went uptown with Gloria to get Norine's present. Norine [only sister] had a birthday party. We had lots of fun.

January 24. Went to school. Semester began. I wrote English in morning. Got 94. In the afternoon didn't have to go. Jean came down to dinner. We helped Sister Roberta in afternoon.

January 25. Went to school. Wrote Latin in morning. Got 86. Wrote History in afternoon. Got 92. In evening studied for geometry test.

January 26. Went to school. Wrote Geometry test. Haven't got my grade yet. In afternoon went down to Gloria's. We went down to school. Went riding uptown in Irene's car.

January 27. Fooled around. Our gas stove got on fire. Called the fire department. Went skating with Poochie in afternoon. Went up with her and Harold. [Hilarious fire details, page 158]

January 28. Went to Church. Read the funnies. Ate dinner. After dinner I went to Gloria's. We went riding. After supper Stephanie came over.

January 29. Didn't go to school in morning. Too cold. After dinner I went to school. After school came right home. After supper I studied my English and Latin.

January 30. Went to school. After school came home. After supper I studied and played cards with Catherine and Loretta. They came over for awhile. Went to bed.

January 31. Went to school as usual. Looked in some of the stores after school. After supper I studied and went to bed.

February 1. Went to school again. After school Gloria and I went uptown. Came home, went to the store. After supper I studied and went to bed.

February 2. Went to school and brought my dinner. Went uptown at noon with Maggie. After school went over to Charlie's. Gloria came down after supper and we made candy.

February 3. [Brother Jim's 21st birthday] Went to school. I'll take it back. It was Saturday. Fooled around. After dinner I went to Church. Pooch called me up. I went to show at State and saw *Half Baked Truth* with Catherine and Alberta.

February 4. Joe [Pedrucci, early boyfriend whose father owned the local movie theater] tore this page out trying to read it when he was over July 17, 1935. George [Fritscher] tore this in two trying to read it February 27, 1935. [Each page in this diary had room for five entries for five consecutive years.] Went to Church. Saw Gloria, she told me she had a date for the Prom. Catherine, Buddy, Harold, and I rode Bud's bike. We got some candy.

February 5. Went to school as usual. After school I had Glee Club. I went over to Kathryn's house after supper and went over to Loretta's.

February 6. Went to school again. Brought my dinner to school. After school came home, went over to Charlie's. After supper I got my lessons.

February 7. Went to school again. After school I had Glee Club. After supper I studied and went to bed.

February 8. Went to school. After school went over to Catherine's. After supper I stayed home and studied.

February 9. Got up. Got sick. Went back to bed. Stayed home from school all day. Mrs. McGinnis came down in afternoon.

February 10. Sat. morning. Stayed in bed until about noon. Still sick. Stayed home in afternoon. In nite Mom, Harold, and I went uptown and I got some new things. We got some candy.

February 11. Went to Church. After dinner Catherine and I went roller skating. Gloria came by for me to go to Jean's. After supper went down to Gloria's.

February 12. Went to school again. After school I had Glee Club. Walked home with Loretta. Studied at nite. Went to bed.

February 13. Went to school again. Gave out some comical Valentines. After school came home. Gloria stayed all nite. We studied and went to bed.

February 14. Ash Wednesday. Beginning of Lent. Gloria and I got up at 5:30 and went to Church. Ate breakfast at her house. Went to school. Went to Church at nite.

February 15. Went to school as usual. After school went to Church and said "Stations of the Cross." Gloria took me a piece home. Studied at nite at home.

February 16. Went to school again. After school for Lent said the "Stations" at Church. Went to Church at nite with Gloria. Went to basketball game. We beat.

February 17. Went down to play basketball with Gloria at Liberty Hall. Went down to Gloria's after supper. Made candy, stayed all nite with Gloria.

February 18. Gloria and I went to 8:30 Mass. Ate breakfast there. It snowed. Gloria ate dinner down at our house. After dinner we made candy. Went to Church.

February 19. Went to school again. Had Glee Club after school. I went to Church after school. After supper I studied my lessons.

February 20. Went to school. After school came home. Gloria took me a piece home. After supper Mamma, Harold and I went to show and saw *Mert and Marge*. It was swell. Joe [Pedrucci] got my World's Fair bracelet. He wears it all the time. Looks cute on him. He's cute anyhow.

February 21. Went to school as usual. After school had Glee Club. I ate supper with Gloria and then we went to Church.

February 22. Went to school. After school came home with

Loretta. Went to Church and after supper went over to Loretta Lonegan's.

February 23. Went to school. After school went down to O'Meara's with Daddy to write insurance. After supper stayed home. There was a b. b. game.

February 24. Mamma was sick. Went down to play b. ball in morning with Gloria. After dinner went sleigh riding. Went to bed rite after supper.

February 25. Went to Church. After Church I went to the store and went sleigh-riding. After dinner Harold and I went again. We got some candy.

February 26. Went to school. After school we had Glee Club. Gloria and I went to Church. Came home. After supper studied and played bridge.

February 27. Went to school.

March 5. Went to school. After school I picked Catherine's presents. Went to her party at nite. I bought her a box of candy. We had a good time.

[March 9. Younger brother Harold's 13th birthday]

March 13. Went to school. After school Carl Rief said he would come down in nite. We went to dance at D.P. Had a swell time. Afterwards went to Peacock Inn.

March 16. Carl Rief, Ed Cox, Gloria, Jim C [Chumley who would marry Norine], Norine, and I were going to dance. They were coming down, but Carl couldn't come. Rest did come. Carl came next nite.

March 17. In afternoon went uptown to look at formals. In

nite Frank W, Carl, Ed, came down. We went up to Gloria's house to dance.

March 18. Went to Church. Catherine and I went up to Gloria's in afternoon and we went riding. Went to Church at nite. Saw Carl.

March 19. Went to school as usual. After school we had Glee Club, but I didn't go to school in afternoon. Went uptown to get my formal. Catherine and I went down to Gloria's in nite.

March 20. Went to school again. After school made my appointment for my permanent. After supper I washed my hair. Loretta wanted me to come over.

March 22. Stayed home from school. Got a permanent in the morning at Ambassador for the Prom. Went to school in afternoon. All the kids liked it.

April 3. Prom! I went with Carl Rief. Double-dated Gloria and Ed Cox, Bud Simon and Margaret Cain. Had a grand time. Went riding afterwards.

No entries made in the ten months between April 4, 1934, and February 4, 1935

1935

Age 15, will turn 16 on 12 July 1935, begins dating

February 4. I was "Mrs. Pendleton," the old cleaning lady, in play called *Daddy Long-Legs*. Had my first date with Joe Pedrucci after the play. Had a good time. He sure is cute! We went riding with B. Belz, R. Smith, J. Corbett, L. Mallen. Joe wanted to X me [kiss me]. Tried, but I wouldn't let him. It made him mad.

[Marginal note written later: "Joe tore this page out trying to read it when he was over July 17, 1935. George tore this in two trying to read it February 27, 1936."]

February 26. I got my 3rd note from Joe. We write one a day to each other. Had fun in Lab and also in Latin. Going to have Chem. test tomorrow.

March 1. Went to school. After school Jack H. asked Joe and I to go to his party that nite. We went. Had a swell time. I let Joe X me [kiss me] for the first time.

March 2. Went to dentist. Eustacia came up. We went uptown in afternoon. Jean and Gloria came down in the nite for awhile.

March 3. I went down to Gloria's in afternoon. After supper Joe called me up. He came down. We went to show with Jim and Norine to see *Gilded Lily*.

March 4. I wrote Joe a note. Had lots of fun in religion [class]. Nothing exciting happened. We worked for the Prom afterwards.

March 5. I got a note from Joe saying that they could go to the Boarders' party at Gloria Hanley's. [The Boarders was the name used for the athletes like George Fritscher who lived at the boarding house run by Routt College, which was a two-year college with a high school.] I went to the play called *As Thousands Smile*. Joe was a girl in the play. I met him after the play. We went to the party and danced. Had a keen time. I let Joe X [kiss] me [in exchange] for his picture.

March 6. Went to Church. Joe gave me his graduation picture. This morning in the hall. It's swell. We talked again at noon. The principal caught us. I wrote a note to Joe. Gave it to him at noon.

March 16. Joe came down. Jim and Norine were here getting ready to go to a dance. Joe brought me a different picture. Had a swell time.

March 17. Joe came down. We went out to Smith's. Had a keen time. Took a walk. Went down to Merrigan's. Then came home.

Always Virginia

March 22. Joe and I came down to see the auto wreck from school. We went skating in the nite all over town up and down streets. Had a swell time.

March 23. Joe and I, Beulah and Jome [nickname for "Jerome"]. Barry, Rosemary, and Billy all went skating all over town. Then we came down at my house. Swell time.

March 24. Went to Church. In eve. Joe came down after Church. We stayed home and talked. Had a swell time.

No entries from March 25, 1935 to April 23, 1935

April 23. Prom. Went with Joe Pedrucci. Had a grand time. Had a swell corsage and a swell formal. Double-dated Ed Cox and Jean Hoecker. Did we have fun?

April 28. Had a date with Harry Buoy to go see *Roberta*. Went with Carl Weidlocker and Beulah Draper. Good time. In evening had a date with "Joey." We came home and danced. Grand time.

April 29. Boarders [of whom scholarship athlete George Fritscher was one at Routt] went on a strike because their cook was fired. None of them came to school. Father Formaz made them come 6th period. More fun. They were in the basement of the boarding house yelling, etc.

May 2. Joe's birthday. I didn't know it though until it was over. I sent him a belated birthday card. It was right cute.

May 3. Joe and Skeets came by and wanted me to go skating. We went by for Mary Baban. Had lots of fun. We fell about 6 times.

May 4. Joe went skating with M. Baban. I went with J. O'Neil. Joe got mad and took Mary home right away and came with O'Neil and me. More fun. Was he mad?

May 5. Joe and Jim came down for supper. Came down about

3:30. We went to see *Reckless*. Had a swell time. Came home [with] them until time for Joe to go.

May 6. Went to school. Joe wrote me a note. Told me he had a swell time. In the nite we went to the library. Had lot a fun.

May 7. After school went to library. Joe took me home. After supper went to French lecture at D.A.R. [Daughters of the American Revolution Hall] It counted as our test. Ed Cox and H. Buoy brought Margaret Cain and me home. Good time.

May 8. Went riding on bicycle with Harold. Lacy took me a ride. Then Joe did. Keen time. Came home. Beulah and I went to library. Came home with Belz and Corbett.

May 9. Didn't go to school in morning. Went to dentist. Joe introduced me to his cousin. He came after Joe because his grandmere was sick. Joe's cousin is awful nice. Went skating in eve.

May 10. After school we played baseball. After supper we went skating. Beulah and I dodged the cop at College. More fun. Laughed and laughed.

May 11. Had my pictures taken in my formal to give to Joe for graduation. One big one tinted for mother. Little one for Joey. Mother and I went to Merrigan's.

May 12. Beulah and I went down to Davison's in evening. Was with C. Weidlocker and Bud Simon. Joe was home. No date.

May 15. I got the proofs for my pictures. Pretty good. They had a hard time deciding which one they liked the best.

May 18. Joe and I kinda mad. He thought I was mad at him. We didn't have a date. He wrote me a note next day and explained.

May 24. Joe asked me to go to *Wag* staff party with him (Friday,

May 24). We went. It was also a dance. Had a grand time with Joey and everyone.

May 25. Went to dentist all morning. In afternoon Beulah and I went walking. Went down to Merrigan's. In evening went uptown with Beulah.

May 26. Sunday. Played ball in afternoon. Routt vs. Winchester. They beat. I played for Winchester. Wally said I was a swell player.

May 27. Monday. Semester exams start. I'm mad at Joe on account of Sunday nite—with M. girls at Davison's. He said I snubbed him. Had Latin test.

May 28. Tuesday. Had French test in A.M. at noon. Joe and I made up. Had English in P.M. Joe called me up in nite. Talked a long time. More fun. (I wrote wrong from May 24. They are supposed to be a day ahead. I was a day off.)

May 29. Norine, Beulah, and I went to dance at park. All seniors came out after their party. I danced with all the kids. Danced with Joey most of evening. Went walking with him in park.

May 30. Beulah and I went to dance again. Joe was out there. I danced with him. We were kinda mad about nothing. Had a good time though. Came home with Chumley's.

May 31. Went to school to get our grades. I passed. I'm a senior now. Joe and I made up. I pressed his cap and gown for him. He came down in evening. We went to Davison's twice, the Silver Jewel, and Merrigan's [where brother Jimmie worked]. Grand time.

June 1. In afternoon Mother and I went uptown. Got my new suit for Joe's graduation. Got my pictures to give to him (a big tinted one). Everyone thought they were swell. Went uptown again in evening.

June 2. Went down to Davison's with kids in afternoon. In evening Joe called me up. He came down. We stayed home, took a little walk around block. I gave Joe his present. He was crazy about it. Kissed me right in front of Jim and Norine. He X'ed me goodbye about 20 times.

June 3. Stayed home in afternoon. Was expecting Joe's parents. Didn't come though. In evening Joey graduated. He introduced me to his parents, sister, aunt and I already knew his cousin. Very nice. I almost cried. Joe said goodbye and said he would write.

June 4. Tues. nite lonesome without Joey. Went skating with J. Sweeney, M. Hefferman, A. David and G. Hanley. Went to Davison's. Had keen time.

June 5. Went on picnic at park with Beulah, Sweeney, Heffie, Gloria, C. Priper. Grand time. Good eats. Watched them dance. Paul Chumley brought us home.

June 6. Norine, Beulah, and I went uptown. More fun acting nuts. They got new dresses. In evening Beulah and I went to show, *4 Hours to Kill*. Grand, scary. More fun and how!!! [Seven years later, on this date, June 6, 1942, she gave birth to Bob Fritscher.]

June 7. Went uptown and looked for a job. In evening Gloria and I went up to Angela's. We went down to Davison's. Had fun. Mildred [Mildred Horn, who became an English teacher and eventually married Jimmie Day] came home with Jimmie and stayed all nite.

June 8. Beulah didn't go to school. In afternoon we went uptown. She got a new pair of shoes. We got some ice-cream cones. Swell time. In evening went riding with Dad and Mom.

June 9 and 10 missing. The following item was written as entry on page for June 8.

George [Fritscher] tore out June 9 and May 24. Those pages said, "I got a darling letter from Joey. I went out to Margaret Cain's in afternoon and rode horseback. Joe was supposed to go to Europe in 2 weeks."

June 11. In afternoon went up to shop with Beulah. Miss Benson was going to cut my hair, but she didn't get time. In evening went skating again with same kids. Went to Davison's.

June 12. Jome and Lil Mallen and Orville [whom she later dated when George left to go back to Minnesota] came up from Hardin. Jome had a date with Lil and I had a date with Orville. Went to dance at park. Swell time. He's a keen dancer. He wanted to X me. I wouldn't let him. He begged.

June 13. Wrote a letter to "Joey." Asked him to come over Sun. Went to dentist in afternoon with M. Cain and Viola. We went to Hamilton's and Matthew's.

June 14. Went uptown with Mother to get her a dress and shoes. In evening Beulah, Norine, and I went walking. Went to Hamilton's Confectionery. We had lots of fun.

June 15. Beulah, Norine, and I cooked dinner. Mother went to Springfield. In afternoon, Beulah and I went uptown. In evening we went riding with Dad and Mother. Then we went to Davison's with Jim and Norine.

June 16. Joe didn't get to come over. It rained terribly hard. In afternoon Beulah and I went to sleep. In evening Jean, Gloria, Beulah, Harold, and I went riding with Mary & C. Abraham. Went to dance at Woodland Inn. On way home we had a flat tire.

June 17. In afternoon I went up to Angela's. She treated me to a Coke. In evening Virginia Smith came down. I took her a piece home. We had fun. Norine was in Carrollton.

June 18. In afternoon I went up to Gloria's. We went uptown. It rained. In evening we went riding with Dad. Oh yes! In afternoon I learned how to drive the car.

June 19. In evening went on weiner roast with J. Sweeney, J. Horchen, M. Hefferman, and Gloria. In evening we went to dance. I danced 9 dances with Johnnie Watkins and 1 with Paul Chumley.

June 20. Went down to Kampsville. Had lots of fun. No one knew me, hardly. Everyone said I was cute. I got a letter from Joe in the morning. Darling letter from a darling boy. [Three years later on this date, June 20, 1939, she gave birth to Jack Fritscher.]

June 21. Charles Ford was up all day. In the evening I got 2nd lesson in driving the car. I drove all the way out of town and in. In evening Frances Lacy and I went bicycling.

June 22. Mother and I went uptown. I got a new dress. In the evening we—Gloria, Jean and I—went to the dance at the park. Danced all the time. Grand time.

June 23. In afternoon Angela and I took a long walk. Had lots of fun. In evening the Shanahan girls, Harold, and I went riding. We followed cars all over. Fun!

June 24. Went down to Kampsville. I stayed with Aunt Mag, while Dad, Mom, John went to Hamburg. Had swell time with the twins. Aunt Mag and them wanted me to stay. I couldn't.

June 25. Wrote 2nd letter to Joey.

June 29. Went to work at Woolworth's at 11 o'clock. First time. I had a keen time. Beulah came to meet me then we went riding. More fun with Paul.

June 30. Went up to Angela's. She treated me to a soda. We went walking with Gloria. In evening Beulah and I took a walk. Went to Hamilton's and swiped about 100 napkins.

July 1. Went uptown and got a new 3-piece pink dress. Cute. Went to Angela's. Forget what we did in evening.

July 3. Beulah and I went uptown. Walked all around in colored glasses. Went to Merrigan's. In evening I played ball on our team.

July 4. In morning went bicycling with Vivian Connolly, Gloria's g.f. from Rockford. In afternoon got a darling letter from Joey. He sent me a darling picture of himself. In evening went to dance. Swell time.

July 5. Bud came over again. He looked cute. He said I was getting better-looking every day. In afternoon Marty, Lil, Joe, Gloria, Angela and her girl friends and I went on a picnic out to Jean's. I took pictures with my camera.

July 6. Beulah, Gloria, Vivian, Patty and I went to dance last nite. Danced with a darling guy from St. Louis. He danced swell. Frankie Smith wanted to give me some ice-cream.

July 7. Angela came down and Beulah and Angela and I took pictures. In the evening Beulah and I took a walk. Went to Hamilton's. Saw Frankie.

July 8. Beulah and I went uptown. I got a new white purse. Went to Hamilton's. In evening we went riding with Mary and Catherine.

July 9. Went uptown. Got my pictures I had developed. Beulah and I went to Majestic to see *The Ghost Walks*. We had a lot of fun. It was scary. I wrote a letter to Joey and sent him a picture of myself in shorts.

July 10. Went up to Angela's in afternoon. In evening Frances Lacy, Beulah, and I went to park dance in Yellow Cab. More fun. Charlie Scott wanted to take me home.

July 11. Beulah's sister came after her. She went home. We cried and so did she. In nite went to Fox-Illinois Theater to see *Charlie Chan in Egypt* with Charlie Scott.

16th Birthday
Three years later she was married on this date

July 12. [sixteenth birthday] Stayed home. Gloria came down. Gave me a pair of gloves for my birthday present. In evening we went riding. Went down to Swift's Cone Shop.

July 13. Norine and I went uptown. In evening we went riding. Didn't do much.

July 14. Mildred was up. We went swimming in afternoon. Got sun-burnt. In evening we went to show, *Ginger*. Swell show. Then we went down to Merrigan's and got a sundae.

July 15. In afternoon Mildred and I went up to see Jimmie [who worked] at Merrigan's. He gave us a great big soda. In the nite I went to bed early.

July 16. Went up to John's office. Had lots of fun. Went to Angela's. In evening Mildred and I went to show with Harold, *The Quitter*, at the Majestic. Good show.

July 17. [Brother John's 23rd birthday] In afternoon Joey called me up. He came down to see me. He looked swell. Said I did. We had a grand time. Went to Merrigan's and Davison's. He hated to leave. Wanted to stay all nite. I hated to see him go. In evening I came to Carrollton. Stayed all nite with Eustacia.

July 18. Mildred brought me to the river [to cross to Kampsville]. I came over in the little boat. Ate dinner with Beulah. In afternoon was with the twins. In evening with Beulah.

July 19. Went to post office with twins. I got a letter from Mother. In afternoon went riding in Clark's old Ford. Clark said

I sure was good-looking. In evening went to show with Beulah to see *Tomorrow's Youth*. Grand show.

July 20. Went up to picnic with the twins. Ate dinner there. Rode on Ferris-wheel. Good time. We met a cute kid from St. Louis. In evening went to dance with Cecilia, Joe, Beulah. Keen time.

July 21. Went to Church in K'ville [Kampsville]. In morning went to picnic at beach. Ate dinner there. Had a swell time. In evening had a date with Tom Ballard. Went to beach again. Came home [to Jacksonville] with Jimmie.

July 22. In afternoon Mr. Benson asked me to work for him. I went to work in evening at 6:30. Made 60 cents. I like it fine.

July 23. In afternoon I took a nap. In evening I worked. I made 61 cents. Came home with Imojean Williams.

July 24. Margaret Cain came in afternoon. We went down to chicken supper for awhile. Went to work at 6:30. Made 86 cents.

July 25. Rosemary and L. Lonergan came down. We went bicycle riding. In evening went to work at 6:30. Made 36 cents because Norine worked too.

July 26. In afternoon the shell-man wanted Norine to work for him and give out souvenirs. He saw me and wanted me to work also. He hired me because he said I had a "Quaker-Oat smile."

July 27. Mildred and I went swimming in afternoon. Had a keen time. In evening I worked at cone shop. Made 62 cents.

July 28. Mother and I went uptown in afternoon. I went to work at 4 o'clock. Worked inside. Had a good time. Made 75 cents.

July 29. Tuesday morning. Got up. My jaw was all swollen up. Went to dentist. I couldn't work that night. Went riding in evening.

July 30. My jaw still swollen. Slept most of the day. In evening we took a ride. Went down to cone shop. Bill and Mr. Benson came to see me all the time.

July 31. I didn't do anything. Didn't work. My jaw still swollen. In evening I took a ride. In afternoon got a card from Margaret Cain in St. Louis.

August 1. I didn't work. Got a card from Joey in Chicago. Went to dentist. He said if it didn't go down he'd have to lance it. Went out to Rosemary Smith's in afternoon. Took a ride in the evening.

August 11. Rosemary, Ginny Devlin, Virgilene Easily, Frances Craig, Edith Lonegan and I went out to airport. Rosemary and I went up. Then we went to Margaret Cain's. Bud drove me home racing at 75 miles an hour. More fun.

August 20. John [brother] called up and said he had found a job for me. I went up and interviewed the man from the Ideal Bakery. Said he'd call me for eve. I went to hotel and Miss Murgerman and Brown explained it to me. Eustacia came up.

August 21. Started to work. We went to Roodhouse and gave out samples of "Youth Breath" and took orders. Miss Murgeman, M. Keller, Thompson, M. Rutherford, and Riley and I worked.

August 22. Part of us went to Carrollton and part to White Hall. Hazel and I went to Carrollton with Mary. Had lots of fun. Ate dinner there.

August 23. Finished up at Carrollton. We ate dinner with Mr. Hale and Mrs. Connors at Linsay Hotel. Then we went to Jerseyville and started working there. Fun.

August 24. Went back to J'Ville and finished up in morn. In afternoon demonstrated in McGuire's stores giving out samples of bread and jam. Came home with O. Harris, sales manager.

August 25. Harold and I went to show to see *Broadway Gondolier* at Fox-Illinois with Dick Powell and Joan Blondell. Swell. In evening went down to Bill's and got a cone with Mildred. Also to Merrigan's.

August 26. We didn't work. I got a permanent from Dolly. Neato perm. I like it. M. Cain came in. We went to dentist and then went with her to pick out a present. In evening Mildred and I went to Merrigan's.

August 27. Mr. Hale and Mr. Mack went with us. Mary didn't go. We went to Virginia in morning and Chandlerville in afternoon. We had lots of fun sampling and everything.

August 28. Mack and Mr. Hale took us. We went to Tallula and Petersburg. Swell time walking up and down hills in Petersburg. Came home rather late.

August 29. Jack Mack went with us to-day. We went to Havana. Had a good time. Swiped 2 watermelons on way home. Went to Millie's and ate one. Then Mack took all of us to the show, *Front Page Woman*. Swell time.

August 30. First we went to Greenview. I drove the Dodge all around town. Next to Mason City, then to Easton. I went with Mack. He's swell. Had a good time. Ate the other melon on way home.

September 20. Went to Springfield. Ginnie and I went with Howard Anderson. We cheerleaded. Played Springfield. It was broadcasted. The announcer told how we were dressed and how much pep we had. We lost 19 - 0. Had a good time. Howard asked me for a date but I wouldn't go.

September 21. Bud Simon came over after school. He introduced me to Jim Nolan. Darling. He's going to send me Catholic newspaper. He autographed my books.

September 23. We went upstairs after school to try out for cheerleaders. Father Johnson said he'd pick them next day. More fun waiting!!!!

September 24. Was chosen as cheerleader out of about 20 kids that went up. Practiced yells after school. Played softball in evening on team.

September 29. In afternoon M. Cain and I took a walk. Raphael Behrens and Lowell Gwinn took us home. We had my dog, "Speed." Everybody though he was darling. In evening Raphael came down. We took Gloria and Jean a piece home and came back.

September 30. Had our first "pep" meeting. Did pretty good. Father Johnson wanted to know what I did Sunday! Ha! Ha! He! He!

October 1. Sister Ernestine tried to take a letter I wrote to Joe away from me, but I wouldn't give it to her. Was she mad? Not much! After school I met Bob Thomas uptown. He bought me a soda and brought me home.

October 2. (Mother's birthday) I went to see *Top Hat*. Next evening came down again. Bob Thomas, said that Boarders [at Routt, including George Fritscher who has yet to enter the diary] said M. Cain and I were the best-looking girls in Routt. Came down again in evening.

October 3. In evening I had a date with C. Ryan. M.C. Wacker, H. Selimann, L. Zellen and F. Weidlocker went with us. Good time. Bob came down again. We took my dog walking.

October 4. Didn't have to go to school in afternoon. Jean, Gloria, Angela, Marg. and I took my dog walking. Had fun. Gloria and Angela came down in evening.

October 5. Worked all day at Montgomery Wards. Had fun.

In evening V. Smith, Norine, and I went down to Merrigan's after work.

October 6. Came up to Angela's and had dinner and supper. Went to Winchester with Bonensingers. Got a letter from Joey who said that anybody who had a date with me was lucky.

October 7. Senior weiner roast. Had a date with "Curly." Went riding with George Wagner. Followed kids all over town. Grand time. He's nice.

October 31. Went to Halloween party at school. Had grand time at dance. Went to midnight show with Lowell Gwinn. Had a good time.

November 1. Went to party at Angela's. Grand time. Swell refreshments. All the kids over there. We started a club.

November 2. Went to work about 3 o'clock. After work went to Hamilton's.

November 3. Slept all afternoon. Gloria, Jean came down. We went down to Davison's. Had fun as usual.

First mention of George Fritscher who is 19 and a scholarship athlete boarding at Routt

November 4. In History, Geo. Fritscher told me to keep an open date for Friday nite. Wrote me a note at noon, asked me for a date Friday and Homecoming.

November 5. I answered the note and said I'd go. He wrote me another one. He's real cute. Thrills!!!

November 8. Had a date with George. I was supposed to go to "Jo" Johnson's party. F. Weid. and V. Easily went with us. George had a radio in his car. Swell time!!

November 9. Margaret and I went to library. Then went around to look at formals. Had fun.

November 14. Marty had the club. We danced all evening. Had a grand time. Came home about 11:15. Next time we meet at Lil's.

November 15. Homecoming. Played I.S.D. in afternoon. Got beat. In evening George and I went to dance. I got a new dress and shoes. C. Pike went with us. They came by at 8. We rode around an hour, then went to dance. Grand time. I like George a lot. He asked me for a date for Sunday nite next week.

November 18. I got a note from George. He told me if I went with C. Ryan he was through with me. I don't know why yet. [They had been dating for only two weeks.] He said he had something to tell me what S. Girard said about him and me. Sister Girard said Sister Isabel wanted me to come Saturday for junior play.

November 22. No school. I went up town in afternoon with Norine. George came up in evening. We went to show *Anna Karenina* [for two movie fans, their first movie together]. Greta Garbo. Good. Swell time. I think he's swell.

November 23. George came down in afternoon. Routt rushed the show. ["To rush" means a group of people, usually young, who all decide to crowd into a place like a theater, harmlessly helter skelter, for the fun of it, like a Flash Mob, without paying—as in this case, a bunch of Routt students having a good time in a small town where everyone knew each other.] We went together to see *Every Nite at 8*. He's swell. After show went down to Davison's.

November 24. Stayed home all day. Dorothy and Lee McGinnis came down in evening. We ate hamburgers. We called up George and kidded him. More fun.

November 25. Next morning he (G) asked me if I called up

and I said no. He wrote me a note and told me all about it. Did I fool him?!!??

November 26. George wrote me a note and told me the varsity Letter-Man's dance was Monday nite. He asked me a long time ago to go. Marty and Harry are going with us.

November 27. George wrote me a note wanted to know what we would do during vacation. Said he'd call me up before to come down.

November 28. Eustacia stopped by on her way to Champaign. I stayed home in afternoon. In evening Ruyles came again. Stayed all evening. Good time.

November 29. Friday nite. Gloria's party. I was getting ready to go. George came up. Norine and Jim went with us. [Both couples soon married.] We went riding. Went down to Merrigan's. Grand time.

November 30. I worked from 2 to 9. George called me up at the store. He wanted me to get off work. He met me after work and we went to the show with Charlie Barber and and Betty Hoops to see *In Old Kentucky* with Will Rogers. George gave me his basketball "R" [varsity letter, eight inches tall, five inches wide, half-inch thick, wool, purple on gray]. Gee, was I glad. Swell time.

December 1. Went to show in afternoon with the girls to see *Smilin' Thru* for the third time. Went to Matthew's afterwards. In evening stayed home. Fooled around.

December 2. I wore my "R" to school. George and I really got razzed. He said he didn't care so long as he had me. Boy, some of the girls were jealous. Was I proud?

December 3. George wrote me a note and said if I didn't come to b. ball [basketball] game Sat. he couldn't play. He asked me for my picture. He said he had something important to tell me when we got together again.

December 6. Went to b. ball game. Routt vs. Ashland. We won 14-13. Saw Georgie play. He made 5 points. When I'd give a yell, they'd all yell "Fritscher." His brother [Clarence Pieschel] was there and laughed so hard when the kids razzed George and me. After game George and I had a date. I met Geo. Elliot. He had the car. We rode around, came home. Swell time. George is swell.

December 7. Went to ball game. We lost 35-6. George only made 1 point tonite. He came down at Davison's after me. Geo. Elliott had the car. He came after us. We went riding. Went out to Wagner's. Had swell time. George is keen. G. Elliott is nice too.

December 8. We rode out to George's house. Then he came by here and honked. We girls went down to Davison's in afternoon. In evening M.L. Maloney, A. McGinnis went with George and me. George told me what he had to tell me. He said [what he said is written in shorthand which she learned in high school]. We went to Winchester at a hotel and danced. G. said if we fell out it wouldn't be his fault. He came in for awhile. Keen time.

December 9. George wrote me a note and asked me if I believed what he told me last nite. He said I acted cold. Cute note. He was going to try to sneak out and come down tonite, but he couldn't get out. I stayed home.

December 10. George came down at 6:30. Stayed till 8:00. He was 15 minutes late for study. We had fun. I met Weezie [Louise] and Norine and we went to Davison's. Fun!!

December 11. Norine, Weezie, and I went up to Merrigan's. Then down to Davison's. We met Pat and Corby from the college. Walked home with them. Had fun.

December 12. I wrote George a note and Sister Gerard got it.

He wouldn't give her permission to read it. He sneaked out at 9:15 and we went with M.L. Maloney and Albert. They went to dance. We rode around in the Packard while they were there. Came home at 11:30. Swell time!!

December 13. George wrote me a note and said Father Formaz didn't know he was out [of the Boarders' House after curfew]. Skeets fixed everything up. I had my club in evening. Angela couldn't come. We had a good time. George said he was going to break up the party.

December 14. I worked from 11 to 9. George played b.b. in Springfield. I promised him a X for each point he made. He said he hoped he was lucky. He wanted the odds 10 to 1.

December 15. Cathedral beat 26-10. George made 4 points. Albert and M.L. Maloney went with us. George and I went to the show, *Barbary Coast*. Pretty good. Went riding afterwards. Good time as usual.

December 16. George wrote me a note and asked me what I wanted for Xmas. In evening Norine, M. Eliz., Dorothy, and I went uptown. Then we went to Davison's. Had fun.

December 17. George sneaked out. He came down. Then Albert and M.L. came by for us. We went riding. Had lots of fun. George put cardboard in door [of the Boarders' House] to get back in.

December 18. George wrote me a note and asked me if I was trying to make him sore the way I acted last nite. I answered and explained everything. He didn't have b.b. practice after school, so he met me and came down and stayed till supper time. Fun!!

December 19. George met me as soon as I came to school and told me they didn't have study tonite. We packed candy after school for our Xmas party. He came down at 6:25. Stayed till 9:40. He made Harold [age 14] tell him what I wanted for Xmas. We had fun. Stayed home. Too cold to do anything.

December 20. George made 10 points. We played Quincy, lost 21-22. Had our Xmas party at school. I was an angel. George made me laugh. He had my name [for the gift drawing]. He gave me a bottle and nipple and a hot-water bottle. He gave me his present—candy too. B. ball game in evening. George met me at Davison's. The Quincy fellows congratulated George in his choice in his girl and told him to bring me along when he came to Quincy. G. Elliott came after us. Swell time.

December 21. George came in the store and said we were going to the show with Charlie and Betty. We saw *Storm over the Andes*. Swell show. We went riding and out to Julienne afterwards. We laughed and laughed. George told me he bought me something. Swell time.

December 22. George and Al came by. We had George's car. Went out for M.L. Went riding. George and I had an argument. Was he ever sore at me. He said I was too touchy and I didn't care for him. Finally we made up. We went to Wagner's then brought M.L. and Al home. George came in. He was swell then. Had fun. He brought Jim home.

December 23. Worked till 9. Then went out to party at Gloria's. Was supposed to go to a potluck supper time. We exchanged presents. I got a little box of guest puffs from Angela. Came home about 11. Good time.

December 24. Christmas eve. George was supposed to have a date with me after work, but Albert McGinnis didn't come by for him and didn't let him know he wasn't coming until too late. Was I mad? Stayed home. Got lots of nice Xmas presents. George was mad too.

December 25. Christmas. Marty, Gloria, and I went to see *Collegiates* at Illinois Theater. Swell show. Gloria ate supper here. I stayed home in evening. In afternoon Jim came in. All of us kids went to Hamilton's. They love my watch.

December 26. Lil, Gloria, and I went uptown. I got a new wool skirt. We went to Matthews. In evening George called me up. He came up. Explained everything about Tuesday. I got a 5 lb. box of candy from him. I gave him his muffler and my picture. He liked them. We stayed with Harold until Daddy and John came home. Then we went out to Wagner's. Swell time. He wanted to go to Springfield.

December 27. Mildred, Norine, and I went up to Merrigan's. Had lots of fun. George came by and honked and honked. We came home with Jimmie and Jack Shumny after they closed up. [Should not be confused with "Chumley" into which family her sister Norine married. Jack Shumny, who lived next door to Virginia Day, became George Fritscher's roommate. He invited George to move into his house which was next door to the girl next door. His name is sometimes spelled in diary as "Shumley."]

December 28. George is nice. Lil, Gloria, and I went up to Matthew's. Lil invited me down for supper, but I didn't go. After supper Jimmie, Mildred, George, and I went to show, *Frisco Kid*. Had swell time. We went after George and brought him home. Swell time. Went down to Merrigan's. I won 2 packs of candy.

December 29. Mildred and I went to show in afternoon, *Annapolis Farewell*. Swell show. Went down to Merrigan's in morning. Stayed home in evening.

December 30. George came up at 8. We went to the alumni dance with Al and M.L. Went to Davison's afterwards. Swell time. I wore my new blue dress and George wore his new suit.

December 31. George and Charlie came after me at 7:30. We went after Betty. Went out to Wagner's. Then went out to Charlie's house, played pinochle, danced. Had fun. Then we went to midnight show. Grand time. After show went to Moore's. George told me what he had wished on my ring after the show. He said, "He hoped things keep going on like they have been."

End note: End of good old '35 when George and I had our first date on November 8.

1936

Age 16, turns 17 on 12 July 1936
Has known George Fritscher for six weeks

January 1. We went down to Ruyle's to spend the day. Eustacia Ruyle and I went riding around town in afternoon. Then we took her aunt and uncle to the river. Had a good time. Got home about 9.

January 2. Marty, Lil, Gloria, all the gang and I went uptown. Went to Matthew's. Marty wanted us to come out in eve, but, I didn't go. Stayed home and played cards.

January 3. All of us kids went uptown again. Went to Matthew's. Stayed up until about 5. In eve. we all went out to Gloria's. Came home in a taxi. Good time.

January 4. George called me up about 2:30. He and Jim came up for supper. We went to the show, *It's a Great Life* with Joe Morrison and Paul Kelly. We went down to Merrigan's afterwards. George bought me a little Santa Claus. Grand time. George threw Joe's picture on the floor and upside down and everything else. I kept picking it up until he got mad so I left it lay. Mother picked it up next morning.

January 5. George came home with me after Church. Stayed till 11:30. Called a taxi, went home. Beulah came up in afternoon. Was I surprised? Marty and Gloria and all the kids came up. Beulah left about 5. George came up at 5:30. We listened to the radio and then went to show, Shirley Temple, *The Littlest Rebel*. Grand, grand time. George told me I should put Joe's picture away and not in my room. More fun! George asked me to go to the Prom with him.

January 6. School started again. George was talking to me at noon. Said Father didn't say anything yet about him not staying at [moving out of] boarding school. After school I gave him my history notebooks. He had to practice it.

January 7. George asked me if he could come down in eve. He came down about 7. We stayed home. Played pinochle. Some fun!!!

January 8. I stayed home and studied until 10 o'clock. Then I went to bed.

January 9. Sister Ernestine tried to get a note from me. I tore it up before I gave her the pieces. George came down in eve. We went to Davison's with Weezie and Norine.

January 10. At noon, Sister Ernestine had pieces of note pasted together and put up on bulletin board. George took it off and put an answer back. George went to Hannibal to play b.b. He made 11 points. He called me up after the game.

January 11. In afternoon went uptown with Marty, Lil, and the kids. Then we went to Church, saw the players leaving for White Hall. We went out to Gloria's in eve. Had swell time.

January 12. George came home with me after Church. He stayed for dinner. We went to the show, *The Bride Comes Home*. He stayed for supper too. We stayed home after supper. Swell time.

January 13. Went to school. George was talking to me at noon, asked me to do some Latin for him. He wanted me to call him up in eve. but I wouldn't do it. Stayed home and studied.

January 16. George came home with me after school. Stayed

til about 5:30. Had fun. Stayed home in eve. and studied for semesters.

January 17. Marty, Lil, and I went to the game in eve. We played I.S.D., got beat 35-14 or something like that. George made 10 points. We had a date after the game. Went to Davison's. Then came home.

January 18. George came down a little while before supper. After supper we went to the show, *3 Live Ghosts*. Swell show, swell time. Went to Matthew's afterwards. G. got mad because I wrote a letter to Joey. He started to go home.

January 19. George came home after Church with me. We studied our history. He called me up about 3:00. Came back up about 7, stayed home. Had fun!!!!

January 20. Our semesters started today. I wrote 8 tests this morn. Geo. came home with me. In afternoon I wrote History. So did George. We girls went to Davison's after tests.

January 21. Today I wrote Typing and Shorthand. George came up in eve. We played pinochle for awhile. Had fun!!

January 22. Wrote French this morn. George and Charlie came after me to bring me home. Boy, is it cold? Geo. called me up about 6:30. Talked a long time. Norine is having a birthday party.

January 23. George came down after school. Stayed til about 6. Didn't do anything after supper. Studied.

January 24. We played Murrayville. Got beat. George made 9 points. Afterwards we went to Davison's. Then came home. Swell time. 23-19 above.

January 25. George came down about 2:30. Stayed til he had to leave for Quincy. After supper I stayed home. Got beat 30-5.

January 26. George called me up about 2. Came up about 2:15. Stayed for supper. After supper we played cards. Swell time.

January 27. Went—no didn't go to school in morn. Geo. didn't go all day. Margaret Cain came over in eve. We went to Matthews. George called me up. Swell time.

January 28. Went to school. In evening George and Jim came up. We went riding. Had lots of fun as usual.

January 29. George and I went to the library. Came home and fooled around. Had fun.

January 30. George didn't go to school. He came up after school. Had a new hat. Did he look cute. We (Daddy and I) took him home. In nite we went to show, *Three Musketeers*. Good. Went to Hamilton's afterwards. Swell time.

January 31. I went to the game, played Cathedral. Lost 26-6. George played on 2nd team. Last quarter of 1st team game. Met him at Davison's. Had fun. Came home. We got mad at each other. Got over it again.

February 1. Went to game. We played Winchester. Lost 17-11. Met George at Davison's. He was going to quit playing, but Wally asked him if he was keeping training, and he said "No." So Wally told him to turn in his suit and he said that was just what he was going to do. So he did come down to Davison's, drank 5 beers, bought everybody hamburgers and beers. Jim came after us. We went riding. George was feeling kinda good. I was mad. He said he didn't blame me. He promised me he'd never do it again. We'll see. [He never did it again in his whole life.]

February 2. George and Jim came up in aft. Too cloudy for me to take pictures with my camera.[Her father gave her a Brownie Box Camera when she was fourteen, and her mother said later, "I couldn't figure why your Daddy gave you a camera when you were such a young girl. I never thought you'd be taking it on your honeymoon."] They stayed for supper. We went to show after supper, *Rose of the Rancho*. Swell. Went to Davison's afterwards. Norine was mad at Jim. I was mad at George. We made up. He said he'd lots rather see that smile of mine than a frown. Had a swell time as usual.

February 3. [Despite George's stopping playing for Routt High School] We went to Letter-Man's party. Swell time. I won an everyday diary. Wally and his sister were chaperones. She tried to get George to play b. ball again. We danced and played all kinds of games. Really had fun.

February 4. Jimmie had a party. Jack Shumny, V.L. Davis, Rob. K., Polly Galke, Mildred, & George. Had a grand time. Played cards and danced. George got the boobie prize (a Valentine heart). He gave it to me. George and I went to see *Midsummer Night's Dream* in aft. Wasn't good. Had fun at show.

February 5. Didn't go to school in morn. Went to school in aft. George didn't go all day. M. Cain, Marty, Gloria, Jean, Angela, Jo, Lil & I went to library. Went to Matthew's afterwards. Swell time. Came home and wrote letters to Joey and Bob.

February 6. The boys had to stay in till 8 o'clock. Then George came by here & stayed. We played cards and fooled around. Had fun. He's swell. How thrilling!!

February 7. Fri. eve George came home from school with me. In nite we went to see Bill Powell in *Rendezvous*. Good. Met Jimmie and Mildred at Merrigan's afterwards. Stayed there for awhile. Came home. Grand time.

February 8. George came up about 7. We went to b. ball game together. We played McCooly. Got beat 16-13. Went to Davison's afterwards. Swell time. Came home, about froze coming back.

February 9. George came up about 2 o'clock. We went to the show, *Tale of 2 Cities*. Swell show. He stayed here for supper. After supper we went out to Charlie's house. Then went to Davison's. Swell time.

February 10. George came home with me after school, stayed for supper. After supper we played pinochle. Had lots of fun. I got a cute letter from Joey in morn. Not bad, eh!

February 11. George told me in a note that Father Coonen said he had too much nite work. Whoa! He wanted to see me after school, but boys had to stay in and girls had Glee Club. Said he'd call me up. I stayed home and studied.

February 12. Went to school. In eve. George came up. Jimmie, Mildred, he, and I went down to Merrigan's. Boy, was it slick out. George and I fell down right in the middle of the street. Had a swell time.

February 13. Went to school. After school went to library. George sent me a lovely big red heart by Jimmie. He called me up. I thanked. Gee, is it swell. He's keen. I love it.

February 14. Valentine's Day. I didn't go to school. Had too bad a cold. Mildred and I went to get George a Valentine. Got him a real cute one. He didn't go to school either. He got mine in aft. He came up in nite. We stayed home with Jimmie and Mildred. We opened our hearts. We had Mrs. Lapping bring us 4 Cokes. Had fun as usual.

February 15. George came up in aft. Said Kennett's [house where he stayed] had scarlet fever. He had to move. Jack Shumny [her next door neighbor who on this date became George's roommate] was over here. Jack said George could room with him. He moved in about 4:45. Swell—neighbors! He came over after supper. We went to the show, *If You Could Only Cook*. Went to Davison's afterwards. Swell time. There was a b.b. game, but we went to show. Harold [younger brother] was in amateur hour. Did swell.

February 16. Went to 8:30 Mass. So did George. He came over about 10:30. Stayed for dinner. Went home. Came back about 6:30. Played cards. Went down to Davison's. George got mad at me, said I acted like I didn't want to go out with him. Gee, we almost broke up. We argued about 3 hrs. He finally said he'd stop it because [line completed in shorthand marks].

February 17. George wrote me a note and said he'd thought it over and thought I ought to explain why I had acted that way Sunday. I told him I wouldn't tell him. He walked home from school with me. We argued and argued. He left and said, "When you decide to give me another date, let me know." Gee, I thought we were through forever, but he came over in the eve. We played cards. He left early. Oh, gee, this is gettin' awful!

February 18. George wrote me a note and said he still wanted to know and he hated to think of it if I didn't tell him. He waited for me after Glee Club, but I didn't walk home with him. He came over, but I wasn't home. He came over in eve. He and Jack. I helped Jack with his French. Jack left at 10:20. George left at 10:30. He didn't tell me good-nite. I don't think he even came to see me. He just came because Jack came. I got Jack's [Shumny] ring.

February 19. George came over. Wanted me to go to show, but I had to study. We stayed home. Fooled around. Made up. Had a good time.

February 20. George and I went to see *Captain Blood*. Good show. Went to Merrigan's afterwards. Jack brought us home. Had fun!

February 21. George and I mad again. He came over and went

uptown with Jimmie. They were uptown for a long time at the garage. Came home. We had lunch, fooled around.

February 22. I was invited to go to a surprise party for "Jo" Johnson Sunday nite. George came over. I asked him if he cared. Said we were supposed to go with Jack and Rita to the show. Dad gave us the car. We bought Jo's present. Went down to Merrigan's. They both got mad at me. I decided not to go. Then G. and I argued awful for about an hour when we came home. Went home mad.

February 25. George had to stay in. Margaret and I went to the library and to Matthew's. George came over in eve. Didn't do anything. Talked. Had fun.

February 26. Got a cute note from George. He walked home with me. He went to Winchester in eve. Stayed all nite. Margaret and I went to Church then to Matthew's. Had fun!

February 27. George didn't go to school. He was here when I came home from school. He got mad at me again, came over in nite. O.K. He read my diary. I got mad. Then we played cards and danced. Then he got mad because I still write to Joe. He read it in my diary. Went home without telling me good night again. Oh gee! I wonder when this is going to let up.

February 28. At school, George would just look at me disgustingly. He wanted me to write him a note. I wouldn't. He didn't write me one either. He walked home from school behind me. I went uptown to get some new shoes. Jack came over, told Mom Geo. wouldn't come. Jack came over and told me that G. was almost ready to bawl, he wanted to come over so bad. He asked me if he could. I said, "Yes." He came over, we made up. He made me promise not to write to Joe anymore. We went to Merrigan's.

February 29. George came over in morning and afternoon. We

went to show in nite and saw *Show Them No Mercy* and amateur show. After show we went to Merrigan's. Had fun as usual.

March 1. George came over when I was eating breakfast. Stayed for dinner. Went down to Merrigan's in aft. In nite went over to Springfield to hear "Horace Heidt." Saw *Exclusive Story*. Had a keen time. They were plenty good.

March 2. George walked home with me after school. Came over in eve. We went down to Merrigan's with Norine and Mildred to meet Jimmie. George got mad at me and went up in front of store. I left and went out to car. Was I sore. We came out pretty soon. Boy was he sore. We made up when we came home. George [shorthand marks]

March 3. George was sick and didn't go to school. In eve. he sent Harold over and wanted me to write him a note. I had one written so I sent it. He came over in eve. We fooled around.

March 4. George is still sick. Didn't go to school. Came over in eve. We played cards. Had fun.

March 5. I didn't go to school and neither did George. He came over. He got mad because I took off my ring that he wished on and he lit a cigarette. He went home. He came over in eve. Had fun, made up. We went to the show, *So Red The Rose*. Swell. Went to Merrigan's afterwards.

March 6. Went to school in morning. In afternoon stayed home. I was so sick I stayed in bed all afternoon. In eve. George came over also in nite. We went to Davison's. He didn't want to.

March 7. George came over in morning and afternoon. In eve. we stayed home. Then went down to Merrigan's about 9 o'clock. Came home. Almost broke up. He said he wouldn't go with anyone else. We just couldn't say goodbye.

March 8. Sun. morning. I walked to Church with George. He came over after Church. In afternoon we went down to Merrigan's. In eve. we went riding, then went after Jimmie. He stayed for supper.

March 9. I went to school, but Sister Wilfred sent me home in afternoon on account of my terrible cold. George came to see me after school in eve. Stayed for supper. Stayed home of course. Had fun!

March 10. Didn't go to school. Stayed in bed all morning. George came to see me after school. Also came over in nite. He treats me swell now while I'm sick. He always does, though.

March 11. Didn't go to school. George didn't go in afternoon. Stayed over here all afternoon. Said he wouldn't go when I wasn't there. Jack comes to see me every eve. George came over in nite too.

March 12. Didn't go to school. George came home because Sister Gerard [one of his teachers] was sick and he didn't have any classes. He came over then went uptown. Came over in eve. We played cards.

March 13. George didn't have to go to school again in afternoon. Came over. Stayed all afternoon. In eve. we went to Church and then shop. Saw *Whipsaw* and *Patty O'Day*. Swell. Came home. Argued over everything mainly because I turned away when he wanted to [shorthand marks]. I told him we saw too much of each other. He went home mad. Went to Blessie's with Jimmie and his girl.

March 14. George didn't come over today. After supper G. Eliot came by here looking for him. I told him he might be at Merrigan's. I went there to meet Norine and Weezie. George, Charlie Bayless, and Clint came in. George wouldn't talk to me. I took a ride with G.E. & Chas. Chas asked me for a date Tues. nite. They brought me to Hamilton's. Met Weezie and Norine. They both were arguing as to who would take me home. OK, me! What next? Poor George, I hope he gets over it.

March 15. I was going uptown. G. Eliot picked me up. In aft. G. Eliot called me up. He asked me to go riding with Charlie and him. I didn't want to. I was sitting in the car with G. Eliot and Chas. B. and George came up and sat in the back with us. In nite I wrote him a note. He came over. We went to the show, *The Country Doctor*. Grand. Afterwards we went to Merrigan's. He told me everything he did. He got mad. We made up. He said he hoped it never happened again.

March 16. George didn't want to go to school. He was here when I came home. In eve. we listened to radio and studied. Also played cards. Had fun!!

March 17. George played b. ball in nite. Came over afterwards. I studied and washed my hair. He stayed til about 11. Fun as usual. George stayed for supper.

March 18. George and I didn't go to Church on account of his ankle. I studied a long time. We didn't do much, played cards awhile.

March 19. Had my graduation pictures taken. V. Smith, Weezie, Norine, and I went to the game to see George play at D.P. [He re-joined the team as it was part of his athletic scholarship.] It rained and snowed. We got down there when the game was over. Went down to Merrigan's. Got a hot dog. Came home. George came over. Stayed till about 11:30.

March 20. We went to Church. George and I came home. Listened to a couple plays on the radio. Ate lunch. Went down to Merrigan's in our car. Took a ride.

March 21. George came over in afternoon. I went uptown and got our proofs. They were terrible. In eve. we went uptown. I got my new coat. Then we went down to Merrigan's. Came home. Everybody liked my coat.

March 22. Went to Church. George and I went up and had our pictures taken over. In aft. we went walking. In nite went to show to see *Mary Burns, Fugitive*. Grand at Majestic. Went to Hamilton's afterwards. Then took a walk. Had fun.

March 23. Went to school. George and I went up to get our proofs after school. They were good. After supper, Jack came over. He's here now. George is playing b. ball. He came over after he was finished. Had fun!

March 24. George and I, Rita and Jack, Bob and V. Lee, and Rex and his wife all went skating. Did we have fun? Went to Merrigan's with our skates on. Came home.

March 25. The Seniors played the underclassmen at L. Hall. I yelled for the Seniors until I was hoarse. Afterwards all of us kids went to Hamilton's. I was supposed to meet George. He and Jack were here when I got home. We went skating. Went to Merrigan's.

March 26. George played b. ball at D.P. Norine, Weezie and I went. They played Routt underclassmen. Won. Afterwards Weezie, Norine, and I went to Hamilton's. Was George mad? He said I was supposed to meet him. I came home at 10:30. George didn't come home. He was at Merrigan's. Came home with Jimmie.

March 27. George was mad and wouldn't go to school. Came over after school and gave me the "dickens." Said Jimmie and he and I were going skating. Well, we went. I fell down and split my head open in 3 places. It bled. Jimmie and George were scared stiff. It knocked me out. I came home. George took me to the doctor's. I said, Please don't cut my hair. George was so sorry. He said it was his fault because he wanted me to race him on Dunlap Court. I almost broke the pavement. More fun!!!

March 28. George couldn't sleep. Came over to see how I was. In afternoon he came again. I went uptown and got a new hat. Boy, is it cute. G. sure likes it even if it is red. [He prefers her in blue.] After supper we went to the show *Music Goes Round*. Good. Went to Merrigan's afterwards. We argued about Joe coming Easter.

March 29. George came over. We took pictures out in back. Took a walk. Went to Cordes. In eve. we played cards. Took a walk. Went to Merrigan's. Argued some more.

March 30. I didn't go to school on account of my head. G. came over after school. Letter-Man's initiation in nite. Came over about 9:30 and we still argued over trifles.

March 31. Didn't go to school again. Mother and I went uptown. Went to Merrigan's. G. came over after school. I told him about Joe coming Easter. He said to write and tell him not to. Finally, he gave in. In eve. we went to Merrigan's. Fun.

April 1. I went to school. Everyone was asking me about my head. G. came home with me. We went up and got our pictures. They were cute. After supper we went riding with Jack and Rita.

April 2. Had cute History test. Jean H. and I went uptown after school. I missed G. after Glee Club. He came over later. In nite we went to show to see *Timothy's Quest* and *Hot Off the Press*. Swell. Went to Merrigan's afterwards.

April 3. George came over and we went to Church. After Church we went to Merrigan's (I think that's what we did).

April 4. I worked. George met me. We came home right after work.

April 5. George ate dinner. He didn't feel so well. We took a walk and went to Merrigan's. We stayed home and messed around.

April 6. George didn't go to school. We went to Carrollton

with Jimmie and Mildred. We went to the confectionery. Didn't stay long. I got a letter from Joey. I told George. Was he mad!

April 7. George didn't go to school. He was here when I came home. In eve. we went to Merrigan's. George went home mad.

April 8. Jean and I went to Church after school. George was here when I came home. In eve. we went down to Merrigan's.

April 9. Jim came home. George, Norine, Jim, and I went riding. Went to Merrigan's. George and I went to Church together in morning.

April 10. George, Harold, and I went out to the lake and shot the rifle. In nite we went to Church. George, Jim, and I went to Merrigan's afterwards.

April 11. I worked. George met me after work. We went to Merrigan's. When we came home there was a great big Easter egg here for me from George with my name on it. It was full of chocolate. John came home.

April 12. George and Jim were here for dinner. After dinner we took a walk. Went out to Wagner's. In nite we went to show, *Callin'*. Good. Came home.

April 13. George came over. We went down to Wagner's. Fun. Jim and Norine went too.

April 14. George and I studied for awhile. Then we went to Merrigan's. Elam's house was robbed. Came home. Went over there.

April 15. George and I studied. Then the police came down to Elam's house, two doors down. We thought there was someone in there, the police didn't find anyone though.

April 16. George told me not to write this in here, but it really showed he cared for me. Joe met me and I gave him my picture.

George sure was burning up. Called me up. Said to come up to Rings Drug Store. We went up. Boy was he mad!! He tried to make me get out of the car. I wouldn't and I came home. He was there. Joe left about 8. Did George and I have it. He got it back from me tho. I skipped school in afternoon to go uptown and get some white shoes. Joe came over in his big Olds. Brought his cousin. When I came home he was here. Was I surprised. I took a ride with them. After supper Norine and I went to Davison's with them. (George wouldn't let me keep this page in here for a long time, but he finally consented and we decided it was best.)

April 17. George was rather hurt at school all day on account of Joe. All the kids were asking me about him. In nite, George and I went riding. Went to Merrigan's.

April 18. George came over in morning. In afternoon we went uptown to get some seat covers for the car. In evening George and I took a ride in the car. Brought some ice cream home.

April 19. George and I went to Church together. He ate dinner with me. In afternoon Norine, Mom, Dad, and Harold and George, and I went to K'ville.[Kampsville] Had a grand time. Took pictures. Ate at Aunt Mag's. Went to dance after supper. Orville Snow asked me to dance. George wouldn't let me.

April 20. Went to school. After school the *Wag* staff seniors had their pictures taken. Played b. ball after school. Seniors vs. Soph. They won 7-6. I made all our 6 points. Boy, was I tired after supper. George, Jimmie, Mildred, and I went to show, *Follow the Fleet*, then to Merrigan's. Took a ride. George went home mad.

April 21. George came over. We studied. He was rather sore because I wouldn't let him see my diary. We took a ride. Had a rather confidential talk. Then we went to Merrigan's. He was swell. We had fun.

April 22. George wrote me a note. Said he wouldn't get mad at me anymore without a very good reason. I played b. ball in eve. Beat freshmen 8-0. I made 3 points. In eve. George and I went to see *Brides Are Like That*. Then we went to Merrigan's. Came home. Show was swell.

April 23. Didn't go to school in morning. Went in afternoon. In evening George came over. We studied. Then went down to Merrigan's. Fun as usual.

April 24. George, Jack, Rita, Jimmie, and I took Mildred home. We went to dance at Carrollton (KC Hall). Swell time. Went to confectionery. Got home about 2.

April 25. I worked all day. George met me in the evening. We went to Merrigan's. Came home.

April 26. George and I went to Church together. He had been trying to see Father Formaz all the time. [He wants to change schools and learn to fly airplanes.] Went over after Church. Ate dinner with me. Saw Father after dinner. Father said he'd do all he could for him. Saw Sister Ana. She said she would too. Father Coonen wouldn't. We went to show in nite *Wife vs. Secretary*. Good. Went to Merrigan's.

April 27. George wasn't going to come to school, but Sister told him to. He did. In evening we studied. Then went to Merrigan's. We played b. ball against Juniors. They won. I made 3 points.

April 28. Went to school. Picked our rings and invitations afterwards. In evening George and I studied. Took a ride. Went to Merrigan's. Had fun!!

April 29. I went out to Marty's with Gloria. We worked on the way. Had fun. George came after me about 10. He was mad because I went. We took a ride. We beat the sophomores 14-9. I made 13 points.

April 30. George wrote me a cute note. I skipped 7th period. Mother and I went uptown. Got a new dress. In evening we studied. Then took a ride.

First mention of marriage

May 1. George, Norine, Corky, Weezie, and I took a ride. Went to Merrigan's. Brought them home. George and I took another ride. He told me that after he took up his course in aviation, he was coming back for me. He said he hoped I still felt the same towards him. He said to write this down as I wouldn't forget it. He's swell. Said some fellow was going to be awful lucky and he wanted it to be him. He's coming to visit me. After he's got a job, he wants to be married if I will.

May 2. I worked all day. George met me after work. Went to the dance at park. (Opening for summer.) Took Weezie and Norine with us. Swell time. Went to Wagner's. I drove. We took a ride. Swell time.

May 3. George and I went to Church together. Came home. Ate breakfast. He stayed for dinner too. In afternoon we went riding. We went down to Carrollton with Jimmie. Went to confectionery. Fun!

May 4. Went to school. Started baseball after school. I pitched. Fun. George came over. We studied.

May 5. Went to school. George came over after supper. We studied.

May 6. Went to school. Played b.b. after school. We got 3rd place in the tournament. George came over in evening. We had fun. Studied.

May 7. George came over. We studied. We took a little ride. Fun as usual.

May 8. We stayed home. Fooled around. That's all I can remember.

May 9. Worked all day. George met me. We went to park dance. Grand time.

May 10. We went to Church. George was over all day. We went to show to see Shirley Temple in *Captain January*. Swell!!

May 11. Played b. ball [baseball] for first time. I pitched. Fun. After supper George and I studied.

May 12. George was over. We studied.

May 13. Studied. Then we took the kids out to the dance. We rode around. Had fun.

May 14. Gloria had her party. We kids went. Had a grand time. George was just sick because I went. He wrote me a long note that evening. He couldn't stand to see me leave. He left.

May 15. We took a ride, I guess, Georgie and I. Anyhow, he was over. I got my permanent. It looks swell. George likes it.

May 16. I worked all day. George and I went to the dance. Had a swell time.

May 17. We went to Church. George was over all day. We went riding in afternoon. I drove. In evening went to show, *Under Two Flags*. We didn't like it.

May 18. I played b. ball. In evening George and I studied.

May 19. George and I studied after supper. We took a ride afterwards. Fun!

May 20. I got my golden slippers for Prom. We played b. ball. Played the 8th graders. Beat them so bad. In evening George and I went to the dance. Swell time.

May 21. George and I studied awhile. Then we took a ride.

May 22. Prom! Got home at 3:30 A.M. Went with Georgie! He sent me a grand corsage. He looked grand. Said I did. Grand time at Prom. After Prom went to "Puddy's" at Springfield. Swell time.

May 23. Worked all day. Didn't go to dance afterwards. Was too tired. George and I took the kids out. Took a ride. Fun!

May 24. George was over all day. So was Weezie. Mom and Dad went to St. Louis. George and I had a fight over my diary. He took it. In evening we went to show, *Small Town Girl*. Good.

May 25. We play baseball against Winchester. The old ladies played us. They won. Got home about 6:30. After supper George and I studied. I drove the car.

May 26. Had Glee Club. George and I studied in nite. I drove George down to Davison's. In nite we took a ride. Fun as usual.

May 27. Semesters started. Wrote English in morning and History in afternoon. George was here for dinner. After supper I took Mom and George for a ride. Went to dance after supper. Swell time.

May 28. Didn't have to go to school in morning. Mom and I went uptown. Got my new dress. Took Shorthand in afternoon. George was here for dinner and supper. After supper we took a ride.

May 29. Took Typing test in morning and French in afternoon. Practiced after school. George was here for dinner and supper. After supper *Wag* gave seniors a dance. George and I went. Grand time. After it Coxie, Marty, George, and I went to Springfield—Puddy's Inn. Swell time. Got home about 2.

May 30. Didn't work. Decoration Day. George was over all day. We went riding. After supper went to dance. Grand time.

May 31. George went to early Mass. Our class went to

Communion in a body. The Juniors gave us a breakfast afterwards. It was swell. Father Formaz gave us all a Missal [prayer book]. George was here for dinner and supper. After supper we went riding. We took pictures at Lil's in afternoon.

June 1. George and I went down to school to get our grades. In afternoon we went riding. After supper—graduation—got lots of nice presents. I [...entry inked out].

June 2. Fool around all day. George and I went to the Carnival. I won a little dog. We rode on Ferris Wheel. [...rest of entry cut off with scissors]

June 3. George and I took a ride in afternoon. We didn't go to dance. Stayed home. Had fun!

June 4. George and I had the car. We went out to Cain's. Shot around with the rifle. Had fun. Mary asked us to come out Monday. After supper we went riding.

June 5. Harold, George, and I went out to lake and shot around. Had fun. After supper we went down to Silverfrost. Jim and Norine too. We all had hot-dogs and it was Friday! Came home. Had fun!

June 6. I didn't work. I stayed home with George. We went to Church together. In evening I got a ducky new hat from Norine for graduation. We went to dance. Had a keen time. Went to Wagner's afterwards.

June 7. George and I went to Communion together. I wore my white suit and hat. We went on a picnic after Church. Jim, Norine, and us. Went swimming, boat riding—played ball. Jim had a cabin. Grand time. We got sun-burned. After supper we went to show, *Showboat*. Grand. Swell day.

June 8. George and I had our first date 7 months ago. George was over for dinner. After dinner we went out to Cain's. John took us out on his way to Springfield. We rode horseback. Swell time. After supper we went riding. Went down to Silverfrost. He went home mad. George got a spec. d [special delivery letter]. He has to leave Thursday [on the bus to see his brother, Clarence Pieschel, in Dixon, Illinois, up north near Chicago. Clarence was the son of George's mother, Amelia Haberman Pieschel Fritscher, whose husband before Joseph Eugene Fritscher was a man named Pieschel who died of typhoid around 1902 in Heron Lake, Minnesota.]

[June 9 and 10 are missing. The following note is hand-written at bottom of June 8]

"June 9 & 10—George tore out [the pages] because Joe's name was on them."

June 9. George and I went swimming. Swell time. Afterwards we went to the hot dog shop. We went to dime show, *Secret Patrol*. Had fun. Went to Merrigan's afterwards.

June 10. [Written on June 11 page] George packed all his things. We went swimming and riding in afternoon. In evening we went to the dance with Jim and Norine. Grand time. The last dance they played "The Beautiful Lady in Blue" and "It's a Sin to Tell a Lie." George told me to wear my blue dress. He liked the bows. We went boat-riding and over to the dance with Charlie and Betty. When we were leaving the dance they played, "If I Should Love You." We went to Wagner's afterwards. Last thing we drank together was a milk-shake. When he left that night he cried and cried. I felt so sorry for him I cried too. I couldn't hardly stand it. Neither could he. He's coming over in morning.

George Fritscher leaves on June 11, 1936, to go to Dixon, Illinois

June 11. George came over at 8. We had breakfast together. Went uptown. Told Jimmie, Daddy, and everyone goodbye. We ate dinner together. Then I took Georgie up to the hotel in the car. He drove up, I back. He cried when he told Mother and everybody goodbye. We were both crying while sitting in the car. He kissed me goodbye so much. The last thing he said was, "Goodbye, darling." Then he hollered "bye" again on the bus. He kept waving from the bus. (over) [On June 12 page, June 11 entry is continued] I could hardly drive home. I cried and cried when I came home I was so lonesome. Everybody misses him—neighbors, everyone. Margaret Cain came in afternoon. After supper I went to Church with the kids. Gee, was I lonesome. I love him so! He said he wished we were going on our honeymoon. He said how he wished we were going away together.

June 12. I went to show with the kids to see *Desire* and *Florida Special*. Swell. After supper Mother and I went to Merrigan's with Jimmie. Came home. Went to bed.

June 13. I got my first letter from Georgie. Darling letter. I worked at dollar store from 4 to 9. Came home—went to bed early. Lonesome for George.

June 14. I went to Church with Norine. It seemed so funny without George. Finished his letter. Weezie, Norine, Virginia Smith, and Margaret Cain came by and took me riding. In evening I stayed with Mother and Daddy. Missed George.

June 15. Went out to Gloria's. Came home. I was so lonesome for George. I cried. Bill and Rosemary came by. I went to Matthews with Lil and Jo and Marty. Went out to Gloria's in evening.

June 16. We, all the kids, went out on a picnic to the park. Went swimming and boat-riding. Missed Georgie. In evening we went to Church and then went up and got a milk-shake. I went up to Merrigan's with Jim and Norine.

June 17. Stayed home. Went to hospital with Mother to visit

Aunt Mag. In evening went to Church with the kids. Went to milk-shake place. Came home, went to bed.

June 18. Went out to Margaret's and spent the day. Rode horseback. Swell time. In evening went to Church with the kids. Came home. Went uptown with Jim and Norine.

June 19. Stayed home. Went to hospital with Mom in afternoon. Aunt Mag went home. In evening Norine and I went to cone shop and Hamilton's.

George makes a surprise return to Jacksonville.

June 20. I went to work at 4. Surprise! George came down at 6:30 with his brother Clarence. I didn't even know he was coming. He stayed here till I came home. They sent me out to the kitchen and there he was. I yelled, "George!" I was never so thrilled in all my life. He looked darling. I could have cried with joy. Clarence has a brand new Pontiac and we got to use it to go to the dance. Was it swell. It seemed like heaven again to be with him. We went to Merrigan's and after the dance we went to a place on So. Main. He's still swell or sweller than ever. He stayed here all night. He left his car here.

June 21. We went to Church at 7:30 in the car. Went out to his brother's. He sure is nice. Then G. Elliot and George and I went swimming. Cold! Fun! Came home. Ate dinner. Then Jim, Norine, and George and I went to show, *Private Number*. Grand. George and I talked and talked. He asked me if I would [shorthand mark] in the show again. He's swell. He had to leave at 6. Neither of us could hardly eat a bite of supper. We went out on the porch and waited for his brother to come. It was hard to part from each other, but we did it (barely). I was so lonesome. He said he was too. I went uptown with Jim and Norine. Charlie Bayless called me for a date. I refused. Said he'd call again. George doesn't want me to go with Charlie and I won't.

George leaves Jacksonville

June 22. Went to dentist in morning. In afternoon I made a cake. Pretty good, ha! In evening I went to Merrigan's with Norine and Weezie. We took Frances McGinnis home. I wrote a letter to George.

June 23. Stayed home in evening. Margaret came in in afternoon. I got a letter from George in morning. Answered in afternoon. We went uptown. In evening I stayed home. I was so lonesome I went to bed and cried myself to sleep.

June 24. Baked some cupcakes in morning. In afternoon went to sleep. In evening went to dance with Weezie and "Jo." Pretty good time. Missed George too much to have fun. Beulah and Jane were there too.

June 25. Went up and got my dresses from cleaners. They look swell. Got a darling letter from Georgie. Was over at Mary's and Catherine's all evening. Wrote a letter to George, I think.

June 26. I didn't do much all day. In evening took a walk with Mary and Catherine. Went to Davison's.

June 27. I worked at Grant's from 1 to 9. I like it. I work in the candy department. John and I went uptown and got us a Coke after work. Missed George as usual.

June 28. Eustacia came up. We went riding in afternoon. Missed Georgie. Went to Merrigan's. In evening I wrote him a letter. Went riding with Mary and Catherine.

June 29. Joe came over in afternoon about 12:45. I didn't know he was coming. He called me up first. He and his cousin came. We went out to Liberty and danced all afternoon. Had fun but not as much as if it had been Georgie. He brought me a nice graduation present. They left about 4. In evening Weezie, Norine, and I went to Merrigan's in eve.

June 30. I worked at Mace's [a local drug store] from 9 A.M. to 10 P.M. Had fun. Mother, Dad, and Harold and I went riding afterwards.

July 1. Worked at Mace's again till 6. In evening didn't do anything but write a letter to my honey. I got one from him in morning.

July 2. Worked at Mace's from 8 to 12. Finished up. Made $4.60. Mildred and I went uptown in afternoon and spent it. I got my new dress.

July 3. In morning Bud Simon came over in his cute truck to see me. Said he just came to see those he was interested in. I worked from 1 to 9. Were we busy. Came home with M. Helena and Paul. Went to Davison's.

July 4. Mildred and I took a ride. We went out to State with John. Saw dull parade. Went on too long. In evening went up to meet Jimmie. We went to park for dance. Then went to Liberty. Came home. Was I lonesome for George.

July 5. Norine and I went riding. Lil and I went to see *White Fairy* in afternoon. Swell. In evening went up to Angela's. Bob Austin wanted a date in afternoon.

July 6. Mildred [Horn] and I went down to Merrigan's. In evening we took the car and went down to meet Jimmie.

July 7. Mildred and I went down to Merrigan's. I stayed home in evening, I guess. Can't remember what I did!

July 8. Margaret had a party. Had a swell time. Got home about 6. Stayed home in evening.

July 9. Didn't do anything in afternoon. In evening, Harold and I went to see *The Ghost Gets His Wish*. Swell.

July 10. Went up to Angela's in afternoon. Didn't do anything in evening. Took a ride.

July 11. Worked at Grant's from 2 till 9. We were expecting George to come down. I got a letter from him. Cute. We then took a ride.

July 12, 1936
17th Birthday

July 12. (My 17th Birthday) Margaret came in and stayed all day. We went riding in morning. In afternoon we went swimming. I got a new swim suit for my birthday. Cute. In evening went up to Angela's. Came home and wrote George a letter.

July 13. Went down to hospital with Margaret S. to see Mary. In afternoon Weezie, Norine, and I went down to Merrigan's. Went to cone shop. Came home.

July 14. Went up to Angela's in afternoon. In evening we went riding. Nothing to do since George left. Miss him a lot. Got a letter from Joey in morning.

July 15. Weezie and I went swimming. I had the car. Brought Mahlon Gaumer and some other kid home. Went down to hot-dog stand. Stayed home in evening.

July 16. Mother and I went riding in afternoon. In evening we all went riding. Went down to Silverfrost. Came home. Norine and I went uptown.

July 17. Aunt Della [Lawler, wife of Mary Pearl's brother, Uncle Jim Lawler], Bob, and Boots came up [from St. Louis]. Stayed all day. In afternoon I went up to Angela's. In evening Weezie and I went up to Merrigan's. Had fun!

July 18. I worked at Grant's. Afterwards I went to the dance. Danced all evening with Don Baptist and Luke Zeller. Came home with Luke, Bob, and Marty. We went to Davison's. Had fun. He asked me for another date. (I missed George.)

July 19. Went down to Eustacia's. Ate dinner at Mildred's. In afternoon we played games at the Church. In evening I had a date with Dean McPherson, Eustacia with Jack Drew, and Janet with Popeye. Went to Jerseyville and Greenfield. Seemed funny without George. Went riding with Jouett in V8 to river and all over. He wanted to take us to dance in evening. I wouldn't go.

July 20. In afternoon Eustacia and I played croquet with Betty. In evening went riding with Jouett and another kid. Had pretty good time.

July 21. I was sick all day. Eustacia and I went to the show to see *Laughing Irish Eyes*. Good, but I was so weak I could hardly stand up.

July 22. In afternoon we went to 4H-Club style show. In evening we went riding with Neil Simonds. He took us to the confectionery. Met the kids. Had fun! Went to river to fish.

July 23. Went to Jerseyville. Came home about 6. In evening Jimmie, Norine, and Jim came after me in our new Plymouth. Was I surprised? I didn't know they were going to get one. They got it Wed. I came home in evening. I got a real important darling letter from George.

July 24. I wrote George a letter in afternoon. Took a ride in our new car. In morning I drove it. It's keen. After supper walked uptown.

July 25. Went to work at 1. Came home after work and Mother and I went uptown. Went to Hamilton's.

July 26. Worked at cone shop in evening. Made $1.08 counting 25 cents I found. Got a letter from Joe. I had the car all day. Norine, Virginia Smith, and I went riding. Went to Wagner's. In evening we went to K'ville. Went to dance. Danced with Jouett, Raphael Behrens, and everyone. I stayed all nite. Jouett wanted to take me home, but I wouldn't let him.

July 27. I sent George a real cute birthday card. Were with Kamp twins all morning. Had fun. In afternoon I came home. Went uptown, got a new dress. In evening all the kids came down. We went to Merrigan's and to skating rink. Had fun!

July 28. Lil and I went to show to see *The Crime of Dr. Forbes* and *The Moon's Our Home*. Swell. Went to Hamilton's afterwards. In evening went riding.

July 29, 1936
George's 20 Birthday

July 29. George's birthday [his twentieth]. I had the car. Mother and I went uptown. Then we went for a long ride. In nite, John, Dad, Mom, and I went to see *Little Red Schoolhouse*. Swell. Went riding afterwards.

July 30. Can't remember what I did. In evening took a ride.

July 31. I got a letter from George and Edwina Kamp [one of the twins in Kampsville] and Eustacia. In afternoon Mother and I went out to Margaret's. She and I rode 5-1/2 miles on horse. Grand time. Was with Angela in evening.

August 1. Worked at Grant's. In evening came home and Mother and I went uptown.

August 2. I went to see Shirley [Temple] in *Poor Little Rich Girl* with Marg, Jean, and Angela. Eustacia came up. I wrote to George. We went to skating rink and Davison's and Black Cat.

August 3. In afternoon Eustacia and I went uptown. Went to Merrigan's. In evening Norine, Eustacia, and I went to skating rink and Merrigan's. We rode 20 miles in our car. Charlie called me up.

August 4. Mother, Eustacia, and I went uptown. Went to Merrigan's. In evening Eustacia and I went skating. Keen time. Went to Hamilton's. Went riding with Paul Chumley. Went to Wagner's.

August 5. I worked all day at Monkey's [Montgomery Wards]. In evening Eustacia and I went to potluck supper at Gloria's. Keen time.

August 6. I worked all day. Eustacia went home. I stayed home.

August 7. Worked all day. Stayed home in evening. Had been expecting a letter from George all week. Am I mad??

August 8. Worked. Went to bed early. Still no letter. I guess he's forgotten me. I told him he would.

August 9. Went to St. Louis to see my Aunt [Della]. Keen time. Got home about 11 o'clock. Went the new way.

August 10. Worked all day. Went up to Angela's in evening. Jean was there. We went to the skating rink.

August 11. Angela came down. We went uptown. Fooled around rest of evening. Worked all day.

August 12. Didn't work. We had McNulty's from St. Louis to spend the day. Margaret and I went uptown in afternoon. In evening I went to dance with Jim and Lil.

August 13. Went on a picnic to park. Swam, played tennis and everything. Did I get brown. I learned how to float on my back and also went down slide. Keen time.

August 14. Mother and I went uptown. I got a new dress and

a new pair of shoes. Wrote to George. I got a special-delivery letter from him and a letter from Joe.

August 15. Jimmie came home from Colorado. Fooled around in morning. Baked a cake in afternoon. In evening Lil and I went to the dance. Had a good time. Jim and Norine came after us. We rode around. Went to hot-dog joint.

August 16. Had the car in morning. In afternoon, Mary came in. We took a walk. Went to Davison's. In evening Lil came up. We went skating. Had fun.

August 17. Lil came up. We went to the dentist. In evening we went riding.

August 18. I had my hair fixed. In evening we went riding. Went up to hot-dog joint.

August 19. I had the car all day. Mother, Harold, and I went riding all afternoon. Had lots of fun. In evening we went riding with Jim.

August 20. I had the car. Mother and I went riding. In evening Harold and I went down to Merrigan's. We got caught in the rain.

August 21. I slept in the afternoon. I was mad because I didn't hear from George. Margaret came in. The telephone rang and it was a telegram from George. Was I thrilled. I went up the office after it. I can hardly wait to see him. I took Mother, Norine, and Harold on ride in nite. Then Mother and I went walking.

August 22. Couldn't hardly do anything I was so excited waiting for George. Mildred and I went down to Merrigan's. In evening we went riding and Mother and I went uptown.

August 23. Went to early Church. Norine and I went riding in morning. I couldn't wait till George comes. In nite he called me long-distance and said he was at Monmouth and would see me in the morning. Glad he called, but I was disappointed. Still something to look forward to.

George returns to Jacksonville

August 24. Harold and I went uptown after my belt. George came meanwhile. I didn't think he was coming till noon. I came home he kissed me in front of Mother. He looks keen. I'm so glad he's here. Did I miss him??? George and I went riding in afternoon. In evening we went to show to see *Suzy*. Had fun. Went to Merrigan's.

August 25. George and I rode around all day. In evening we went riding (Jim and Norine too). We went to Wagner's. Keen time. George is still the same. George and I took Father Andy 8 miles east of Carrollton for a sick call [to take Communion to the sick]. Had fun coming back. Stopped at Carrollton.

August 26. George bought me the most beautiful vanity set I ever saw. I love it. He picked it and then took me along to get it. He's a darling. We went to show in afternoon. Saw *Jailbreak* and *It's Love Again*. Everyone loves my vanity set. In nite we went to Carrollton with Jimmie, saw Shirley Temple again. Good.

August 27. George and I went riding in afternoon, went to milk-shake place. In nite Charlie, Betty, Joyce Wilday and Archie DeSollar, and George and I went to Liberty. Had lots of fun. It rained and rained.

August 28. George and I went to show to see *Message to Garcia* and *My American Wife*. In evening we went to Carrollton.

August 29. George and John and I went hunting. In nite we went to the dance. Had lots of fun. Were with John and Betty awhile.

August 30. We ate dinner in Carrollton with Mildred. George

and I and Jimmie and Mildred went to St. Louis to ball game. Saw Dizzy [Dean] pitch. Went out to Aunt Della's afterwards. Had oodles of fun. Ate supper in Alton. Grand time.

August 31. In afternoon we went riding. In nite we went to see *To Mary Watkins*. Swell. Afterwards we went riding. Went out to Wagner's.

September 1. We went riding. In nite we went to Carrollton. Had fun as usual.

September 2. Some fellow bumped me on the square. Cost him $3 to repair our fender. In afternoon we went riding. In evening we went to the chicken supper. It was out to the State hospital. We went to the dance. Had fun.

September 3. Took the car up to have it fixed. Went riding. In evening went to Carrollton to Fair. Swell time. Mildred and I walked about 2 miles. Then we got in the car and locked George, Jimmie, and Norine out. Was George mad. We made up. Had lots of fun.

September 4. In afternoon saw President Roosevelt. In nite went to show to see *Straight From the Shoulder* and *The Bride Walked Out*. Went riding afterwards. Fun.

September 5. George went hunting [squirrels and pheasants] in afternoon. In evening we went to the dance with Jimmie and Gwenn. Then went riding. "Swell time."

September 6. Rosemary Lambert [cousin] and all of 'em came up from St. Louis. In afternoon we all went riding. In evening went to show to see *Texas Rangers*. Swell.

September 7. George went hunting. In evening we went to Carrollton with Jimmie. Had lots of fun.

September 8. We went out to Margaret's. Rode horseback. Had a swell time. In evening we rode around. Had fun.

September 9. In afternoon we went to see *Let's Sing Again* and *Case of Velvet Claws*. Swell. We went to dance in evening. Larry Thompson's orchestra. Swell. Afterwards went riding till real late with Jim, Norine, Gwenn, and Jimmie. Went to hot-dog joint. Swell time.

September 10. George went hunting in afternoon. In evening we had the car. Went out to Wagner's. Rode all around. Had a keen fight. Got Mother from her party. Fun.

September 11. In afternoon we went to see *China Clipper* and *Hollywood Boulevard*. Swell. Went to Merrigan's. In evening Chick and Pat, Jimmie, Gwenn, George, and I went out to Snyder's and danced. Then rode around. Swell time.

September 12. I had my carbuncle lanced twice. Dr. Norris did it. [In June 1939, Dr. Norris delivered George and Virginia's first child, Jack, while the entire multi-generational family lived at 517 S. Church Street.] George and Mother went with me. In evening we went to the dance. Had a swell time. Went to Wagner's afterwards.

September 13. Went to show in afternoon to see *His Brother's Wife*. Swell. Went to Merrigan's. George is mad now. He wants to help me write in my diary. He wanted to make up so we did. We went uptown and fooled around.

September 14. I worked at Deppe's [the department store—in Jacksonville on the square—where she was paid 25 cents an hour, and bought her wedding dress]. George worked with Chumley's [construction company]. In evening we went to Carrollton with Jimmie. Fooled around. Went to confectionary.

September 15. I worked. In evening Jim, Norine, and George

and I went riding. Went down to Silverfrost. Fun as usual. Fight as usual.

September 16. I didn't work. In evening Jimmie, Gwenn, Bob K., Ethel Heurty, and George, and I went out to Snyder's. George and I went to the dance first. Swell time.

September 17. I worked. In evening Jimmie, Gwenn, George and I went to show to see *Half Angel* and *Love Begins at 20*. Met Jim and Norine and we all went out to Wagner's. Had loads of fun.

September 18. I worked. In evening George and I went to the show to see *State Fair* and *Three Cheers for Love*. Went to Merrigan's afterwards.

September 19. I worked. Got off at 8:30. Got a new hat and a new pair of shoes. George and I went to the dance. Fun. Came home and Norine and Jim and we went to Julienne. Rode around. Fun.

September 20. George and Mildred and I went to see 3 hr. picture, *The Great Ziegfeld*. Pretty good. In evening we rode around and went up and got Jimmie.

September 21. Jimmie worked at Merrigan's. We went up to get him. Rode around. Went to Wagner's and came home.

September 22. George and I went to the show, *Kelly the Second* and *High Tension*. Swell. Went to Merrigan's.

September 23. George and I went riding in the rain. Went up to Silverfrost. Had lots of fun. Good fight.

September 24. George and I worked. Mother and I went riding. George and I had a fight. I told him [short-hand marks]. He didn't X [kiss] me once today. He went to bed. Mom, Norine, and I stayed up a long time.

September 25. George got up and was going home. He wouldn't

even speak to me. He went uptown and came home and wanted me to make up with him, so I did. Everybody's happy now. Ha.

September 26. In the morning fooled around. I went to work at $ store [the dollar store, a 5 and 10 cents variety store] at 2. We went to dance afterwards. Swell time. Went to Julienne.

September 27. Mother, George, Norine, and I went to see *Gorgeous Hussy*. Good. In evening we kids stayed home. Fooled around.

September 28. In afternoon, Mom and I went riding. George worked. In nite we saw *His Second Wife* and *King of the Royal Mounted*. Swell.

September 29. George worked. In afternoon, Mother and I went riding. In nite we had the car. Went riding.

September 30. In afternoon George worked. Mother and I went riding. Jimmie came home and gave us the car. We went riding. Went down to Creed's.

October 1. In afternoon, Mother and I took a ride. In nite George and I went to see *Devil Doll* and *Back to Nature*. Swell.

October 2. (Mom's 48th birthday) George ran a nail in his foot working at Chumley's. Doctor in afternoon. Went riding. Home in evening.

October 3. Mother and I went uptown. George stayed here. In nite we saw *Bengal Tiger*. Swell. Went to Merrigan's. Mildred, Jimmie, George, and I went down to Creed's.

October 4. Norine, Mildred, Jimmie, George, and I went to Champaign to see Jim. Had a wonderful time. Ate chicken dinner at Perkin's restaurant. Swell place. Went to show in afternoon, *Swing Time*. Grand! Ate supper at Stanley's restaurant. Swell joint. Came home about 12:00 o'clock.

October 5. In afternoon George and I went to show, *Sing, Baby, Sing*. Good. In evening, Shorty, Louise Gilmore, Jimmie, George, and I brought Mildred home. Had lots of fun. Went to confectionary.

October 6. Rode around in afternoon. In nite we had the car. Had a fight. Went out to Julienne. Made up. Came home early.

October 7. Went to show in afternoon, *Yours for the Asking* and *Front Page Lady*. Good. In evening Shorty, Jimmie, Gwenn, Kay Kerger, and George and I went to dance at Palace ball room. Had fun. Gwenn and I left. Went to Merrigan's. Was George mad. He wouldn't go to the dance anymore. Stayed in car.

October 9. Went riding in afternoon. In evening, we went out to Liberty. Shorty, Jimmie, Gwenn, W. Lendie, George, and I. Had swell time. Gwenn told orchestra to play "Beautiful Lady in Blue" for Mr. and Mrs. George Fritscher. Were our faces red! [Friends begin teasing the couple who seem suited to marry.]

October 10. I worked at Grant's. George was still sick. Stayed home after work.

October 11. Shorty, Jimmie, Marg. Cain, Mildred, George, and I went to weiner roast at park. Swell time. Then went to Carrollton.

October 12. Gloria [Hanley] came up. She's going to be a nun. Came home from school. In evening we went with Daddy. Then went to a party out to Gwenn's. Fun!

October 13. We took a ride in afternoon. In evening went to show *End of the Trail* and *Grand Jury*. Good.

October 14. In afternoon Mother and I went riding. In evening we went to Carrollton with Jimmie. Went to confect. and out to see Mildred's school. Had fun. We got to Carrollton in 25 minutes. Raced Paul Chumley. Was I scared?

October 15. Took a ride in afternoon. George and I walked uptown. Came home. Made candy.

October 16. George and I washed and Simonized the car. Looks swell. In evening, Weezie, L. Gilmore, Shorty, George, and I went out to Liberty. Had fun.

October 17. (Daddy's 49th birthday) I worked. Went riding—Jim, Norine, George and I after work.

October 18. George, Mom, Dad, Harold, and I went to see John [at Kenrick Seminary]. Ate at Dolphy's. George and I went riding in afternoon. Had lots of fun. Got home about 8:30.

October 19. George slept. I went uptown and got a new "overnight bag" (yum!). In the evening went to show, *Thank you, Jeeves* and *Spendthrift*. Swell. Went riding afterwards.

October 20. The club gave Mother a surprise party. George and I had to fill in. Played pinochle. Fun.

October 21. Went to Carrollton with Jimmie. Fooled around. Went to confectionary.

October 22. George, Gwenn, Shortie, Norine, and I went out to Liberty. Had fun!! As usual.

October 23. George and I, Jimmie, Mildred Ash, Shortie, and Norine all went out to Liberty. Good time. Went riding. Came home.

October 24. I worked. After work George and I went to the party at Grant's. Swell time. Went to Wagner's.

October 25. Went to show, saw *Big Noise* and *Alibi for Murder*. Good. I got sick that night. Scared George stiff.

October 26. I was sick. Stayed home. We played pinochle. I won every game but one.

October 27. George, Mom, Dad, and I went to Kampsville. Mom and Dad went to Hamburg. We saw Beulah and the twins. George and I ate at Aunt Mag's. I had my hair set.

October 28. Went to Carrollton with Jimmie. Saw *Satan Met a Lady*. Went to confectionary. Came home.

October 29. Mom and I went uptown. I got a new skirt. Shortie, Jimmie, George, Norine, Gwenn, and I went out to Liberty. Swell time.

October 30. Jimmie, Bernice, Mother, Shortie, Norine, and I went out to Snyder's. Swell time.

October 31. Worked at Grant's. After work went to a party at Gwenn's. Had treasure hunt and weiner roast. Swell time. Got home about 2.

November 1. Went to Carrollton with Jimmie. Went to Jerseyville. Saw *My Man Godfrey*. Rotten. Ate supper with Mildred. Went up to confect. after supper.

November 2. George slept. I went uptown and got a my new shoes. In evening went to show *Cain and Mabel*. Grand. Went to Merrigan's afterwards.

November 3. In morning George and I went uptown. In afternoon we took a nap. Took mother uptown. In evening went to the show *Women Are Trouble* and *Sea Spoilers*. Good.

November 4. In afternoon went riding. In evening we played cards. Mother made hot choc. Had fun! Gwenn stayed all nite.

November 5. Jimmie, Thelma Graves, George and I, and

Shortie and Norine went out to Liberty. Had lots of fun. I got my new coat and hat. George thinks its swell.

November 6. Shortie, Norine, Jimmie, George, and I went to Carrollton after Mildred. Came home. Went to Merrigan's. Then George and I went riding.

November 7. I worked. George met me. Rode around and then went out to Julienne. Came home. Went to bed.

Inside the front cover of the Diary, is a tiny scrap of a yellowed clipping torn out of the Jacksonville newspaper, dated November 10, 1936. The headline reads, "To Return North." The four-line text reads, "George Fritcher [misspelled] expects to leave this week for his home in Heron Lake, Minn., after spending several days with relatives and friends here." Virginia's note on the clipping, handwritten in ink, says, "Jimmie's trick," meaning her brother Jimmie Day, who, to tease the young dating couple, had sent in a notice to the Jacksonville social column.

Dating for a year, George leaves for Minnesota to attend Mankato State College from November 1936 to return in the summer of 1937 when he came back to Jacksonville to become engaged to Virginia, and worked for three months with future brother-in-law Jim Chumley's dad's construction company. Jim was the son of Alderman Thomas C. Chumley, 1231 South Clay Avenue, Jacksonville. In the fall of 1937, George returned to Minnesota, and in the early winter of 1938 his fiancée Virginia took a train to Mankato and stayed a month with George's sister, Agnes Tschohl, and her husband Harry, and their children. She paid special attention to their then youngest, Bill, on whom she doted. That month cemented the positive certainty of the relationship. George returned to Jacksonville on April 12, 1938, the very day Aunt Mag (Day-Stelbrink died) and George said, "Let's get married on July 12 on your birthday and your parents' anniversary." So he got a job at Producer's

Dairy where he worked when their first child, Jack Fritscher [John Joseph Patrick Fritscher], was born June 20, 1939.

1936 continues

November 8. George and I have been going together a year today (Swell). We went to show in afternoon to see *Pigskin Parade*. Grand. In nite played cards and went riding. Had a fight.

November 9. Went riding in afternoon. In nite stayed home and popped corn. Fun!!!!!

November 10. In afternoon I slept. In evening we went riding. In nite played cards and then Shortie, Norine, George, and I went riding.

November 11. Armistice Day. In morning we saw parade and went riding. In afternoon my honey, Georgie, and I went to show *The Road to Glory*. Swell. This is probably the last show we'll see together for some time. I sure hate to see him go. [Notes in shorthand] tonight?? We took a walk and then played cards. We won the tournament. Ha! Last time we'll tell one another goodbye for a long time. We kissed each other on the steps as usual. That night we both broke down. We just can't say goodbye. We both love one another. Went to bed about 1 A.M. I guess this is the last time George will help me write him into my diary for a long time. He hates to leave, but we guess it's for the best.

George leaves 12 November 1936 until June 1937

November 12. George and I got up early on account of his leaving. Went up and told Jimmie, Shortie, and Mrs. Holmes goodbye. When he told Norine goodbye, he cried like a baby. I felt so sorry for him. I started in then too. He said he hated to leave me and our crowd. He kissed Mother goodbye and told Dad goodbye. (I wrote George a letter in nite.) His eyes just filled up. I couldn't take it. I took him up to the bus depot. He kissed me several times. I cried and so did he but we managed to smile goodbye to one another. I came home and cried and cried. I miss him so much. In afternoon Mother and I went uptown. Took a ride. In evening I wrote my darling a letter. Then went with Dad and mailed our letters.

November 13. I got a letter from George, card from Charlie. We went to Springfield to take Norine over. I drove. In afternoon we fooled around in the stores. In nite I wrote him a letter and Mother and I went up to mail it in the car. Missed George so much.

November 14. I got another letter. Was I troubled? I worked in afternoon. Mother met me. Then we took a ride and went after Jimmie. Missed George not meeting me.

November 15. Went to Church. Missed George. I wrote him a letter. In afternoon Gloria and Marg. came up. Went to Hamilton's. In nite went to Springfield after Norine with Jimmie, Shortie, Mother, and Mildred. Missed George an awful lot tonight.

November 16. Mother and I went riding in afternoon. In evening I went up to Merrigan's with Norine and Weezie. Had the car. Took V. Smith, and M.E. Spaulding home.

November 17. I got a letter from my sweetheart. Mother and I walked uptown. In evening I wrote my "Georgie" a letter. Mother and I went up and mailed it. Took a little walk and came home. I always miss George every place I go.

November 18. In afternoon Mother and I took a ride. In evening we went to Carrollton with Jimmie. Ran into a surprise party at Eustacia's. Fun. As usual, miss George.

November 19. I got a nice letter from George. In afternoon Mother and I wrote George a letter. Norine and I went up and mailed Jim's and George's letters. Went to Merrigan's. We both missed our honeys. Jack Shumny called us the two "widows."

November 20. Mother, Dad, and I went to Springfield. I drove. I got a darling new sweater. Mother did a little Xmas shopping. Went to Sugar Barrel. Got home about 5:30. In nite Norine and I wore our little sweaters and went up to Merrigan's with Dot. I had the car. Norine was with Shorty. Did I miss George?

November 21. Got the most gorgeous special letter from Eustacia. Gee, it made me feel swell. In afternoon I worked. Mother met me. We went up after Jimmie. Came home, went to bed. Guess I'll always miss ole "Georgie."

November 22. Went to Church and Communion. Missed George. In afternoon Mother and I went to see *Dimples*, with Shirley Temple. Got his picture. It was darling. Made me cry. Missed George at show. In evening wrote George a letter.

November 23. In afternoon Mother took me to the doctor with my toe. He said I'd have to go to the hospital. I was scared stiff. Took a ride. Wish George was here to go with me.

November 24. Went to the hospital at 8. Made me go to bed and put an operating gown on me. I took a hypo. I was on the table over a half hour. The gas made me sick. In afternoon Margaret came to see me. In nite Shorty and Johnnie came down. I got a letter from George. Sure miss him.

November 25. Stayed in bed practically all day. I was sick. Mother wrote to George. I sure miss him. Gloria called up.

November 26. Thanksgiving. Thought I'd get a letter from George but didn't. Jim was up for dinner and Mildred was up for supper. I was blue all day. Missed George.

November 27. I got a darling letter from George. He wrote to know what I want for Xmas. Mildred took Mother and I for a ride in afternoon. Went and got a Coke. Wrote George a letter. Miss George terribly since my foot is sore.

November 28. Couldn't work. Sure seemed funny. Stayed home all afternoon. In evening we went with Daddy. Went up to get Jimmie. Got a swell special letter from George. Wrote to him. Miss him more than ever since I was operated on.

November 29. Couldn't go to Church. Jean, Gloria, and Margaret came in. Stayed all afternoon. We took a ride after they left. Played cards in evening. Wrote George a letter. Missed George.

November 30. Mother and I went up to the doctor's. They dressed my foot. Then Mother and I came back uptown. I drove first time since I was operated on. Picked out George's robe. It's darling. Expected a letter. Miss him so much.

December 1. Washed my hair. Expected a letter again today. Boy, he'll wait till I write to him!! He must care a lot! He'd bad. I miss him. Why doesn't he write?

December 2. Mother and I took a ride in afternoon. When I came home there was a darling special from George. He asked me if I wanted a ring with a watch for Xmas. In evening Shorty, Norine, and I went up to mail my letter I wrote to George. Went to Merrigan's. Missed George.

December 3. Mom and I went to the Doctor's. He took the stitches out of my foot. Did I yell? Auntie and Angela came down. Stayed till 12. Had fun!!

December 4. Dorothy came in. Brought little Barbara Ann. I played with her. In evening I went down to Merrigan's with Norine and Beulah. Rode home with Jimmie. Had fun. Miss my little George. I always do and always will, I guess.

December 5. Wrote George a letter in afternoon. In morning got a lovely special letter from him. He's so sweet. In evening Mother and I went with Daddy. Cold and raining. Missed George.

December 6. I cooked dinner. Made some pumpkin pies. They all liked them. Mom is sick. Jean, Rosalind, and I went to show, *Love on the Run*. Grand. Missed George so much because we always went. I wrote George a letter in nite and got a cute special from him asking me why I didn't write and I always do. Gee, I hope it didn't get lost.

December 7. Mother and I went up to the Doctor's. In morning I wrote George a letter. Weezie came over and we played cards. Missed George as usual.

December 8. Went to Church. In afternoon Mother and I went uptown. Aunt Mag and Cecilia and Joe came up for supper. Wrote George a letter in morning. In evening stayed home. Got a darling special-delivery letter from George.

December 9. Roths came up. Stayed all afternoon. In afternoon wrote George a letter. In evening stayed home. Missed George.

December 10. Wrote George a letter in morning. In afternoon Mother and I went to a party at Maurer's. Got a letter from George. In evening stayed home. Missed George. Got my shoe on for the first time since I was operated on.

December 11. Went uptown in afternoon Mother and I. Got a letter from George. In evening Jean came in. We and Joe went walking. Went to Hamilton's.

December 12. I went to work at 12. First time since my foot was operated on. Got a lovely special from George. Mother and Norine met me. Went to Hamilton's and Black Cat. Missed George meeting me.

December 13. Wrote a letter to George. Marty came up in afternoon. Went down to Merrigan's. In nite Norine and I went riding with George Brainerd.

December 14. Went to work at 12. In morning I got a letter from George. Wrote to him in evening. Norine and I had the car. Went and mailed it. Got M.E. Spaulding. Went to Merrigan's.

December 15. Got a darling letter from a darling boy. Worked from 12 to 5:00. In evening wrote to George. Norine and I had the car. Went to Merrigan's. Was with Jimmie and Shorty.

December 16. Did some of my Xmas shopping. Went to work at 12. Wrote Georgie a letter and got a darling one from him. He thinks I'm mad but I'm not. He didn't even owe me any. He's so sweet. I can't wait till I get my watch.

December 17. Stores started staying open till 9 o'clock. I worked from 12 till 9. Mother met me. We went and got a Coke, came home. Wrote to George in morning.

December 18. Wrote a letter to George. Worked from 12 till 9. Mother met me. We went and got a Coke. Came home.

December 19. Worked from 12 to 9. Mother met me. We went and got a Coke. Got cigarettes for George's robe [to hide as a gift in the pocket].

December 20. Went to Church. Washed my hair. In afternoon I wrapped George's presents. Joe came up in afternoon. We went to Hamilton's. In evening wrote to George. Norine and I went to Merrigan's.

December 21. I had Daddy mail and insure George's package. I hope he gets it Wed. I wrote him a letter. I get one from him every day. It's sure swell. I worked from 12 to 9. Mother met me. We got a Coke. Came home.

December 22. Worked from 12 to 9. Mother met me. I got a special from George. He said I should get my watch the same time as I get the letter, but I didn't. I was so excited. Mother and I got a Coke. Came home. I couldn't sleep I was so excited.

December 23. Wrote George a letter. Worked from 12 to 9. Gee, I thought I'd get my watch, but I didn't. I was so disappointed. In evening Mother met me. We went and got a Coke. Came home. I couldn't sleep.

December 24. Christmas eve. I wrote George a letter, mad too, and got one, but still my watch didn't come. I guess it's lost. When I came home from work to supper, it was here. I couldn't wait to get it open. It's simply darling. George is so sweet. He had the cutest card with it.

December 25. Christmas. Gee, I got lots of lovely things. Everything I wanted, but Georgie. I missed him so much. Everybody loves my watch. I got a blue satin negligee, blue pajamas, blue town sweaters, blue powder jar, and boudoir brush. Darling!

December 26. Fooled around in morning. In afternoon Mother and I went uptown. I got a new pair of sno-boots. Darling. I got a letter from George. I wrote him one. In evening Gloria had a potluck supper. Played bingo. Had a keen time. Everyone loves my watch.

December 27. Went to Church. In afternoon we went to a coffee at Margaret's, in honor of Gloria [who's off to the convent to become a nun]. We all gave her a goodbye gift. She cried. Came home, we all went down to Lillian's. Had fun! Went to Hamilton's.

December 28. I got a letter from my honey. Went to Angela's in afternoon. In evening Norine, Weezie, and I went down to Merrigan's. I wrote George a letter. We mailed it.

December 29. In afternoon I went up to see Angela. Slept awhile. In evening Jean, Gloria, and I went to Majestic and saw

The General Died at Dawn and *Ticket to Paradise*. Swell. Missed Georgie. Went to Hamilton's afterwards. 2 A.M.

December 30. Had the car in afternoon. Aunt Mag and Joe came up. Aunt Mag has to go to the hospital again. In evening, Jean and I went walking out to Gloria's and to Merrigan's. Had lots of fun. Real cold.

Aunt Mag Day Stelbrink dies 100 days later on April 12, 1938, the very day George returns from Minnesota to propose marriage.

December 31. Aunt Mag was operated on. Joe, Cecilia, and Uncle Cap [Stelbrink] were here for dinner. John and I went to the b.b. game in Roodhouse v. Routt. Took Jimmie and Mildred to Carrollton. Sure missed George. I was with him a year ago tonite.

End note written inside back cover
"End of 1936, the most wonderful year, I believe, I ever spent. George and I went together the whole year. Wonderful times. And I got my wrist watch from George this year (Xmas)."

George Fritscher and Virginia Day,
Kampsville Locks, April 19, 1936

Always Virginia   145

Top. In 1934. George Fritscher, born of immigrant Austrian parents on a farm in Heron Lake, Minnesota, was, at age 17, a star player for Heron Lake High School when he was recruited by a sports-scholarship scout from Routt High School in Jacksonville to start in August 1935. **Bottom**. In 1948, he was continuing his love of sports on the basketball team of his employer, the *Peoria Journal Star* newspaper.

ROUTT HIGH SCHOOL VARSITY LETTER
On November 4, 1935, Routt varsity letterman George Fritscher asked Routt cheerleader Virginia Day to be his date for Homecoming. This is the first mention of him in her "Diary." On November 30, he gave her his Routt Rockets varsity letter which she sewed onto her letter sweater. He played and lettered in football, basketball, and baseball, and she was the literary editor of the school magazine, *The Wag*.

The Wag

EDITOR - - - - - - - CHARLES MAGNER
ASSOCIATE EDITOR - - - MARDELLE THOMPSON
BUSINESS MANAGER - - - - JOHN KENNEDY
ASSISTANT BUSINESS MANAGER - - - JACK HANLEY

LITERARY EDITORS
VIRGINIA DAY   ANGELA DAVID
MARY MARGARET RING   LEE McGINNIS

JOKE EDITORS
JOSEPHINE JOHNSON   GLORIA HANLEY
WILLIAM MONAHAN

EXCHANGE EDITORS
LILLIAN MALLEN   LUCILLE SCHWABE
RAPHAEL BEHRENS

FACULTY ADVISERS
SISTER MARY EULALIA, O. P.
SISTER MARY MAURICE, O. P.

SPORT EDITORS
HOWARD ANDERSON - - - - - JOHN MAGNER
ALUMNI EDITOR - - - - - PAUL A. KAISER

CIRCULATION
HARRY BUOY, JOHN LAIR, ROBERT RING, PAUL BERGSCHNEIDER, ARTHUR HULL, FRANCIS MALONEY, BERNARD SHANAHAN, JAMES LONERGAN, VINCENT TOBIN, JOHN DeVOS, FRANCIS CASEY, ROBERT LAVERY.

CLASS REPORTERS
AGNES MERNIN, EDWARD COX, CATHERINE JORDAN, CHARLES PIKE, VIRGILENE EASLEY, ROBERT JOHNSON, ANN DEVLIN, ROBERT DeBARR.

FIRST CLASS HONOR RATING—NATIONAL SCHOLASTIC PRESS ASSOCIATION, 1934-'35

INTERNATIONAL FIRST PLACE HONOR AWARD— QUILL AND SCROLL, 1934-35

ALL CATHOLIC HONORS—1933-'34, 1934-'35

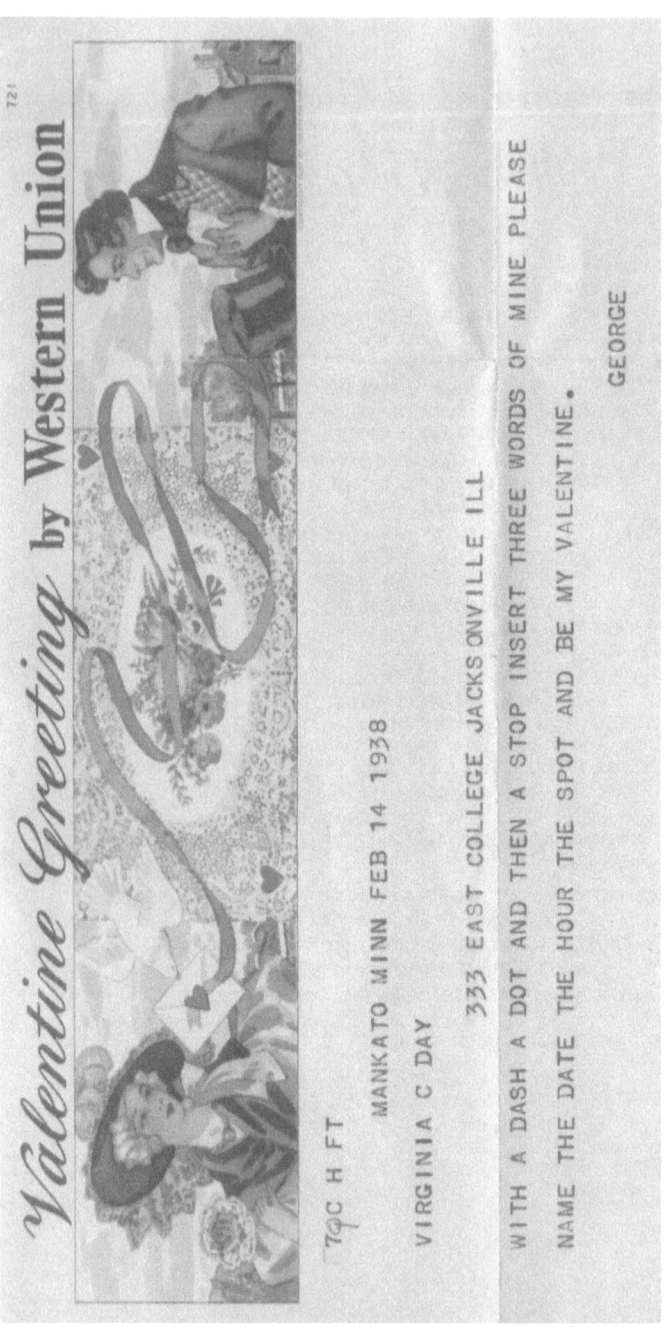

February 14, 1938, Valentine telegram to Virginia in Jacksonville from George in Mankato, Minnesota. After graduating Routt, George returned home to improve his prospects for marriage by studying accounting near his family at Mankato State College. Two months after this telegram, he returned to Jacksonville on April 12, and proposed they marry on July 12, Virginia's birthday and her parents' wedding anniversary. As a new husband, he worked as an accountant for Producers Dairy in Jacksonville.

July 12, 1938
Harold Day, George and Virginia Fritscher, Norine Day

Mr. and Mrs. George Fritscher, July 12, 1938

THE WEDDING
Jacksonville Journal and Courier
July 12, 1938

Virginia Day Weds
George Fritscher Here This Morning
Ceremony Performed at Church of Our Saviour
Before Large Audience

Virginia Claire Day, daughter of Mr. and Mrs. Bart Day, 517 South Church Street, and George Fritscher, son of Mr. and Mrs. Joseph E. Fritscher of Heron Lake, Minnesota, were married Tuesday morning at 8:00 o'clock at the Church of Our Saviour in an impressive ceremony. Rev. John B. Day, brother of the bride, and assistant pastor at St. Peter and St. Paul's church, Collinsville, officiated at the ceremony and the Nuptial Mass.

Miss Day was attended by her sister, Miss Norine Day, as maid of honor, and Harold Day, brother of the bride, served as best man for the groom.

Miss Stella Ring presided at the organ and gave a short recital as the bridal party entered and left the church. During the Mass, Mrs. Edward J. Flynn sang the following solos: "Ave Maria," Charles Gounod, and "Panis Angelicus," Cesar Franck.

The bridal party entered from the rear of the church with the maid of honor preceding the bride who with her father was met by the groom at the altar, where the bride was given in marriage. The maid of honor was met at the sanctuary by the best man forming an impressive group before the altar.

The bride was attired in white marquisette over white satin, designed floor length, princess style with long train. The puffed sleeves, pointed over the hand were trimmed with inserts of butterflies. She wore a long veil of tulle arranged in bonnet effect with orange blossoms and pearls. The bride's flowers were a large arm-bouquet of white lilies, baby breath, and white roses tied with a bride's bow of white tulle.

Miss Norine Day, as maid of honor, wore a peach-colored net dress over taffeta with white slippers, made floor length. Her short veil in halo arrangement was of peach color and transparent. Her arm bouquet was of tea roses and baby breath, tied with blue tulle.

The groom and his best man were attired in white and wore boutonnieres.

Following the ceremony a wedding breakfast was served at the Dunlap Hotel to 25 guests, the members of the wedding party, the immediate family, and a few friends. The color scheme carried out was peach and white, arranged on the tables which were T-shaped with the bride and groom, also with the attendants, with Father Day, at the head of the long table. A bride's cake in two lovely tiers was cut by the bride who served it to the guests.

After the breakfast, Mr. and Mrs. Fritscher left for a wedding trip to Minnesota. The bride wore for her going-away outfit a light blue lace dress over satin with white accessories.

Both Mr. and Mrs. Fritscher graduated from Routt college. Mr. Fritscher later attended Mankato Business college in Minnesota. He is employed at the Producer's Dairy in this city as an accountant.

Out-of-town guests were: Miss Mayme McNulty of St. Louis; Mrs. Hasen Mueller, Davenport, Iowa; Mr. and Mrs. W. Horn, Mrs. E. Ruyle and daughter, and Mrs. W. C. Cross, all of Carrollton.

Virginia Day Fritscher and Norine Day Chumley, Sisters
Peoria, Illinois 1942

Jack, George, Virginia, and Bob Fritscher
Christmas 1943

Jack, George, and Bob Fritscher, and Brownie
September 1954

George Fritscher
1948

OBITUARY
George Fritscher
July 29, 1916—November 6, 1976
Peoria Journal Star
Monday, November 8, 1976

Services for George Fritscher, 60, of 921 Willow Lane, will be tomorrow at Wilton Mortuary and at 10 at St. Philomena's Catholic Church, with the Rev. John M. Lohan officiating.

Visitation will be from 7 to 9 tonight at the mortuary where the Rosary will be recited at 8.

Mr. Fritscher died at 1:20 p.m. Saturday, November 6, in St. Francis Hospital where he was admitted October 23, after many such admittances during a twelve-year illness.

He was born at Heron Lake, Minn., July 29, 1916, the youngest son of Joseph Eugene Fritscher and Amelia Haberman Pieschel Fritscher. He married Virginia Day on July 12, 1938, in Jacksonville.

He last worked for Trend Kitchens where he was employed since 1969. He was a former manager of the Carson Pirie Scott & Co. appliance department for 18 years.

Mr. Fritscher was a member of St. Philomena's Catholic Church and the Men's Club of the church. He was treasurer of the Boy Scout troop at the church and was on the board of directors of the St. Vincent de Paul Society.

Surviving are his wife; two sons, Dr. John J. of San Francisco, Calif., and S.Sgt. G. Robert of Washington, D.C.; and one daughter, Miss Mary Claire of Berkeley, Calif.

Also surviving are three half-brothers, Henry Fritscher of Santa Rosa, Calif., Arthur J. Fritscher of Long Beach, Calif., and Clarence Pieschel of Dixon; two half-sisters, Mrs. Theresa Kummeth of Cogswell, N.D., Mrs. Agnes Tschohl of Mankato, Minn., and one sister, Mrs. Beatrice Brooks of Columbus, Neb., and three grandchildren. Three brothers preceded him in death.

Eulogy for Virginia Day Fritscher
July 12, 1919—November 14, 2004
December 4, 2004

Jack Fritscher

"Here we are as in Olden Days,
Happy golden days of Yore.
Faithful friends who are dear to us
gather near to us once more..."

My mother was a force of nature. She was good, smart, witty, and sophisticated. When alive, she lived. She had two declarations of independence: "I want to go where I want to go and do what I want to do." And, "I don't care what anyone does as long as they don't expect me to do it." She loved her parents who named her Virginia Claire Day, after the Virgin Mary and after County Clare in Ireland. She loved her three brothers and sister. She loved her husband through sickness and health. She was his care-giver for 12 years, from 1965 to 1976, during his 22 operations and six months at a time in ICU at the same time she raised a daughter from 6 years old to 18. Many of you here witnessed that 12-year ordeal and you were there to support my Mom and our family. Without you, faithful friends who are dear to us, this family could not have survived that 12-year tragedy and its post-traumatic stress. I have thanked you before, and I thank you again in the same way my Mom remained always grateful to you.

In adversity, she never lost her cheerfulness. From the age of 15, selling hosiery for 10 cents an hour at Mace's Drug Store, through the Commercial Bank and Block and Kuhl's in the 1950s, up through her career in marketing until she was 80, she was a working woman with a job and her job always involved talking with people. She was one of the world's great talkers. I listened to her on the phone nearly every night for the last 40 years. She loved the telephone. She was also a prolific writer of thousands of letters, most of them to me, and I have saved them all.

She was a photographer since she was 15; her last roll of film was shot 70 years later this last October 31 at a Halloween party where she won first prize for best costume. She was a cook and a baker who was famous for her banana cream pies with six-inch meringue. Her house was white-glove clean. She was a fashion plate who collected clothes. My father's favorite color for her was blue. So blue was always her favorite color. She modeled her wedding dress at a fashion show for charity here at St Philomena's thirty-five years after her wedding. She donated her dinner-dance dresses from the 1950s and 1960s to the costume department of a community theater group. For years, at the orphanage out on Heading Avenue, she weekly volunteered to hold unwanted babies in her arms. In 1954, she took a foster son into our home to care for him. In the 1960s, she was caregiver to her grandchildren Scott, Dianna, and Laura.

She loved movies and plays and the actress Alice Faye and Andy Williams. She was an Irish princess whose father had a rare blood condition found only in Irish kings. When she was 73, she flew to Ireland and she hung upside down by her heels, out of a castle window, ten stories up, to kiss the Blarney Stone. She bragged, "Irish and Catholic, thank God." Yet she understood that for a thousand years before her family was a thousand-years Catholic they were Irish Druids. She knew who she was and she accepted her identity.

Like many of you, she was a St. Philomena pioneer who helped found and build this parish with funds and volunteer work. I was one of the first St. Phil's altar boys for 16 years from 1947-1963, and when I needed a ride to early mass when I was too young to drive, my mom who never liked to get up early, drove me to serve. She was afraid of cats and mice. Even though she lit up her house on Willow Lane with so many spotlights that we called it "Virginia's Little Waco," she was a progressive person.

She was an intelligent woman who changed with the changing times of the complicated world of today. She was a progressive

Democrat who voted 12 days before she died. She marched in the streets against war carrying a sign that read "No Blood for Oil." She was a progressive Catholic who said the rosary, made Cursillos, and prayed nightly novenas. She stood for individual rights for each person. She was free of bias based on religion, race, and gender. She believed racism and sexism and homophobia are mortal sins; but she judged no one while accepting everyone. She didn't tell you, or me, or anyone, what to think, but she'd sweetly tell those who asked what she thought. She taught me tolerance. She taught me to be myself. No matter what.

She was always upbeat, positive, and the life of the party. She was a musical-comedy kind of woman who was a complex and real human being. Her parents adored her. Her brothers and sisters loved her. You, her friends who are indeed so dear to us from our auld lang syne, enjoyed her because she was never boring. She was a great care-giver who, at times during her life, needed some care which was given by her granddaughters Laura and Dianna who called her almost nightly; by Becky Mohn and her parents Chuck and Dot; by Pat Mullane; and especially by Pam Perrilles and her family, Marie and Jennie.

People sometimes joked that I was her only child, but for the last 26 years she was also cared for by the son-in-law she loved, Mark Hemry, who, most people said, looked more like her than anyone. I am so thankful to see my mother-in-law, Claudine Thomas, here today.

I took care of my mom from the onset of my father's illness 40 years ago, but really she took care of me from our wild adventures before and during World War II to the present day. She was and always will be my Irish good luck charm. The last thing she said to me before she went into her last surgery was, "I love you, honey. Thank you for everything." She was a lovely, glamourous person to whom I can only say, standing in front of you all as witness…she was a lovely lady to whom I can only say thanks, my dear, my mother, my mom, I love you. "Angels guard thee, Sweet Love, till morn."

Funeral Program

Alive, She Lived!

Virginia Claire Day Fritscher
July 12, 1919 - November 14, 2004

A Mass of Eternal Life
Saturday, 11 AM, December 4, 2004
Reverend John Patrick Day, C. P.,
cousin of Virginia Day Fritscher, Celebrant
St. Philomena Church
3300 Twelve Oaks Drive
Peoria Illinois 61604
309-682-8642

Inurnment
Noon, December 4, 2004
Resurrection Mausoleum
7519 N. Allen Road
Peoria Illinois 61614
309-645-2500

Gathering of Friends and Family
at the home of Virginia's dear friend, Pam Perrilles
1 PM Saturday, December 4, 2004

Entrance Carol
(Recorded)

"Seacht Suailci na Maighdine Muire"
("The Seven Joys of Mary")

14th Century Christmas Carol, *A Real Irish Christmas*
Gaelic Singers, Ronan Browne, Sean Corcoran, Desi Wilkinson
English Lyric Translation ©2004 Jack Fritscher

The first joy of Mary was her woman's joy
to see her Blessed Baby Son
on Christmas born.
Mary's further joys
were to see her Son
make the lame to walk,
to make the blind to see,
to make the unloved loved,
to make the young and old
safe and secure,
to comfort the sick
and make the dead to rise.
Mary's seventh joy
was that her Son
carried her to heaven.
Glory to the Father, Son, and Holy Ghost.

Sung Live
Camille McCarty, Soprano
"On Eagle's Wings," Michael Joncas
"Ave Maria," Charles Gounod, J. S. Bach

Virginia Claire Day Fritscher
Holy Mass, Celtic Celebration of Life,
December 4, 2004
Father John Patrick Day, C. P.

Farewell Carol (Recorded)

"Angels Guard Thee"
Benjamin Godard (1849-1895)
Kenneth McKellar, Irish Tenor

Beneath the quivering leaves where shelter comes at last.
All sadness sinks to rest,
or glides into the past.
Her sweet eyes prismed now, in the soft, silken boughs.
O, My Love, calm she sleeps
beneath the trembling stars.
Ah! Wake not yet from thy repose.
A fair dream spirit hovers near thee,
weaving a web of golden rose
through Dreamland's happy isles to bear thee.
Sleep, Love, it is not yet the dawn.
Angels guard thee, Sweet Love, till morn.

How from the noisy throng, by songbirds lulled to rest
where rock the branches high, by breezes soft caressed.
Softly the "Days" go on,
by sorrow all unharmed.
Thus may life be to thee: a sweet existence charmed.

Angels guard thee, Sweet Love, till morn.

Final Carol (Sung Live by All)
"Auld Lang Syne"
Robert Burns

Mr. and Mrs. Bart Day and son Rev. John B. Day, Christmas 1953

MARY PEARL LAWLER DAY
Interview by Jack Fritscher
May 8, 1972

This interview of Mary Pearl Lawler Day, mother of Virginia Claire Day Fritscher, and grandmother of Jack Fritscher, who conducted the interview, was recorded on audiotape at Virginia's 921 Willow Lane home, Peoria, Illinois, on May 8, 1972, seven months before Mary Day's death on December 6, 1972.

Present at the taping: Mary Pearl's daughter, Virginia Claire Day Fritscher (age 52), and Virginia's daughter, Mary Claire Fritscher (age 14).

Mary Pearl Lawler Day speaks, with great humor and warmth, in a lilting South Midland Dialect, in which "or" is pronounced "ar." Her grandson, Jack, as an infant called her "Nanny" and the name became another one of her names. To some, she was "Mary." To others, "Pearl," a name she hated. To others, as the wife of Bart, or the mother of the priest, Father John B. Day, she was "Mrs. Day." To her grandchildren, she was "Nanny" and "Nan."

Mary Pearl Lawler, born October 2, 1888, married Bartholomew Day, July 12, 1911, and was widowed February 13, 1954.

Of her five children, three are mentioned in this interview. Her daughter, Virginia, with whom she lived in Peoria when she was not living with her other daughter, Norine, in St. Louis. Her son, John, was a Catholic priest with whom she lived from 1948 to his sudden death in the St. Cabrini Parish house rectory, May 9, 1967, Springfield, Illinois.

A short story partially based on information in this interview is "Silent Mothers, Silent Sons" and appears in the fiction anthology, *Sweet Embraceable You: 8 Coffee-House Stories*, written by Jack Fritscher, published in May 2000. Other incidents in this interview appear fictitiously in the novel, *The Geography of Women: A Romantic Comedy*, written by Jack Fritscher, and published in 1998. It was the Finalist Winner of the National Small Press Book Award for Best Fiction 1999. *The Geography of Women* was translated into Greek and published by Periplous Publishing, Athens, Greece, in December 2000.

The "voice" of the narrator in *The Geography of Women* grows out of the combined dialect, speech patterns, vocabulary, and stories of both Mary Pearl Lawler Day and Virginia Claire Day Fritscher. The interviewer, pointedly, knowing all these family stories by heart, directed the thirty minutes of these questions to accommodate the energy of his eighty-three-year-old grandmother. This transcription is absolutely accurate.

May 8, 1972

Jack Fritscher: [John Joseph Patrick Fritscher]: Nanny, thank you for doing this little interview. Tell me where you were born and anything else you wish to say.

Mary Pearl Lawler Day: I was born in St. Louis on Virginia Avenue, October 2, 1888. I had four brothers and no sisters. I always had a very happy life. Everybody was always good and kind to me and still are. I don't see why lots of people say they wish they were dead. I don't. I'm getting old. I'm almost 84. I am old. And I'm still happy to think I'm living. I have lots of good friends and all my relatives. I could live with any of them, and get along and be happy. Well... [She laughs.]

Jack: Tell me about your mother and father.

[John Patrick Lawler, born c. 1857 in St. Louis of parents from Ireland, died (age 63) 1920, in St. Louis and Honorah Anastasia McDonough Lawler, born 1861 in north St. Louis of parents from Ireland, died (age 63) 1924 in Kampsville at the home of her daughter Mary Pearl Day who cared for her.]

Mary Pearl: My mother and father were very good to me. My mother was a little on the jealous side, because my dad just idolized her. If she said we were wrong, we were wrong; even if we were right, we were wrong. Our dad always stuck with her, and that's the way it went. As far as my dad went, I don't think there was a better man ever lived, or better father. He was just wonderful. My mother was good, but she didn't believe in sparling [spoiling] me. I did all the work.

Jack: What did you do when you wanted a dress and your mother wouldn't give it to you?

Mary Pearl: Go to my dad and he'd say, "Now what does my little pet want?" He always called me his little pet. I'd say, "Well, Dad, I'm going to a dance and I'd like to have a dress." He said, "Tell your mother." I said, "I did and she said that I got a dress before the last dance I went to." He said, "Well, is it still good? Did you tear it?" I said, "Nope, but I don't want to wear the same dress, because it is going to be the same crowd." So I would get the money for a new dress. Then my mother would get mad and say to my father, "Sparl her, just sparl her." He would say, "She's my only little girl and I'll sparl her if I want to."

Jack: Were those the nights he would throw his hat in the door?

Mary Pearl: Yes, he did that sometimes when they had a big argument. I don't know about what. He never would argue with her. We lived near a little public square with a little park and he would go over and sit in that park for a half an hour or so, until he figured she had gotten over her crabbiness and then he would come back and throw his hat in the door first. If she threw it out, he wouldn't come in. He'd go out and fool around in the yard a little while. But she never threw his hat out but once I think. When it was okay, he would say, "Well, I guess I can come in." And she would say, "Oh, you damn fool." He really was a wonderful man. I imagine nobody ever had a better dad than we did.

Jack: What was his name?

Mary Pearl: John Patrick....John Patrick Lawler. And both his parents came direct from Ireland. And of my mother's folks, my Grandma McDonough—I don't think she came from Ireland. I know my grandfathers did. My mother said her mother was born somewhere in north St. Louis. We're all Irish all the way through. Irish and Catholic, thank God. There was never anything but Irish in us, so we're really Irish—not the shanty Irish—the lace curtain Irish. Daddy used to say we were descended from Irish kings, because he one time had that blood disease only royalty gets. What's it called, Virginia?

Virginia: Hemorraghica purpura.

Mary Pearl: Where the blood just comes out of your pores. Daddy was in the hospital for six weeks and they cured him by giving him horse serum and he was never sick again. [When she put Bart in the hospital, the doctor said, "You'll be a widow by morning."]

Jack: Tell me about the World's Fair [The Louisiana Purchase Exhibition, 1904, St. Louis]

Mary Pearl: I was 16 when we had that fair in St. Louis. I was always small for my age, so whenever they had a kid's day at the Fair I would go and get in free. Nobody ever knew I was 16. A whole bunch of us would get in. Only spend maybe a dollar or two all the while we were there. They had the Pike that had shows on each side with the hula-hula dances and just everything. It was great. That was in 1904, I think.

Jack: That was when they invented ice cream cones.

Mary Pearl: And the ice cream machines, we would all stand and watch them turning out the ice cream. We thought that was wonderful.

Jack: How much did the ice cream cost?

Mary Pearl: I think only 10 cents. Everything was cheap in those days, because nobody made good salaries. It was good accordingly, but not good like today.

Jack: Do you remember the first movie you saw? Or any actors?

Mary Pearl: Oh no. I'm trying to think of that woman's name. She was a real rough talking thing.

Mary Claire: Mae West?

Mary Pearl: No.

Virginia: Marjorie Main.

Mary Pearl: That was the one. There was a show with a whole bunch of kids and their pop was an engineer and they kept hollerin', "Pop, can I blow the whistle?" That movie, that was good.

Jack: Did you like Charlie Chaplin movies?

Mary Pearl: No. I didn't like him then and I don't like him today.

Jack: Why didn't you like him? I don't care for him either.

Mary Pearl: I don't know. Just something about him. I'm that way. I just like you or I don't like you. Nothing in between.

Jack: Tell me, Nanny, at the World's Fair, didn't you ride in gondola boats?

Mary Pearl: Oh yes, they were beautiful, the way they curled up in front. They had "lagoons" they called them at the Fair. We had a lovely time. I got in free because they thought I was twelve years old.

Jack: What was living in St. Louis like at that time?

Mary Pearl: Just about like it is now. I can't see much difference. Of course, there is more to go and see now. I'd go to see my girl friends and they'd come to see me, and they'd stay til 10 o'clock and we'd walk each other halfway home. You wouldn't do that in St. Louis today. But we did then and we weren't worried about it, and our parents weren't either, because nothing ever happened. But now it's like every other big city.

Jack: Nanny, will you sing "Meet Me in St. Louis, Louie"? You did the other day.

Mary Pearl: I can't sing no more.

Jack: You sang for me the other day.

Mary Pearl: I was just foolin' then. Jack.... [Spontaneously, she sings.] "Meet me in St.Louis, Louie. Meet me at the Fair. Don't tell me the lights are shining anywhere but there. We will dance the hootchy-kootchy. You will be my tootsie-wootsie. Meet me in St. Louis, Louie. Meet me at the Fair." [They both laugh.]

Jack: Very good. [Their laughter continues.] Tell me your wonderful story about Francis Devine.

Mary Pearl: Ooooh. [Laughs at the memory.] That was my old boy friend. I went with him for practically two years. We were engaged, then I met the man I married.

[On July 12, 1911, she married Bartholomew Day, born October 17, 1887, in Hamburg, Illinois, of parents John Day (c. 1824-1900) and Mary Lynch (1844-1924), both born in Ireland; Bart died February 13, 1954 in Springfield where he lived with Mary Pearl and their son, John Bartholomew Day, in the rectory of St. Cabrini Parish where he was pastor, and himself died when he was 55, April 9, 1967, as Mary Pearl held him in her arms. She was 78 years old.]

Jack: What year was that when you had both Francis Devine and Grandpa in love with you?

Mary Pearl: Oh gosh. I was married in 1911. About 1910, the winter of 1910, around Christmas 1910 all this happened. I think I knew him [Daddy] about six months before we got married July 12, 1911.

[She always called her husband "Daddy," because he was the father of their five children; and he always called her "Mom."]

Jack: How did you meet Grandpa?

Mary Pearl: Visiting up in Hamburg, Illinois, at the Jones's home, my mother's cousins.

Jack: How did you travel up there?

Mary Pearl: On the boat up the river. We'd get on at 4:00 o'clock in the afternoon in St. Louis. We'd dance all night, and get up to Hamburg the next noon. I used to love those boat trips, with a band and a dance. Really nice.

Jack: Did you have a room to sleep in on the boat?

Mary Pearl: Yeah. What'd they call them? Berths, cabins, something like that. My mother and I went up there two or three times. We had lots of fun like that.

Jack: And what happened? The story I've always heard is you were driving along in a horse and buggy coming from the boat with your cousins and you saw a red-headed man walking across a field, and you announced, "That's the man I'm going to marry," and your cousins said you couldn't because you were engaged to Francis Devine, and you said, "Not any more."

Mary Pearl: No. We visited my mother's cousin, Mrs. Jones, and she said to me, "I know a nice young man who would be nice for you to meet." I said, "I know lots of nice young men." She said,

"Well, he and his mother are coming up tonight." And when they came up, well, I must have fell for him right away and he for I, because I broke my engagement to Francis as soon as I went back home. Six months after, we were married. We only went together six months.

Jack: Didn't Grandpa go out west for awhile?

Mary Pearl: Yes, between the time we met, and before we got married, to Portland, Oregon. He had a brother, Tom, worked out there. Tom came home with Dad and visited their mother [Mary Lynch Day] for about four or five months and then Tom went back and that's where he died—and got married out there too. [Bart Day had 4 brothers: Tom, Joe, John, and Jim. He had one sister, Margaret who was known as "Aunt Mag."]

Jack: In your wedding story, my Mom always told me that in Hamburg when you saw the man walking across the field, you liked everything about him, but that he had red hair.

Mary Pearl: I never cared for red hair. When Daddy went out to Oregon he had red hair, and when he came back his hair had turned black. And then we got married.

Virginia: Tell Jack about how Francis Devine threatened to kill you on your wedding day.

Mary Pearl: Yes, Francis always said that because I broke the engagement that he'd kill me on my wedding day. I said, "You won't know when it is." We were getting married in secret. [So they could not announce the banns of their marriage.] But Francis found out, and there he was out in front of the church, but I wasn't a bit afraid. He didn't come near me, nor I didn't him. And I never once saw him....well, once, after that, I was going to the bakery for my mother, and I was on one side of the street and he was on the other. I didn't notice who it was walking toward me—'course more people walked in those days than they do now 'cause everybody has cars. I heard somebody holler, "Hello, Pearl," and I thought, who is that, and I looked across and there he was. And I said, "Oh...hi, Francis," and he said, "Can I come and talk to you?" And I said, "That's up to you." So he did, and that was the last time I saw him.

Jack: But I thought Francis Devine showed up on the porch at your house one night when you and Grandpa and Uncle John—when he was a baby—were having supper?

Mary Pearl: Francis did come up. The doorbell rang one night. We had a long glass door. They used to call them French doors, and I could see it was him, and I didn't know whether I should open the door or not, so I did. I said, "Well, what do you want?" He said, "I just heard you lived here and thought I'd come by and see you." I never let anybody scare me. He says, "Can I come in?" I said, "That's up to you. You can if you want to. You're perfectly welcome." So he came in. Then he wanted to see John. John was about six months old. I went and got the baby and showed it to him. He said—stayed maybe a half a minute more: "Well, I only came for one reason, to see if you were happy, and I see that you are very happy, and goodbye." And I never saw him from that day to this. But we went together for over 2 years.

[This story of Francis Devine coming to the porch is the base of a major dramatic scene in the novel, *The Geography of Women: A Romantic Comedy*.]

Jack: When you were a little girl in the 1890s, what were some of your favorite things?

Mary Pearl: I don't know. I was one that kinda liked anything that had a little fun to it. I liked to jump rope. We used to jump rope so much. There was an old French woman used to say: "That Pearl Lawler she makes my Julie jump 116 times. That's too much jumps for my little Julie." Jack, 'cause I could jump so much, and Julie'd say she couldn't and I'd say, "Just go ahead. Keep it up."

And I'd make her jump. [Laughs.] I had the devil in me, like your mom [Virginia].

Jack: What was your favorite dress when you were a little girl?

Mary Pearl: I don't know. I always liked pink. Anything in pink I liked. So my mother would get me pink. I was dark complected, same as you, and it always looked good. I had a good life, Jack. Specially with my dad. "Anything my little pet wants, she's my only little girl, and she'll get it." And my mother would say, "You'll sparl her. Just go ahead and sparl her."

Jack: Did you have any pets when you were little?

Mary Pearl: We had rabbits. I had four brothers. We had everything. Not at once, but at different times. Squirrels, even white rats. Aggh!

Jack: What were your brothers, the Lawler brothers, like?

Mary Pearl: They were wonderful, every one of them, Jim, Ed, Jack, and Will. Course they were all good to me. They were railroaders, all but Jim.

Jack: What did he do?

Mary Pearl: Head bookkeeper at Simmons Hardware Company in St. Louis. The other boys, Jack and Bill, they were railroaders. Of course, Ed, I was gone before he did much of anything, because he was the baby of the family. They would say, "Press my suit today, Sis?" I would say, "Yeah, but you have to pay me for it though." And they'd leave a ten dollar bill in their pants pocket, knowing that I'd find it.

Jack: Sounds like a good racket.

Mary Pearl: [Laughs.] Oh, it was a good racket. They gave me everything I wanted. "That's a wonder!" Dad always said, "I was a little afraid to marry you, because I knew darn well you got everything you wanted." I was the only girl, you see, and they were good to me.

Jack: Did you have any jobs when you were a young girl?

[From 1948 to 1967, Mary Pearl and Bart lived with their priest son John in his parish houses as housekeeper-cook and gardener. When Father John died, Mary Pearl not only lost a son that morning, she also lost a place to live. The story of her later life is used as basis for Jack Fritscher's short-story fiction, "Silent Mothers, Silent Sons," in *Sweet Embraceable You: Coffee-House Stories*.]

Mary Pearl: Yes, I worked at Simmons Hardware Company as a stenographer for six months and at Norville Chapways [*sic*]. Those were the two biggest hardware companies in St. Louis. I worked in the bookkeeping department.

Jack: Isn't Simmons where your brother worked too?

Mary Pearl: Yes, Jim. For a long time, and then he went into the arl [oil] business. He was one of the head men in the Shell Arl Company. And he's got his picture, you remember, Virginia, and what would you call it, a notification or something, citation, all the employees signed it and gave it to him.

Jack: What did you think of the First World War when it happened? Did you know it was coming?

Mary Pearl: Well, I used to hear them talk about it, but we couldn't get out of it. I'll never forget the first morning. They said, "We're at war," and that was it. They shot at one of our ships. Dad didn't have to go because he was married, but if it had lasted another week he would have been gone. He was registered and ready to go.

Jack: What did you think of the 20s?

Mary Pearl: They were very nice, the Roaring 20s.

Jack: What did you do for fun?

[In 1920, Mary Pearl was thirty-two and the mother of four—soon to be five—children. Virginia was one year old. Bart, thirty-three, was a school teacher and a mail carrier on a Star Route with the U.S. Postal Service.]

Mary Pearl: I don't know why they called them the Roaring 20s. I think it was because of the dances. They had these wild dances. We didn't think they were wild then. Nowadays they think they're wild now in their dances, but it's nothing like we danced. We had lots of fun. It was mostly the waltz, the two-step, and the cakewalk. They had those at every dance we'd go to. They really did give a cake to the best two.

Jack: Do you remember the Russian Revolution in 1917 when the royal family was killed?

Mary Pearl: No, I really don't. I guess I wasn't paying much attention. What was that [noise]?

Jack: Just the tape machine squeaking.

Mary Pearl: Oh, I thought it was the dog [Spot].

Jack: What about the Wall Street Crash? Do you remember that day?

Mary Pearl: I remember it was terrible. Everybody suffered from that. I remember the newspapers came out with extras then. They didn't have television like they have now. And that's all you'd hear was, "Extra! Extra! Extra!" They'd charge a quarter or 50 cents and people'd pay them and get that "Extra."

Jack: Where did you go to school?

Mary Pearl: Blow School.

Jack: What?

Mary Pearl: Blow. B-l-o-w. On Leffler and Virginia. It's still there, a great big beautiful building. They still have school there. I went through 8th grade there and then after I graduated I went to St. Mary and Joseph's Academy and took up bookkeeping and short hand.

Jack: St. Mary and Joseph's was a high school?

Mary Pearl: Yes. I went there two terms, and then I went to work at the Simmons hardware company as a stenographer and then at Butler Brothers. And my Dad made me quit. He said my mother needed me at home. He said, "It's too bad if a dad and four brothers couldn't keep a mother and a sister." I wanted to work, because I had lots of fun.

Jack: How did you meet Francis Devine?

Mary Pearl: Being with his sister. She was a friend. I didn't know she had any brothers. Two weren't married and one was. We went as far as being engaged until I met Daddy and I broke it up. Francis Devine's mother and dad came down at Christmas and wanted me to reconsider and go with him, and I said, "No." They said, "You don't know if this other guy loves you or not." I said, "No, I don't; but I know I love him. So that's it."

Jack: What was your house like at the turn of the century? Did you live in the same house all the time when you were a little girl in St. Louis?

Mary Pearl: No, my mother and dad rented for a good while in that one house on Minnesota Avenue for fourteen years, and Daddy [Bart] and I moved to the house [in Hamburg] that Daddy [Bart] bought—in fact, it was his mother's house that we bought. [Grandma Day also owned the house next door where she lived.]

Jack: But what address was that where you lived when you were a girl?

Mary Pearl: 7800 Minnesota. My Dad [John Patrick Lawler] raised the roof, a kind of attic like, and there were rooms up there and two more rooms down the stairs. We had a nice big home for the five of us and our parents.

Jack: Was that the house where the roof caught on fire while you were taking a bath?

Mary Pearl: No, that was in Cannon's house [we rented in Jacksonville] after we were married and had Virginia and all of them. [1932] I don't know how it started. It was a gas stove. I don't really know…I was in the bathroom taking a bath to tell you the truth and I really never did.

Virginia: I was doing the dishes and the flames started shooting.

Mary Pearl: And Daddy took the pan of dishwater, some greasy water, and poured it on it and, of course, that made it worse. So the firemen came down. They were all gonna rush right in through the front room and I wouldn't let them. I said, "Go around to the other door [the kitchen door]. Daddy never did get over that. [She laughs.] He said, "Mom would rather see the house burn down than let the firemen dirty her living room." [Much laughter.] I said, "I'd just house-cleaned." I wasn't gonna let them in. I was a character, I guess. [Laughs.] Oh, my.

Jack: Tell me about where you lived on Pershing Avenue. What that apartment was like. [5536 Pershing Avenue]

Mary Pearl: [She tells instead of Kansas Street.] It was beautiful, brand new. We were the first ones to live in it [1912]. They called them the "Bridal Flats." There were fourteen units, and there really were all just newly married couples that lived there. We had, I don't remember, a kitchen and a bedroom and a hall and a livingroom. 'Course that was enough just for two, you know. They're nice yet. They used to call it Kansas Street, now it's called "Holly Hills." They look as good as they ever did.

Jack: Pershing Street was changed to Kansas Street?

Mary Pearl: No, you're thinking of Pershing Avenue, that was the last place Dad and I lived when we were in St. Louis [during and just after the War, 1941-1946]. But our first place was on Kansas, now called "Holly Hills" so it sounds a little more stylish. When we were first married we moved to Hamburg [Bart's hometown] and then we moved back to St. Louis [Mary Pearl's hometown] on Kansas Street.

Jack: Tell me the story about when Grandpa found the butterfly.

Mary Pearl: Oh God. [Laughing.] Norine was living a block from us in the hotel up there [on Pershing]. She had an apartment. Jim [Chumley, Norine's husband] was still in the service and "across" [colloquial for overseas, fighting the War in Europe] which John [as an Army Chaplain] was also, and Daddy went up to see Norine for a little while in the evening. I don't know. For some reason I didn't go.

Virginia: Daddy went to walk Norine home.

Mary Pearl: Yes, and when Daddy came back he found this great big butterfly. He saw it on the bushes in the front yard of the hotel and he went back up to Norine's and wanted to know if she had a sack, and she said, "Why would you want that?" And he said, "Oh, I saw a great big buttefly down there. I think its asleep on the bush, so if I can get it, I'll bring it home to mom." So he did catch it, and he got it in the sack, and he came home laughing. He came home, and I was in bed, and he said, "Come here. I wanna show you something." So I got up. He opened the bag really easy and he said, "It's gone." I looked at him like he was crazy. I said, "What's gone?" because there he was holding open an empty sack. He said, "I had a beautiful butterfly in there, but it got out." [Laughter.] I couldn't believe him. He said, "Well, you call Norine up right now and ask her." I said, "Norine, is your dad crazy, or did he find a butterfly?" "Oh, Mom," she said, "he brought it home." I said, "No he didn't. He had an empty sack when he got home." It must have got out someways, 'cause he opened the bag and said, "Look at my beautiful butterfly." And I said, "I don't see no butterfly." And he said, "It's gone." I never will forget that. We put him on about that all the time. He said, "Well, you all think you're smart. You think I didn't have any. He said, "Norine knows I did," and I said, "Nah, you just thought you did."

Jack: When you lived on Pershing, during the War when I stayed with you so much, wasn't there a step up into the bathroom?

Mary Pearl: Yes, I'll tell you how that looked. There were two rooms. One was called the dressing room and one the bathroom. You'd go in first to the dressing room and then a step up, and that was the bathroom where the bowl and bathtub was.

Jack: What did you used to drink in there at night in bathroom?

Mary Pearl: Water, I guess.

Jack: No, you used to put something into a glass that would fizz.

Mary Pearl: Ooooh. That was Bromo Seltzer. You went and got Grandpa and you said, "Come on, Grandpa, come quick, Nanny's drinking Duz!" [Much laughter. Duz was the name of a very sudsy soap.] "No," Grandpa said, "that's Bromo Seltzer." I don't ever take that no more. You know you put it in a glass and it would fizz up, and you thought it was suds. You were gonna get somebody to save Nanny from herself.

Jack: What's the first thing you remember when you were a little child?

Mary Pearl: Oh, gosh. I don't know. I remember that mother always bought me little red slippers and I used to love them for the summer. I had a little white dress trimmed in red. Of course, me being the only girl, I got everything that come out as soon as it did come out.

Jack: How did you wear your hair?

Mary Pearl: Curls. I just had long curls, for a long time, until I guess my Mother started to braid it after I went to school awhile.

Jack: What kind of books did you read when you were a little girl.

Mary Pearl: Mother Goose rhymes, such as that. I used to love to read. After I was out of school and my Dad and Mom made me quit working at Butler Brothers, I think I read every book in the St. Louis library, 'cause it was all I did.

Jack: What were some of your favorites?

Mary Pearl: Oh God, Jack....I loved *Ben Hur*. I read that two or three times. I really can't remember all of them. Zane Gray, mmm, I loved that. I had more fun than anything else.

Jack: Did you travel on any trips when you were little?

Mary Pearl: Not much. My mother went to Tennessee one time, but I stayed home. I was old enough to take care of the house while she was gone. My dad had relatives down there [in Tennessee] by the name of Lawler.

Jack: What color was your hair?

Mary Pearl: Always dark, never black, just a real dark brown. My mother had coal black hair, but mine wasn't as black as hers. Now, of course, it's white, and has been since I was 43. [When she had gall-bladder surgery, she said, "The ether turned my hair white."]

Jack: What were the names of some of your friends?

Mary Pearl: Oh, May Devine, Francis Devine, Irma Langford, Dora Friederling, Oscar Eichorn, her [Dora's] cousin—that's how I remember him so much. Oh, I just had lots of friends. Bertha Powell. Some of them would say, "If you go with her, I can't come down. You're with her." I said, "Well, It's too bad that I have to have just one girl friend." My mother would say, "You just go with whomever you want to, it's none of their business. If they don't like us, then stay home." But Irma Langford, I think, was my best friend.

Jack: What was your house like? Can you describe it, coming in the entryway and all that. The one that you lived in when you were a teenager, let's say. About the time of the World's Fair [1904].

Mary Pearl: Well, I guess that time was after my mother and father had their own home [7800 Minnesota]. The house was a big red brick. At that time, they hadn't raised the roof, but it had a lovely attic up there. I mean, sleeping rooms up there. The boys slept up there. We had six rooms. I can see the little gate. And we had these flagstones from the front gate to the front door. We had a grape arbor in the back where we used to come and sit. People didn't have all the advantages they have now, like fans. We went out in the yard to get fresh air. Very nice. That's where I lived when we were first married [and Bart got sick with Hemorraghica Purpura].

Jack: Can you describe what your room looked like?

Mary Pearl: Just an ordinary room with an ordinary bed,

walnut, a single one. A little dresser, a little wash stand, Jack, with a little curtain around the bottom of it, with a cistern with a bowl, and big pitcher, where I could wash my face in the morning.

Jack: Did you have electricity?

Mary Pearl: Yes. First we had gas, for a long time, but the systems were together. Gas was on top and the electric was around it. I think that's the way it was. And so we got the electricity, 'cause everybody wanted electricity rather than gas.

Jack: When did you make your first telephone call?

Mary Pearl: Oh, I don't know. I couldn't begin to tell you.

Jack: Do you remember your first automobile ride?

Mary Pearl: No. I don't even know who I went with. Boy, I can remember standing out in the front yard, and out walking, and I'd say to mom, "Come on, quick! Here comes an automobile down the street." Everybody called 'em automobiles. Nobody called them cars yet. The first ones were electric. And my mother would come out and say, "Well, isn't that nice. Maybe we'll have one someday," she'd say. I can still see an old woman...she used to sit in one like this [sits up very stiff and proper] and then she'd have that thing—what do you call it?—and they pull in and pull it out, and go rrrrrrr! She lived in our neighborhood and she looked like a paste doll. [Laughs] She looked terrible. Mmmmmm.

Jack: What did you and your friends think of sex when you were teenagers. You don't mind my asking, do you?

Mary Pearl: No. I...I guess just about like they do now, Jack. There wasn't a whole lot of difference. That's what I often say. The only thing that I can see that's different: people or kids or youngsters are all more open with things than they used to be. You used to be almost afraid to ask or say it. In those days, you weren't supposed to know nothin'. You were supposed to be dumb, but now they're not—which is better. My mother was fair, though. If I'd ask her, she'd tell me, because she always said, "I'd rather you get the answers from me than somebody else. You don't know how they'd tell it to you." You know. And me being the only girl was kind of tough with four brothers. But I got everything, I have to say. I had four good brothers. Only Jim. Jim was kind of haughty. If he wanted me to do something for him, like he'd come downstairs, and maybe wouldn't bring his cufflinks, and he'd say, "Go upstairs and get my cufflinks, Sis," and I'd say, "Who was your slave girl last year? I'm not gonna do it." He'd say, "Ma, make her go." She'd say, "No. She don't have to wait on you." Then he'd get mad and he'd say, "Just wait until your birthday comes. You think you'll get something from me." I'd say, "Well, keep it. You wouldn't give me enough to put in my eye anyway." And I'd win the fight. We always did, always argued. If we meet today, we'd still do the same thing. He always thought he run the place, but he could never run me. My mother would always say, "Take up for yourself." [Laughs.]

Jack: Do you remember Isadora Duncan?

Mary Pearl: No, I don't.

Jack: Did you have any pets when you were little?

Mary Pearl: Oh yes, my brothers had everything. We had white rabbits, little squirrels.

Jack: I mean any special dog?

Mary Pearl: Oh yes. I had a big Saint Bernard that Aunt Nell gave me. When it came—a little puppy like this, you know—and he grew up to be so big and then he got ferocious. So we gave him to some friends of my mother's down in DeSoto, Missouri, by the name of Long, because as soon as any stranger come in the yard he'd leap for their throat, and a policeman told us we had to get rid of it.

Always Virginia

Jack: What was your dog's name?

Mary Pearl: Don. He was a Saint Bernard. Oh, it was mine. I had him from the time he was a little puppy. He sure was a pretty dog, but he was too mean for the city.

Jack: You started to say your mother said something about him?

Mary Pearl: She told me I had to get rid of it. I couldn't have it. Aunt Nell gave it to me, bought it for me.

Jack: What year did your mother die? [Honorah Anastasia Lawler McDonough]

Mary Pearl: Mmmmmm. I have to stop and think now, when did she die? I don't know, Jack. My dad died first [in St. Louis].

Jack: What year did he die?

Mary Pearl: '53, I guess.

Jack: Your dad didn't die in 1953.

Mary Pearl: No, Daddy [her husband Bart] died in 1953, didn't he. [Actually, Bart Day died February 13, 1954.] Ohhh, Virginia, do you remember when my dad died?

Virginia: When I was six months old. February, 1920.

Mary Pearl: Yes, he died in February—February 11. I remember that.

Jack: And your mother died how much later?

Mary Pearl: She lived with me six years [in Kampsville] and then she died. But she was never happy. I didn't ever think she'd live that long, because—I don't know—my dad just gave her everything. I did the best I could, but I couldn't wait on her hand and foot like he did, 'cause I had five kids to take care of. She came up and lived with me until she died. And she always told me she didn't want to be buried there. I said, "Well, no. I know that, 'cause you've got your lot in St. Louis." That's like me, wherever I live when I die, I'll be buried in Springfield because that's where Daddy and John are, and that's where my lot is. That's where I bought it.

Jack: Could you describe that morning when Uncle John died [suddenly at age 54]?

Mary Pearl: Well, I was down in my room [in the St. Cabrini Rectory]. Millie [Imelda Honerkamp, Uncle John's longtime housekeeper] had got up. I was just about dressed when she come down and she said, "Nan, come quick! Something happened to our father." Our father? It never dawned on me that she meant John. She said, "Father John!" I said, "Well, what happened to him?" She said, "I don't know, Nan," she said, "but come quick." She took ahold me by the arm and we ran up the hall and he was...uh... laying on the bathroom floor. And I got down on my hands and knees, and put his head in my lap, and he just looked at me and smiled, and he was gone. But anyway he knew: I was there. Millie said he was, uh, and when her and Father [Corbett, the assistant pastor] found him—that he was just reaching for the shower to turn it on, and I guess that's what gave him the heart attack. And they laid him on the floor. Then they called me. I'll never forget that day. I can remember now, though, Father Corbett told me, he said, "You got ahold of me and you just beat me in the chest with your hands as hard as you could hit me," and I don't remember it. He said I was just excited and he was holding me tight, you see, 'cause I was screaming and everything and I was just a-beating on him. Wasn't that awful to do that?

Jack: No, people do that all the time.

Mary Pearl: He was nice. He came to see me one time I was at Norine's [in St. Louis], and he and Father Haggerty came and Noreen saw them [the two priests] and just because she had on her robe she wouldn't go and let them in, so I never got to see them and they never came back. I think they knew she was in the house. So do I hear from 'em? I don't anymore. Father Haggerty I do on Christmas and everything, but not Corbett.

Jack: Do you remember when you used to come up to Peoria and see me during the war?

Mary Pearl: I remember coming up. Only you used to sit on the top step when you knew it was me, and you'd say, "What you got for me, Nanny?" [Laughs a lot.] You always knew I brought you something.

Jack: Do you remember one time when you came in and you picked me up and you had on a sharp brooch, and I caught my cheek on it and cut it?

Mary Pearl: Yes, it scratched ya. Oh, I never! Boy, that taught me a lesson. Whenever I was gonna pick up a little baby, I'd take a pin off. They used to wear them—remember, Virginia?—wear a pin or a brooch or something up here, and it scratched poor Jack's face.

Jack: And made me as ugly as I am today.

Mary Pearl: It didn't feel very good getting scratched.

Jack: Who did you say I look like now?

Mary Pearl: Uncle Jim Day. I think you're just the image of him. And he was handsome. I'll say that too.

Jack: Keep saying it.

Mary Pearl: He was one of the Lawlers, of the Days, I mean.

Virginia: He wants that on record.

Mary Pearl: [Laughs heartily.] He really was!

Jack: He was one of the Days. Tell me about him.

Mary Pearl: He was a steamboat captain. He was a good guy. He was married once and his wife died and he never remarried, and he had one child, Howard. I met Howard a couple of times, but I don't know whether he's living or dead, or what now. Of course, naturally, he wouldn't have kept track of me, and I didn't him, because I didn't know how to do that, wherever he'd be.

Jack: Of all the things you remember in your life, what sticks out most in your mind?

Mary Pearl: Oh...I don't know....I can remember when I was 18, though, when my mother knew they were going to bring me a surprise party, but I didn't. I can remember laying there. I just put my head down on the dining room table, and I was half asleep, and I heard the bell, and I said, "There's some funny looking people at the door." And she said, "How do you know they're at the door?" And I said, "Well, I heard the doorbell." And she said, "Well, go and see who it is," 'cause she knew who it was, and when I went, I thought I'd die! They had pans and were hitting on them with spoons and everything else and were making noise.

Jack: Was this for your birthday?

Mary Pearl: My 18th birthday. [October 2, 1906]

Jack: Who were these people?

Mary Pearl: Oh, lord! Dora Friederling and Hattie Austin and Bertha Powell and Francis Devine and George Devine and Jim Hill. I can see Jim yet. He was a little short guy. He was a nice fella.

Jack: Did they bring you presents?

Mary Pearl: No. I think they brought me a big bouquet of flowers. We had lots of fun. My mother knew they were coming and so she had a big cake baked. How she ever baked it with me around I'll never know, unless she sent me someplace. We had a nice evening. That's when I was eighteen.

Jack: What was it like riding on the trolley cars in St. Louis?

Mary Pearl: Oh! I never thought nothing of it, [but those trolley cars] they were open all the way through from one side to the other. They used to call them "Thumb-er" cars. You could get in or out just anyplace you were sitting. When you wanted to get off, you'd get off. They had those even a long time after they put the new ones on. They were very nice. But they have the university cars now. They have the same kind in Canada as we have. They were all so much improved. Well, Jack, I'm [giggles] tired.

Jack: Okay. Thanks, Nan.

Virginia Day Fritscher, Bart Day, Bob Fritscher, Mary Pearl Day, Jack Firtscher, Reverend John B. Day. Peoria, 1951. Bartholomew Day's obituary in *The Jacksonville Journal*, February 14, 1954, identified him as "postman," with burial in the family plot in Oak Ridge Cemetery, Springfield, IL, very near President Lincoln's Tomb. His wife and priest son are buried next to him

Rev. John B. Day, Ordination, April 24, 1938

Mother's Day, May 14, 1939
Sermon Written and Delivered by
Father John B. Day

John B. Day, age 27, was the son of Mary Pearl Lawler Day and Bartholomew Day, and brother of Virginia Claire Day Fritscher, who was seven months pregnant with the family's first grandchild, and his namesake, John Joseph Fritscher [Jack]. On the same Sunday, his brother James Day's wife, Mildred [Horn], was five months pregnant with their son, James Day.

SS. PETER & PAUL'S CATHOLIC CHURCH
207 Vandalia Street
Collinsville, Illinois

This sermon is from *The Collected Sermons of the Reverend John B. Day*, edited by Jack Fritscher, to whom Mary Pearl Day gave the sermon manuscripts the day after Father John B. Day died on May 9, 1967.

> Who ran to help me when I fell?
> Or would some pretty story tell,
> Or kiss the part, to make it well?
> My Mother.

Mother! The sweetest word in all the English language! Try to define it and you cannot find the right words to express yourself. So, my friends, after searching for many years to find the best definition for this beautiful word, I am at last convinced that the most complete expression of what motherhood is and what it means, is found in the verse of the poet I just quoted.

Let us take this verse apart and see how full of meaning is each line.

Who ran to help me when I fell? Does not this line express at once the solicitude that each and every mother holds in her heart for her child? What mother would not risk her life to save her son or daughter from even the slightest harm? Recall your own childhood days. Who alone was there at your every beck and call? No one, but your own dear mothers. At the sight of a stranger, or of a strange dog, at the sound of a clap of thunder, did not each and every one of you instinctively cling to your mother's side. You knew, whatever happened, or whatever danger was near, you knew your mother would protect you.

The second line, of our verse—*or some pretty story to tell?* Ah, my friends, does it not bring back the fondest memories of your childhood days, yes, even of your whole life—to recall the beautiful stories you first heard on your throne as a little king—on your mother's knee? Ah, the sweet stories of the Infant Jesus, of your Guardian Angel, or of the Holy Family of Jesus, Mary, and Joseph! How your dear mother convinced you of what was right and what was wrong, of what was virtue and what was sin. Perhaps she even thrilled you with tales of fairy land. Would that we all could have kept the innocence of our early childhood days.

Who would kiss the part to make it well? My Mother! Suppose you did stub your toe, or cut your finger, or bump your head. It felt as good as new as soon as mother healed it with her maternal kiss. Suppose someone hurt your feelings. Yes, mother would still be your friend. She would understand.

Yes, my dear friends, this is sentimental talk. But who can deny these words, or say they are not true? Yes, every child though he be 6 or 60 knows that his mother really and truly loved him, as bone of her bone and flesh of her flesh.

Is your mother still living? How do you treat her? Are you going to call on her today? Are you going to remember her by some little token of esteem? Don't say you can't afford any gift. Remember, it is not the gift of the lover, but the love of the giver. Suppose your dear mother has passed to her eternal reward. You can still remember her today in your prayers, and ask God to have mercy on her soul.

So far we have been talking about our earthly mothers, but it is impossible to speak of mothers and Mother's Day without our thoughts going to Mary, the Mother of God, and the Mother of Mothers. [He had a lifelong special devotion to the Blessed Mother.]

Just as our earthly mothers take care of our physical needs, so does Mary the Mother of us all, Our Heavenly Mother, take care of our spiritual needs.

Going back to the words of the poet. Who could have told us a more beautiful story than the Divine Romance of the Redemption in which Mary played so prominent a part! And it is Mary who implants the sweet kiss of grace on our sinful brows as she welcomes us again into the charmed circle of repentant sinners.

Yes, Mary in spite of her unique honor as Mother of God, is always in close contact with us. She is just as solicitous for us today, as she was on the occasion of the wedding at Cana, when through her unfailing intercession, her Son worked His first miracle, changing the water into wine, merely to save a bride and groom from embarrassment at their wedding feast. For all that is noble in womanhood, Mary is responsible. She has ever been the pattern of all who wish to live purely, the ideal of Christian motherhood.

On this day commemorating the sublime privilege of motherhood, let the whole Catholic world cry out: "Oh, Mary, Mother of God, conceived without sin, pray for our mothers who have recourse to thee." God bless you all, and keep you all. In the name of the Father, and of the Son, and of the Holy Ghost. Amen.

—The Reverend John B. Day

* * * *

This sermon was written by Father John B. Day, age 27, for Mother's Day, May 14, 1939. Father Day (born July 17, 1912—died May 9, 1967) had been ordained a Roman Catholic priest on April

24, 1938. On July 12, 1938, he had performed the wedding mass of his younger sister Virginia Claire Day to George Fritscher. July 12, 1938, was also the 27th wedding anniversary of Father Day's and Virginia Day's parents, Mary Pearl Lawler (McDonough) Day and Bartholomew Day, who had been married July 12, 1911, in St. Louis, Missouri. Virginia Claire Day was also born on July 12, 1919.

At the time of writing this sermon, Father Day was speaking not only of his own mother, Mary Pearl, but also of his pregnant sister, Virginia Claire, who was a month away from becoming the first sister of Father Day to become a mother, with the birth of Father Day's namesake, John Joseph Patrick Fritscher [Jack Fritscher] on June 20, 1939 who was Father Day's first nephew—before he had nephews or nieces—in a generation in which only Father Day's brothers and sisters would leave issue. Just as important emotionally, his closest brother Jimmie's wife, Mildred, was also expecting their first child, James Day, born October 1939, who became Resident Judge of the Seventh Circuit.

This presentation of Father Day's "Mother's Day" sermon was edited on April 4, 1997, by Jack Fritscher from papers inherited from Father Day on his death at age 54, May 9, 1967.

* * * *

A Brief Biography of the Reverend John B. Day

Born in Hamburg, Illinois, baptized in Michael, Illinois, and raised in Kampsville, Illinois, pioneer pastor Father John Bartholomew Day happened to be, in the lineage of priestly vocations, only the fourth boy born, and raised, in the county to be ordained to the priesthood in the Springfield Diocese.

For many years until his death in the rectory, Father Day was pastor of St. Cabrini's Church, Springfield, where he built the school, the convent, and the new church building itself. Previously, he had been assistant pastor at St. Peter and Paul, Collinsville,

Illinois, and pastor of St. Joseph's parish outside Quincy, Illinois, where his mother and father first began to live with him as housekeeper and gardener.

From 1941-1945, he had served as a much-decorated Chaplain with the United States 5th Army. The Associated Press as well as *TIME* magazine, April 2, 1945, page 27, published a wire-photograph of Father Day saying mass on the front lines in Belgium during the Battle of the Bulge. A fictional account of his death appears in the collection of short stories written by Jack Fritscher, *Sweet Embraceable You: Coffee-House Stories.*

He is buried in Springfield, Illinois, next to his mother and father, near President Lincoln's tomb.

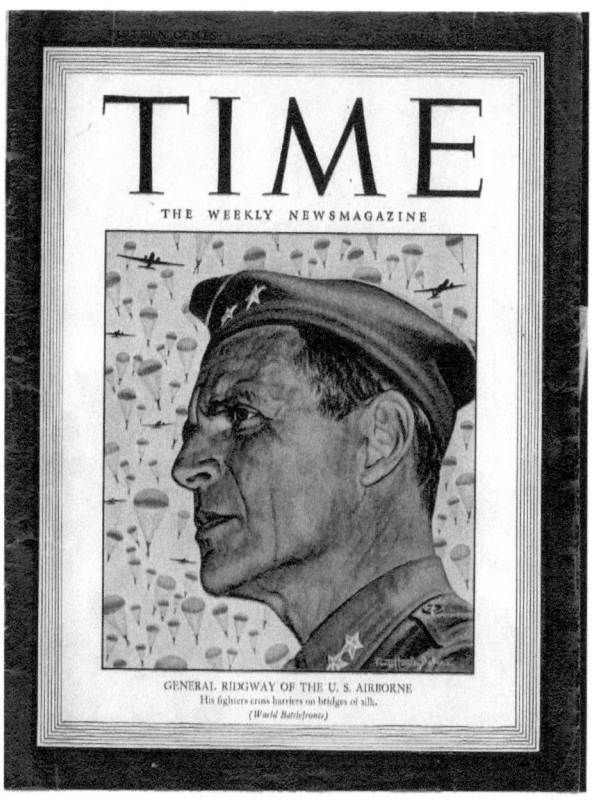

TIME, April 2, 1945

TIME
THE WEEKLY NEWSMAGAZINE

U. S. AT WAR

Vol. XLV No. 14   April 2, 1945

BEHIND THE FRONT IN BELGIUM*
Ahead, a road was opening up.

Associated Press

THE NATION

The Road to Berlin

U.S. troops poured over the Rhine by the thousands—in boats, over bridges, through the air. Now even the most professionally pessimistic observers had to admit that the final round was on. The roads to Berlin had opened up.

At home, the U.S. people took this significant advance in stride. A year ago, such a tremendous push might have started public celebrations. By now, the U.S. people, like their Army, had become more professional in their attitude toward war. They were also, as ever, mindful of the cost.

In the week before the Big Push, U.S. casualties reached an alltime high—19,-908 for seven days. Casualties since Pearl Harbor now totaled 859,587, more than twice the number of World War I. And the battlefront pictures showed the cemeteries growing ever larger (*see cut*).

FOREIGN RELATIONS

The Price to Pay

The Crimea Conference's stern decision

Chaplain John B. Day (right) burying soldiers at the Battle of the Bulge. TIME, April 2, 1945

NEWSCLIPS
from the scrap books of
Virginia Day Fritscher

Jacksonville Journal and Courier, **April 1938**

Father Day's First Mass Here
The First Sunday in May

John B. Day Will Be Ordained as Priest of Catholic Church

Jacksonville Young Man to Be Ordained April 24 at Springfield

John B. Day of this city, who is completing his studies at Kenrick seminary at St. Louis, will be ordained to the priesthood of the Roman Catholic church Sunday, April 24, by His Excellency Bishop James Griffin, D.D., Bishop of Springfield, in the Cathedral of the Immaculate Conception.

Rev. Father Day will say his first solemn mass Sunday, May 1, at 10 a.m. at the Church of Our Saviour in Jacksonville, a ceremony that will be largely attended by members of the parish and friends of the young priest.

A dinner in his honor will be given at the Knights of Columbus hall on East State Street immediately after his first solemn mass. There will be a reception the same evening at the home of Father Day's parents, Mr. and Mrs. B. Day, at 517 South Church street.

Father Day will say a mass at Kampsville Monday, May 2, and at Michael on Tuesday, May 3. He is a former resident of Calhoun county and well known in those communities.

He will be the first priest from this parish to be ordained. A number of relatives and friends will go to Springfield for the ordination service at the cathedral.

Father Day has many friends who have followed his progress

through the preparatory schools and seminary with much interest. He will be assigned to a parish soon after ordination.

He was born July 17, 1912 at Hamburg, Calhoun county, where he attended St. Anselm's parochial school, followed by a year at Kampsville High school. The Day family then removed to Jacksonville, after which he attended Routt High school, graduating in 1930.

Father Day attended first year college at Routt in 1930-1931, and spent his second college year at Quincy college. He entered St. Louis Preparatory seminary in September of 1932 for study of philosophy for two years. In September of 1934 he entered Kenrick seminary for four years' study of theology.

During his student days, Father Day was employed for five summers in various departments of the *Journal and Courier*. He was in the circulation department, worked on the telegraph desk, and did reporting at various times. His versatility made him a valued employee.

He has always shown much interest in athletics and sports, being an ardent baseball fan. He often played with amateur teams and served as manager of some of them.

In more recent years, Father Day worked during the summer as an interviewer for the National Re-employment Service, and county supervisor of the U.S. Department of Agriculture Economics, with headquarters at the court house.

Father Day is the oldest of five children of Mr. and Mrs. B. Day. His brothers are James and Harold Day; his sisters, Norine and Virginia Day.

A number of visiting clergy will participate in his first mass here, as well as in the ordination ceremony at Springfield.

* * * *

Jacksonville Journal and Courier
March 15, 1945

A. P. Correspondent In Belgium Tells of Work of Major John B. Day

by Hal Boyle

Henri Chapelle, Belgium, March 15. —(Delayed)—(AP) [Associated Press Wire Services]

All day long Sgt. Roy Steinhauer, of Fresno, Calif., sits before a wooden table in a small Belgian farmhouse and lists dead men's effects.

Most American soldiers carry three things in to battle—a picture of someone they love, a religious article of some kind, and an American dollar bill.

"This is a typical case," he said and pointed to a handful of objects he was ready to pack for forwarding to the quartermaster depot in Kansas City to be checked again and sent to relatives.

On the table were a few letters, a photograph of the dead soldier's wife or sweetheart, a pocket knife, a Catholic Saint's medallion, a pen and pencil, and a one dollar bill.

Testaments and Rosaries

"It is rare we find a frontline soldier who isn't carrying a religious symbol of some kind," said Steinhauer. "Protestant boys usually have a New Testament in their field jackets and Catholics have a Rosary or a St. Christopher's medal.

"And most of them usually have one or two dollar bills stuck away just for remembrance of the old U.S.A."

From a window he can look out across shining white crosses stretching as far as the eye can see in the largest Allied cemetery on the western front. There are some 16,000 Americans, Belgians, French, British and Poles buried there—although most are

Americans—and nearly 9,000 Germans. Among those 25,000 graves are those for scores of Yanks killed in the infamous "Malmedy massacre" at the start of Von Rundstedt's winter breakthrough.

Also buried there are thousands of the finest Nazi troops who died in that last vast gamble by Hitler for victory.

Over one corner of the American section the Stars and Stripes flies at perpetual half staff.

Memorial Flagpole

"The flagpole was built by one engineering outfit as a memorial to one of its sergeants killed in action," said Lt. John McKenna, of Montclair, N.J., who supervises Allied burials.

Graves are dug by hand by newly captured German prisoners en route to rear areas. Each day a new batch is brought over from the army prisoners cages.

"Once we had a little prisoner who was convinced we were compelling him to dig his own grave," said T/Sgt. A. H. Herberts, of Chester, Ill., ranking non-com for both cemeteries.

"He thought we were going to shoot him when he finished and kept begging that he didn't want to dig his own grave—he just wanted time to write his wife that he had died fighting for the Fatherland. He was still unconvinced at the end of the day. He thought he was being taken back to the prison camp to be shot there."

Combat Chaplain

Major John B. Day, former Jacksonville, Ill., priest, whose parents live at 5536 Pershing Avenue, St. Louis, Mo., is one of the combat chaplains who take turns coming back from the front so that each day the dead soldier can be buried with ministrations of his own faith.

Father Day is a gentle-voiced man with a gentle outlook in life and it saddens him immeasurably to see these remnants of immortality put into the earth. Turning to leave after the last soldier had been buried, he waved across the green and muddy Belgian hills.

"That's what is wrong with war," he murmured. "Those crosses."

Father Day was assistant pastor at SS. Peter and Paul's church, Collinsville, prior to his appointment as army chaplain in March, 1941.

* * * *

St. Louis Post-Dispatch
August 15, 1942

Now Is Captain
Rev. John B. Day

Headquarters 78th Infantry Division, Camp Butner, N.C., Aug 15—

First Lieut. John B. Day, a chaplain assigned to the 78th Lightning Division, received word Thursday of his promotion to a captaincy.

Chaplain Day, a Roman Catholic priest, joined the Lightning Division after serving as a garrison chaplain at Ft. Riley, Kans, for more than a year. He formerly was assistant pastor of the St. Peter and Paul Church at Collinsville, Ill.

A graduate of Kenrick Seminary in St. Louis, Chaplain Day was ordained four years ago in Springfield, Ill.

* * * *

Jacksonville Journal and Courier
May 1940

Lieut. Chumley And Norine Day Reveal Marriage at Party

Jacksonville Young Couple Leave to Make Home at Fort Benning, Ga.

Mr. and Mrs. B. Day, 517 South Church street [where Virginia, George, and Jack also lived from 1938-1941 and where Jack was born], announced the marriage of their daughter Norine to Lieut. James T. Chumley, son of Alderman and Mrs. Thomas C. Chumley, 1231 South Clay Avenue, during a party and shower given last night at the home of the bride's parents.

The date of the marriage, May 1, 1940, was revealed at the beginning of the evening, being concealed on tiny slips of paper in capsules attached to the tally cards.

The evening was spent playing cooty, first prize going to Mrs. Gail Entrikin and consolation prize to Miss Clara Ritter. The bride received many useful gifts. At the close of the evening dainty refreshments were served by the hostess, Mrs. Day.

Lieut. and Mrs. Chumley left at noon Wednesday for Columbus, Ga.,where they will make their home. He is stationed in Fort Benning, Ga.

Those present at the announcement party were Misses Angela David, Jean Hoecker, Rosalind Hoecker, Rosemary Walsh [Harold Day's wife-to-be], Frances Handy, Elizabeth Manz, Clara Ritter, Eustacia Ruyle, Mrs. Thomas C. Chumley, Mrs. Edward Chumley, Mrs. Leroy Gilpin, Mrs. George Fritscher [the bride's only sister, Virginia], Mrs. Jay Mann, Mrs. James Day [Mildred Horn], Mrs. Jesse Garner, Mrs. Eugene Lee, Mrs. Forest Crouse, Mrs. Kenneth Kinser, Mrs. Richard Wade, Mrs. M. Dombrowa, Mrs. Elmore Sutter, Mrs. Gerald Hagen, Mrs. Nancy Lindley, Mrs. Gale Entrikin, Mrs. Bart Day, Mrs. William Hodgson, Mrs. Orville Cox, and Lieut. Chumley.

NOVEMBER, 1935

The Way

ROUTT HIGH SCHOOL
JACKSONVILLE, - ILLINOIS

Routt Graduates Are Qualified For GOOD POSITIONS after attending

BROWN'S BUSINESS COLLEGE

Jacksonville, Illinois

Day or Night School
Business and Music Courses

New Terms Begin—
June, September, December, March

O'DONNELL & REAVY

Funeral Directors

328 EAST STATE ST.
JACKSONVILLE,
ILLINOIS

PHONE—DAY AND NIGHT—1007

VISIT
MRS. KUMLE'S BEAUTY SHOPPE
FOR "SERVICE AND PRICES THAT SATISFY"

37½ SOUTH SIDE SQUARE   PHONE 376

Capps

100% PURE WOOL CLOTHES

All the New Sport Suits

New Styles in Top Coats
and Overcoats

MAC'S
∴ Clothes Shop ∴

JACKSONVILLE BUS LINES

Fast and Dependable
Service to All
Points

New Streamlined Buses

For Information Call
UNION BUS DEPOT
DUNLAP HOTEL
Phone 1775

The WAG

FIRST CLASS HONOR RATING 1934-'35

VOL. VIII. No. I   NOVEMBER, 1935

TABLE OF CONTENTS

November	2
Stamp Collecting	4
Ghostly Goblins	5
Latin Helps Our English	6
Geometry	7
My Last Penny	8
Waglettes	9
The WAG Wins Two First Place Awards and All Catholic Honors	10
Editorials,	
Good Beginning—Now All Together, Reading	11
Some New Books	14
The Development of the Printing Press	16
The Newest Thing in Jewelry	19
Sports	20
Just Among Ourselves	25
Honor Roll	28
Alumni Notes	29
Exchanges	30
Jokes	31

    THE WAG is published four times during the school year by the students of Routt High School, during November, January, March and June. Contributions are solicited from the students. Yearly one dollar; single copy thirty-five cents.

    Entered as Second-class matter, December 12, 1922, at Post Office of Jacksonville, Illinois, under the act of March 3, 1879.

November

Mardelle Thompson, '37

To most people November is just another month of the year, but to good Catholics it means the month dedicated by the Church to the Poor Souls in Purgatory. For, although one special day in the month is called All Soul's Day, the whole month is given over to them and is really All Soul's Month. It is not hard to imagine that the suffering souls in Purgatory wait for their month.

Let us stop for a moment and picture a man thrown on a railroad track, bound hand and foot; he is helpless to free himself, but he can warn others. So, too, the suffering Souls in Purgatory are bound and are helpless to aid themselves; but they may warn others. They have had their opportunity in this life and have brought this suffering upon themselves by their disobedience to God's Laws; consequently, after facing judgment they are now atoning for the stains that marred their souls and kept them from eternal happiness. For if at death the soul is stained with any impurity it remains for a time in a place of expiation, the length of time varying according to the soul's sinfulness.

These suffering souls call to us for aid. If we fail to pray for them we are like the unfeeling person who would pass the helpless man bound on the railroad and refuse him help.

As the man bound and helpless must await the charity of another to free him, so too, must these suffering souls await the charity of their friends and loved ones to free them. The

The WAG

charity to be rendered to them will be in the form of prayers and good works. The Church teaches that the suffering souls are relieved by the intercession of the saints in heaven and by the prayers of the faithful on earth.

Immediately after a beloved one is taken by death, those left behind remember to pray for a while; one then really realizes one's duty to the dead. However, as the passing of time lessens the anguish, do not the prayers become less frequent? Yet the knowledge that we can continue after death to help our loved ones is one of the most consoling of the Church's teachings.

Would you thank someone for rescuing you from suffering? The poor souls thank you when you rescue them by your prayers. However, their thanks to you will amount to more than mere words. Their "Thank You" will be used in getting you out of purgatory and into heaven.

Beginning this month, let us say a prayer each day for the souls in purgatory; let us keep this practice up every day of our lives; let us consider this month not as just another thirty days, but as a special month of devotion to the Poor Souls, who are constantly crying out to us: "Have pity on me, have pity on me, at least you, my friends, for the hand of the Lord hath touched me."

The WAG, the student body and the faculty offer sincerest condolences:

To Herbert and Raphael Behrens on the death of their sister.

To Jack O'Brien on the death of his father.

To Coach Wallace Baptist on the death of his mother.

Stamp Collecting

Thelma LeBeau, '39

Postage stamps are so interesting that the collecting of them has become a hobby with me. Imagine how dignified I felt when I learned that such a hobby has a name, as also has the one practicing the hobby. So I am a philatelist, and I practice philately.

Despite the high-sounding name, there is much of interest and of information to be learned from the collecting of stamps. Then, too, the arranging of the collection is no small task, but if properly done may handsomely repay the collector for the care taken.

First, I am going to tell you about some of the many things to be learned from a collection of stamps. In a pleasant way we shall learn much geography. If we save stamps from many countries, the sorting of the various stamps into their countries fixes in our minds a knowledge of geography. We learn what the countries are like, for many place on their stamps the pictures of cities, mountains, or local scenery.

Also our vocabulary of foreign words is increased. The different countries print on their stamps the money value of the stamp and, of course, all the money values are not written in English. For instance, on a German stamp is printed the words "Deutfches Reich", on an Italian stamp is printed "Poste Italiane", on a French stamp is printed "Republique Francaise", and on an Austrian stamp is printed "Osterreich".

Moreover, the study of history is made more interesting. Countries, even our own United States, print on their stamps pictures of famous men, various scenes, and incidents connected with the history of that certain country. A picture of King Emanuel is printed on a fifty-cent Italian stamp. A stamp of Denmark has the picture of a very old ship, the type of ship in which Columbus crossed the ocean. On a one-cent French stamp is printed the picture of an Indian using a bow and arrow. A picture of Leon Houvqux is printed on a sixty-cent Belgian stamp. On stamps of the United States are pictures, such as many of the presidents, and of Benjamin Franklin. On a four-cent stamp is a picture of the Mesa Verde, the ruins of the clay huts that the Indians used to live in; on a ten-cent stamp is a picture of the Great Smoky Mountains; on a two-cent stamp, issued in 1929, is a picture of Edison's electric light.

Secondly, I am going to give a few pointers on how to make a collection of stamps. In starting a collection ask any of your friends that receive foreign letters to save the stamps for you. This way you may get quite a few stamps, some of which may become valuable. All you need to start a collection is a stamp-album, some stamps, and some stamp hinges. An illustrated stamp-album is best for them for it gives all the information

The WAG

about the classification of stamps. A good way to find some very nice stamps is to hunt among old correspondence. If you cannot get any stamps this way and you have to buy some, it is best to buy an assorted packet of stamps.

Next, in sorting your stamps, be sure to look at the illustrations in the album of the stamps of the different countries. If you find that you have more than one kind of a stamp and wish to trade it with someone else for another stamp, do not trade it until you have found out whether it is the same stamp. Many stamps are exactly alike, except that they have different water marks.

Now, in putting the stamps in the album, always remember to put them in neatly. Do not, above all, paste the whole back of the stamp in the album. This spoils the stamp and takes away the value of it. It also makes it difficult, if not impossible, to remove the stamp from the album if necessary. One should buy the stamp hinges that are made for this purpose.

In taking a stamp from an envelope, do not try to pull it off. Tear the piece of envelope on which the stamp is stuck from the rest of the envelope. Next put it in a saucer of luke-warm or cold water until it has soaked itself from the stamp. But in putting the piece of paper which the stamp is on, in water, do not let the face of the stamp get wet. When the stamp is free from the envelope place it directly on a piece of blotting-paper, face down and allow it to dry.

The most important thing in stamp collecting is to be sure not to cut the perforation off the stamp. This greatly decreases the value of the stamp. Some rare specimens of stamps would be absolutely worthless if the perforations were cut off.

The number of stamps in the world is so great today that some collectors confine their collection to one country or one continent. I extend my collection to every country in the world. For an interesting and educational hobby I choose philately.

GHOSTLY GOBLINS

Loretta Lonergan, '37

'Tis shakin' of the shutters
'Tis bangin' of the doors
'Tis flickerin' of ghostly shadows
On awful creakin' floors.
'Tis flittin' of the shadows
All up and down the hill,
'Tis ghost and goblins spying
On every Jack and Jill.
Ghostly goblins peer 'n glare;
Tonight—goblins is nigh everywhere.

Latin Helps Our English

Irene Bergschneider, '37

Why study Latin? James R. Day, Chancellor of Syracuse University, says, "As a time saver and as a sure road to the topmost round of all things that require strong, critical, and clear thinking, I would urge the patient and untiring study of the Greek and Latin languages." Men who have studied Latin tell us that it has helped them in many ways. However, the purpose of this paper is to show just one of the ways in which Latin repays our study: Latin makes the English language more intelligible. Without Latin, the full meaning of most English words cannot be obtained; without Latin the expression of clear and concise English is hard to attain. The more Latin one knows, the better he can read, spell, write, and understand English.

For two-thirds of the words of the English dictionary are derived from Latin; in our everyday conversation one half of the words are of Latin origin. A small boy on the street might say, "Please give me a cent, Mister;" such a sentence contains one half Latin derivities: please, cent, mister; and one-half Anglo-Saxon: give, me, a. The vocabulary of a person better educated than the small boy would probably contain more than fifty percent of Latin derivities, since usually a better vocabulary contains more words of Latin origin.

Dozens of Latin words have come unchanged into the English—for example: veto, actor, stimulus, camera, apex, radius, ultimatum, dictator, vertex, villa, arena, curriculum, rostrum, index, bonus, momentum, victor, crux, senator, plus, minus, stadium, via, animal, etc. Many of our English words have Latin plurals: radii, data, stimuli, vertices, loci, genera, vertebrae, stadia, minima, alumni, alumnae. Almost every technical term in biology, zoology, geology, chemistry, and mathematics comes from Latin or Greek. Law books are full of Latin terms. In many states Latin is required by law as a preparation for the study of law, medicine, and pharmacy.

Many Latin abbreviations are taken from Latin words: therefore a Latin student should be able to use them intelligently. Not knowing abbreviations sometimes handicaps one. Once there was a University student who, when he saw "Ibid" after some history references, spent a long time looking for an author by that name.

A few years ago, if such a student had seen "123 A. D.," he might have thought it meant 1 2 3 after Dillinger!

Here are some of the most common modern abbreviations that are of Latin origin: A. D.—**Anno Domini**, in the year of our Lord; N. B., **nota bene**, note well; ibid.—ibidem, in the same place; Ad lib.—**ad libitum**, at pleasure; E. g.—**exempli gratia**, for example;

The WAG

id est—i. e., that is; vs.—versus, against; etc.—et cetera, and others.

Many of our modern inventions get their names from Latin. These words are gradually increasing our vocabulary; some of these inventions are: incubator—derived from the Latin word **incubo**—to brood over; automobile—derived from the Greek word—self, and **mobilis**, the Latin word movable. Other examples are: locomotive, motor, radio, pedometer, pulmotor, binocular.

It is altogether likely that if you can't understand Latin and Greek references, such as—"lonely as Prometheus," "hydra-headed despotism," "a Janus faced fact," you will avoid books containing them. But by doing so you will rob yourself of much of the best English literature from Chaucer to the middle of the nineteenth century; for as Dr. Sherman, former Professor of English at the University of Illinois, says, "Every great English writer of prose or poetry from the time of King Alfred to the time of Alfred Tennyson has--almost without exception—been schooled in the Latin languages, has known well some of Latin masterpieces, and, consciously or not, willingly or not, has written under the influence, sometimes indistinct, sometimes over mastering, of the Latin models."

It can be truthfully said, therefore, that Latin is of great practical value, that it makes the English Language more intelligible.

GEOMETRY
Catherine Heffernan, '38

Night in, night out, I scratched and scratched,
G'om'try to get, tougher than tow.
The other day, the chance I snatched,
"Teacher," I asked in a voice quite low,
"Why to G'om'try, such worth attached?"
And she said, "Aw, you're too young to know."

Night in, night out, I try and try,
Next day no solace brings, but woe.
I know teacher is apt to sigh,
"Why, child, where's the G'om'try you owe?"
Would that it weren't bold to reply,
"My dear, aw, you're too young to know."

My Last Penny

Mary F. Schneider, '38

Woe was me! One whole evening left to go before I would get my allowance, and only one cent to my name.

It seemed that I wanted everything that came to my mind, but all of the things were priced beyond my meager fortune. Finally, I tried out the old stand-by, borrowing. The first fellow I accosted was B. Ferry, coming out of the meat market. "Just too late, Schneider," he said. "I spent my last nickle on hamburger for Whimpy (his dog)." Next on the program was Marjorie Y. "Sorry, Mary," she laughed. "Spent my last cent for lipstick." The last fellow I cornered was R. Thomas, the Latin shark. "Da pecuniam mihi," I said in a most pitiful tone of voice and with my saddest expression. "Huh?" he grunted, and walked on. That was the last straw. Evidently I wasn't cut out for a successful career as a beggar, so I gave up the idea.

The thought of cocs, sodas, candy bars, sundaes, and all of the other delicacies that make life worth living, made me tighten my belt and think seriously of ending it all. Of course if I did that, I wouldn't get my next week's allowance, so I decided to suffer it out.

Suddenly I struck upon the bright idea of a stick of gum or a penny candy bar. I wanted the gum worse than anything, but the candy bar ran such a close second, that I decided to take the chances of ruining my good name by sticking a paper wad instead of my penny in a gum machine. If it didn't work I would use the penny as a last resort.

The paper wad went in, but much to my disgust no gum came out. In desperation, I took out my fortune, kissed the candy bar goodby, and dropped the penny into the slot. Lo! and behold! again no gum came out. I was frantic, and was just about to go in to pick a fight with the manager of the store, when I thought better of the idea. I knew he'd find the paper wad, and then my goose would be cooked.

The rest of that evening I was quite down-hearted, resolving that I'd never try to snitch gum out of a slot machine again—at least not with a paper wad!

WAGLETTES

Well, folks, here we are startin' a new school year by gettin' the ole pen a goin' and greasin' the rusty brains for the WAGLETTES "The capacity of the human mind to resist the introduction of knowledge is most impressive" . . . WAGLETTES . . . Why was Lena L. seeking the correct address of Notre Dame? . . . WAGLETTES Paul, have you bought that Chemistry credit for a dime yet? . . . WAGLETTES . . . Art Hull has gone in the taxi business—good car, but can't recommend it for rainy days . . . WAGLETTES . . . R. Behrens boasted a black eye (not from a door knob either)— Oh, but you oughta see the other guy . . . WAGLETTES . . . John Kennedy, you kitten-ish little thing, quit teasin' Joe J. . . . WAGLETTES . . . G. Magner thinks that an Elizabethan sea-dog is Robin Hood . . . WAGLETTES . . . Pike gets a big kick out of reporting himself absent from roll-call—come up and hear him some time . . . WAGLETTES . . . The Freshmen are ambitious—a large squad of them reported for cheer-leading—and football. Keep it up CHILDREN . . . WAGLETTES . . . Is it true, Leona, that Irene B. walks as if she were from the country? . . . WAGLETTES . . . Have you seen "Big" Maloney?—Oh, you mean older Maloney? . . . WAGLETTES . . . "Skeets" after Trinity game: "I've got a scar the shape of a T on my arm". S. Isaacs, p r o u d l y: "That's nothin', I've got the whole alphabet". . . . WAGLETTES . . . If the freshmen would please give their names (also addresses, telephone numbers, e t c.) to the Seniors, it would aid the UPPERCLASSMEN immensely . . . WAGLETTES . . . Did you know the Doctor has ordered Norbert to chew gum?..WAGlettes.. Greg says he is going to be a locksmith—He practiced during English one day (With the teacher's consent) . . . WAGLETTES . . . No white-washing—the freshmen seem physically unable to carry the brooms—Cute though, aren't THEY? . . . WAGLETTES . . . Bill M. insists that all people in the sixth study hall are intelligent— I suppose he includes himself . . . WAGLETTES . . . Wonder why Red L. comes to school—We know somebody else who wonders why, too . . . WAGLETTES . . . Lee McGinnis is thinking about starting a shoe store in Ethiopia—Wish you luck, Lee . . . WAGLETTES . . . Mr. C. to detention squad: "I am going to excuse you now."— Yes, the bell rang as we got to the door . . . WAGLETTES . . . Gee, next year October 4th will fall on Saturday — Seniors should worry . . . WAGLETTES . . . Trees seem to have a magnetic power over Bob Ring—They draw him right to them . . . WAGLETTES . . . As I was a sayin'—"The goblins will getcha if you don't like our WAGLETTES."

The Wag Wins Two First Place Awards And All Catholic Honors

Mary Louise Maloney
Editor

Joseph Mandeville
Business Manager

Again THE WAG has triumphed, gaining three high journalistic ratings: an International First Place, a National First Place, and an All-Catholic rating.

THE WAG, rated as a quarterly magazine, has been awarded a First Class Honor Rating by the National Scholastic Press Association of the University of Minnesota. Every magazine entered in the Association is carefully graded and scored, checked for errors in design, arrangement of matter, and quality of material. This honor award rated the magazine as excellent.

THE WAG was also given International First Place Honor Award by the Board of Judges of the Quill and Scroll Society, with headquarters at Northwestern University. In this instance the publication was judged "a magazine of high achievement."

More dignity was added to the publication when the Catholic School Press Association of Marquette University announced that our magazine had won All-Catholic Honors for the second successive year.

This year's staff hopes to equal and if possible to excel the record made last year; that is to attain the highest award—"All-American" rating.

To the 1934-'35 staff, headed by Mary Louise Maloney, Editor, and Joseph Mandeville, Business Manager, we say CONGRATULATIONS!

10

The Wag

EDITOR	CHARLES MAGNER
ASSOCIATE EDITOR	MARDELLE THOMPSON
BUSINESS MANAGER	JOHN KENNEDY
ASSISTANT BUSINESS MANAGER	JACK HANLEY

LITERARY EDITORS

VIRGINIA DAY	ANGELA DAVID
MARY MARGARET RING	LEE McGINNIS

JOKE EDITORS
JOSEPHINE JOHNSON GLORIA HANLEY
WILLIAM MONAHAN

EXCHANGE EDITORS
LILLIAN MALLEN LUCILLE SCHWABE
RAPHAEL BEHRENS

FACULTY ADVISERS
SISTER MARY EULALIA, O. P.
SISTER MARY MAURICE, O. P.

SPORT EDITORS

HOWARD ANDERSON	JOHN MAGNER
ALUMNI EDITOR	PAUL A. KAISER

CIRCULATION
HARRY BUOY, JOHN LAIR, ROBERT RING, PAUL BERGSCHNEIDER, ARTHUR HULL, FRANCIS MALONEY, BERNARD SHANAHAN, JAMES LONERGAN, VINCENT TOBIN, JOHN DeVOS, FRANCIS CASEY, ROBERT LAVERY.

CLASS REPORTERS
AGNES MERNIN, EDWARD COX, CATHERINE JORDAN, CHARLES PIKE, VIRGILENE EASLEY, ROBERT JOHNSON, ANN DEVLIN, ROBERT DeBARR.

FIRST CLASS HONOR RATING—NATIONAL SCHOLASTIC PRESS ASSOCIATION, 1934-'35
INTERNATIONAL FIRST PLACE HONOR AWARD—QUILL AND SCROLL, 1934-35
ALL CATHOLIC HONORS—1933-'34, 1934-'35

Good Beginning— Now All Together

Congratulations, students! You have made a good start by your improved cooperation in the study hall and corridors. Still better observance of all school regulations would increase the comfort and freedom of all of us. Most of us have discovered that those who push and knock their way through the halls are selfish and deservedly unpopular; and that when a collision with a passing student

The WAG

accidentally occurs a courteous apology makes the offender seem less awkward. During this newly begun school year why can't we do things which are not asked us—the little things which in themselves are not important, but which contribute much toward neatness and order? In going up and down stairs, for instance, everyone should keep moving, but not running, and stay on the right side of the stairs to avoid unnecessary delay; don't throw paper on the floor—it's just as easy to throw it in the waste basket; why insist on putting books out of place in the library? —spend another half minute and put them in their proper places; don't chew gum in class —it hinders your thinking and annoys the other students; why not take better care of the laboratory equipment? If you want to know something about your supplies, ask your instructor—don't try to find out yourself and break the instruments.

Another item of interest for the Routt student might well be an improvement in the methods of freshman initiation. The word initiation should give you a mind picture of a specific week known as "Freshman Week". Why can't Routt have such a procedure instead of the usual way of "doing a little" every day for two or three weeks? This "bit by bit" method interferes with school work and is very unpleasant for the freshmen. What do you, as a Routt student, think of introducing this plan? Give the freshmen a break.

The main part in a pleasant, successful school year is played by the students, so why shouldn't you, Routt students, take your side seriously?

12

The WAG

Reading

"Some books are to be tasted, others to be swallowed, and some few to be chewed and digested; that is, some books are to be read only in parts; others to be read, but not curiously; and some few to be read wholly, and with diligence and attention."

One might be tempted to think that Lord Bacon gave his three purposes in reading for the Routt students alone. For truly his purposes cover the varying aptitudes of our students, whether it be the superficial reader, or the intensive reader.

Do not these three types of readers include every Routt student—at least, every English student, who has to read a certain number of books every year and report on each? Some students think of book reports only as extra assignments which are useless. Other students regard them as something to "kill time". But there is more to be gained from this use of books than that. The volumes read are of different types of literature—history, drama, short story, and poems. This is the variety that Lord Bacon mentions in the above quotation. The books should give the students something to think about, should increase their desire for reading, and should also yield some sound facts. Why do students grumble about book reports? The reason is clear—they don't understand the real benefits to be derived from such requirements.

SOME NEW BOOKS

Are you among the number of those who have a tendency to keep away from lives of the saints because you think them dull reading? If you are, the chances are you haven't read any of the books on this list. During November, the month in which we celebrate the feast of All Saints, and during December, the month in which we prepare for the coming of the Model of all the Saints, why not read one or two of these books and demonstrate to yourself how interesting biographies of Saints may be? In addition, you will perhaps discover that the saints are not dull people at all, but very human, very likeable—very much like ourselves.

EDMUND CAMPION by Evelyn Waugh. This work of one of the most brilliant of English novelists will be a surprise to those who have not yet shed the old fashioned notion of what a saint is.

THOMAS MORE by Daniel Sargent. The publishers, Sheed and Ward, remark that More is the first member of the English House of Commons to be canonized, adding: "We trust that we may have the honor of publishing as good a book on the first Congressman to be raised to the altars." The **New York Times** says: "Daniel Sargent has made us see a great man in all his greatness; he has made us see how truly great it is sometimes vouchsafed humans to be."

THOMAS MORE by Christopher Hollis. Another deservedly popular biography of the author of **Utopia.**

St. JOHN FISHER by Vincent McNabb. This is an historical portrait of the famous bishop who, like his friend Sir Thomas More, had his head cut off by Henry VIII and who, with Sir Thomas, was canonized last May.

THE ANGEL OF THE SCHOOLS by Ruissa Maritain. This is the life of St. Thomas Aquinas written for young people. **America** says: "It would be a great blessing if all the

The WAG

saints were written about with the scholarship and enthusiasm Ruissa Maritain has poured into this beautiful life."

PETER CLAVER: A SAINT IN THE SLAVE TRADE by Arnold Lunn. The N. Y. **Herald Tribune** says: "It will give a new horizon to your mind and imagination."

ST. THOMAS AQUINAS by G. K. Chesterton.

St. FRANCIS OF ASSISSI by G. K. Chesterton. Those who know the gifted Mr. Chesterton will want to read these two books.

St. CATHERINE OF SIENNA by Alice Curtayne. A most readable life of a most remarkable woman. The girls who pass St. Catherine's statue every day shouldn't miss this book.

SIX O'CLOCK SAINTS by Joan Windham, for very young readers.

MORE SIX O'CLOCK SAINTS by Joan Windham. Here the author introduces us to St. Lawrence, St. Barbara, St. Dorthea, St. Anthony, St. Margaret, and St. Joan of Arc.

THE ENGLISH WAY includes biographical studies of St. Bede, Alcuin, St. Boniface, Alfred the Great, Thomas a Becket, Thomas More, John Fisher, Edmund Campion, Newman, and other outstanding Englishmen remarkable for sanctity. Among these authors are such interesting writers as Belloc, Chesterton, Bede Jarrett, and Christopher Dawson. Students of English Literature should take time to read and enjoy it.

THE IRISH WAY, edited by F. Sheed, gives sketches of Irish saints.

Most of these books have been published, within the last two or three years, by Sheed and Ward, an English firm that has had a branch in this country since about 1933.

—Gloria Hanley, '36

The Development of the Printing Press

Mary Rose Mollenbrok, '38

The press by which the many million newspapers, magazines, and books have been printed, folded, and made ready for use has a most interesting history. The days when Roman scholars copied the great orators and philosophers by hand, or even several centuries later when medieval scribes labored over manuscripts with such pains seem far removed from the present. In some countries rude methods of printing came into use earlier than in others. At the early date of 900 B. C., the Chinese had organized an unskilled method of printing in ink on paper but not by engraved blocks, although it was almost 1000 years later that printing in this manner was extensively used. Also in Europe, Spain, and Italy, crude methods of printing took place. The first step in modern process was to invent a type which could be adjusted at will and would provide for any number of copies. Such a press was invented by Johannes Gutenberg around 1440.

Letters of Indulgence, printed by type cast in a mould and issued from his press at Mainz, are thought to be the first printed matter. This famous press was rudely constructed from two upright timbers with cross beams at the top and bottom. The letters were fastened securely to its bed and inked with soft leather balls. The paper was dampened and

The WAG

laid upon the type which was pressed down with a lever. After a few minutes the lever was raised and the paper hung up to dry. This simple method continued in use for almost one hundred and fifty years. In fact there was little change until the early seventeenth century, when Blaew experimented with putting the screw through a wooden block from which the platen was suspended. He also invented a plan for rolling the bed in and out under the platen, and improved the hand lever for turning the screw. This press was widely used, for almost two centuries, every where in the world for printing small books.

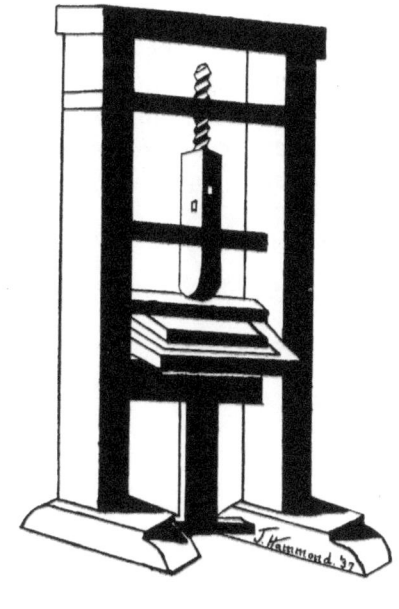

As time passed and printing assumed an important place in the cultural life of the people, there was a demand for a faster press. The first speedy press was brought out by Isaac Adams of Boston. His machine printed six hundred sheets per hour and might be operated by a child. Soon after came the cylinder press of Frederick Konig with a capacity of eight hundred impressions per hour, to be followed shortly by the Hoe type revolving machine. This style attained a production of twenty thousand sheets per hour but printed on one side only. The Web press, patented by Bullock, printed from a continuous roll of paper but still on only one side. This difficulty was finally overcome by the Rotary Perfecting Press which printed on both sides at the same operation and turned out the newspaper ready for use.

Soon after the newspapers had arrived at this degree of

excellence, it seemed probable that the printing of magazines might be improved. The present press assembles, posts, cuts, separates, and folds again the papers and delivers them ready for use. The whole operation consists of three different activities but each may be performed separately, even to individual delivery of the papers.

The color press is just coming into its own. By skillfully dividing colors in the ink fountains and combining by overprinting, very beautiful effects can be produced. One Christmas picture has been printed with thirty-six different colors.

Thus we see that the machine which prints the thought of man has passed through many interesting phases. To try to measure its influence on civilization is almost impossible, for there has been so much of good and evil coming from it, but whatever else it has done, it has brought knowledge and learning to the poor, as well as to the rich.

The Newest Thing in Jewelry

Eileen O'Meara, '39

One day as I sat idly watching the girls and boys in the Study Hall I was struck with the amount of jewelry they were wearing. All of the girls around me had on rings and bracelets; three had ear rings and many of the Sophomore and Junior girls had colored beads and necklaces. Here and there I saw combs and bandeaus and tiny little ribbons in their hair. Many of the boys were wearing wrist watches with wide ornamental bands, rings with wide sets, and bracelets.

"They think they are very up to date; don't they?" I said to myself. "But really they are only wearing the same things that the Egyptians wore four thousand years ago."

In those ancient times the women strung beads of blue and green stone on linen strings and wore them looped gracefully around their necks. Wide bands of gold and silver, ornamented with hieroglyphics served as bracelets and were worn both on the upper and lower parts of the arm. Egyptian rings were all signet rings, with the name of the reigning pharaoh inscribed on them. Many of these rings are preserved in the American and English museums today. Ear rings were introduced into Egypt by foreigners, and both men and women wore them. The first styles were broad, ornamented discs of silver and gold.

Great attention was given to the hair and after it had been carefully waved it was decorated with ribbons and wreaths. The men used wigs a great deal though they never had the length that the French wigs had.

The royal family had a special covering for the head. In his palace the king wore a crown of gold and on the battle field he had a metal helmet. The queen wore a large headdress made of silver and gold on which the sacred bird (for the protection of the king in battle) appears to spread his wings over the head of the queen.

So for all our seeming modernism, we have things much the same as the Egyptians long before the twentieth century.

COACH BAPTIST'S CALL FOR RECRUITS
LO, THE ANSWER

With a determination of a bigger and better football team, Coach Wally Baptist opened the season by issuing equipment to 38 football aspirants. The large number of players did not mean veterans; only eight veterans were present, leaving a remainder of heavy, young, and inexperienced recruits.

The season opened with intensive work. With a very light backfield and a line of inexperienced recruits rapid development was not expected. In spite of this sad story Routt Rockets are off to a happy start for 1935.

U. HIGH FAILS TO STOP ROUTT RALLY
ROCKETS WIN 13-6

Both teams battled evenly during the opening half, with first one eleven threatening to score and then the other. As the second half opened, the U. High lads drove over for a touchdown, but failed to add the free point. The Rockets suddenly came to life then and with a few passes and end runs, sent Lawrence over for their first counter. Lawrence also tallied the extra point on a plunge, to take the lead as the period ended. In the final quarter the Rockets added another touchdown to put the game on ice, this time Ring lugging the oval across the goal.

Score by periods:

U. High	0	0	6	0	6
Routt	0	0	7	6	13

Scoring: Touchdowns—Routt: Lawrence, Ring. U. High—Pierson.

Point after touchdown—Routt—Lawrence (plunge).

ROCKETS TUMBLE TRINITY IN SEASON'S OPENER 14-6

Battling against a veteran Trinity High team and Old Sol's blistering heat, Routt's Rockets came through with an impressive victory in their opening game. Trinity drew first blood, banging over a touchdown in the second quarter, when Gleason, Trinity quarterback, picked up 31 yards, and then Lacey slipped over the final stripe. The try for the extra point failed.

The Rockets scored in the second and fourth periods; both times Lawrence breaking off tackle for the pay-off. After each touchdown, the Rockets opened up a hole for Lawrence to slip through and add the gift points.

The fourth quarter was mostly a period of blocking and good ball handling, with neither team scoring.

The lineup:

Pike	L. E.	Sweeney
Beerup	L. T.	Schmidt
R. Lonergan	L. G.	T. Leeson
Doherty	C.	C. Baldini
Roth	R. G.	McCambridge
Fritscher	R. T.	Ulbrich
G. Gaitens	R. E.	Nelson
Buoy	Q. B.	Gleason
A. McGinnis	L. H.	Lacey
Isaacs	R. H.	Yeagle
Lawrence	F. B.	Stolze

Substitutions: Routt—Ring for Buoy, Balkan for Pike, Lair for Isaacs.

Trinity—Deutsch for Schmidt, W. Leeson for Ulbrich.

Score by periods:

Routt	0	7	0	7	14
Trinity	0	6	0	0	6

Scoring: Routt Touchdowns—Lawrence 2. Trinity touchdown—Lacey.

Points after touchdown: Lawrence 2.

Referee—Young; Umpire—Rose; Headlinesman—White (All of Bloomington).

ROUTT FALLS BEFORE McCOOEY HIGH 19-0

The Rockets dropped their first decision of the season, when they went down before a blocking McCooey High team 19-0. McCooey scored in the first quarter by a lateral pass breaking King, McCooey halfback, for a 30 yard run across the goal line. Routt neared the goal in the second quarter, but was checked by McCooey's stern wall on the 20 yard line. McCooey recovered a Routt fumble on the Rocket's 30 yard line. Then with a 15 yard gain on line plays, Hull with a pass from Crim galloped over the final stripe for another touchdown.

Crim slipped through for the gift point. McCooey again recovered a Rocket's fumble on Routt's 45 yard line and passed the 20 yard line at the close of the third quarter. A couple of line plays brought up Crim, McCooey fullback, for another McCooey touchdown. Although Routt piled up a few more first downs than McCooey, still they could not get beyond that 20 yard line. The breaks seemed to be against the Rockets during the entire game.

Substitutions: Routt— Kindred, Balkan. McCooey— Hedges, Palhunus.

Score by periods:

Routt	0	0	0	0	0
McCooey	6	0	7	6	19

ROUTT BOWLS QUINCY ACADS OVER FOR SECOND STRAIGHT 27-0

The Rockets tacked victory number two on their season's work when they journeyed to Quincy and took a 27-0 decision from the Academy eleven.

Routt brought their scoring machine into action in the first quarter, taking the opening kickoff and driving to their first touchdown. Lawrence plunged for the extra point. In the third quarter the Rockets took advantage of a fumbled punt on the Quincy 15 yard line, turning the break into another marker with Lawrence again converting the extra point.

The WAG

Then came the longest run of the game, the Rockets breaking Isaacs through tackle for a 60 yard touchdown run. Isaacs took a pass from Lawrence for the free point. Buoy's pass to Lawrence scored the final Rocket tally in the closing quarter.

Substitutions: Routt—Lair, Ring, W. Gaitens, DeVos, Kindred, Wiedlocher, Cox, Tapscott, Balkan, Maloney. Quincy: Ascheman, Ramer, Kuse, Schneir, Bowen, Bicks, Hathaway.

Scoring: Routt touchdowns—Lawrence 2; Buoy, Isaacs. Points after touchdown—Lawrence 2 (plunges); Issacs (pass)

ROCKETS DUMPED BY CATHEDRAL
FIRST TIME IN RIVALRY 19-0

For the first time since their rivalry began in 1932, the Routt Rockets were defeated by the Cathedral Cyclones 19-0. It was also the first time the Routt goal line had been crossed by a Cathedral ball-carrier. Both teams battled evenly in the first half, with neither scoring.

Cathedral banged over their first touchdown early in the second half when Isaacs fumbled, Cathedral recovering. A pass from Holmes to Miller was completed, Miller stepping over the pay stripe on the next play. The kick for extra point went wide. Their next counter came shortly after, this time Frisch knifing his way through the Rockets for a nineteen yard run and a touchdown, after a Rocket punt had been partially blocked. Reynolds plunged over to add another point. In the last period, when a Rocket penalty carried the ball to the one foot line, the Cyclones added their final marker as Reynolds went through guard. The try for the extra point failed. Routt threatened in the closing minutes but the gun ended the rally.

Score by periods:

Routt	0	0	0	0	0
Cathedral	0	0	13	6	19

Scoring: Cathedral— Touchdowns— Miller, Reynolds, Frisch. Point after Touchdown—Reynolds (plunge).

Officials: Referee — Gibbs; Umpire — Ken Richards; Headlinesman—Hap Troy.

Routt Rocket's Racket

"It takes Mandeville to show them how"—
"How to do what?"
"How to sleep—ask the Rockets."

R. R. R.

Samuel, a game can be won without getting on the good side of the referee by lending him your pen. Eh, Samuel?

R. R. R.

Signals—"Formation 30" (Beerup — after listening to police calls) "Formation, calling all cars, 38, 56, license number 50, -94, shift,—go to corner of Michigan Ave. and Madison, 1-2-3-4. Man robbing house—hike, shoot to kill. Formation 30."

R. R. R.

(Wally, proudly) "This year's team is the lightest and greenest (not the color light green) team I have ever coached; but let me tell you although they are green, it is not from lack of brains, but lack of experience."

(Wally, grinning from ear to ear.) "And they're coming along fast; and won't we have a team for years to come?"

R. R. R.

Routt's unbalanced line—Charles Pike, left end; and "hoped-to-be" right end, Robert Lavery, Freshman.

Always Virginia

Just Among Ourselves

I.

Without much campaigning the following Freshmen were elected to office:
 Class Advisor—Sister M. Gerard.
 President—Paul Mandeville.
 Vice-President—Helen Schumm.
 Secretary-Treasurer — Paul Pieper.

If any of the upper classmen have a little extra money, would they please lend it to the Freshmen? We're thinking about buying a microphone in order to make S. M. G. hear us.

Be careful; don't call these Freshmen green; we aren't. Look at our football player on the first team: "Ted" Beerup. We also have the honor of donating James Tobin as a cheer-leader.

The first night we, the Freshmen, had a class meeting, Paul Mandeville, the president, said, "I just called this meeting tonight to inform you there will be a meeting tomorrow night."

Fate met Jeanette Johnson at our first social meeting, a weiner roast. She sprained her ankle and was walking by the aid of crutches.

Wanted: In Algebra Class Section A, an erasing teacher for Mary Jane Looker.

Is Ann Devlin afraid some one will steal her coat? She has worn it every day since school re-opened.

ROUTT'S BABIES AND GROWN-UPS

First row—Robert DeBarr, Teresa Sponski, Sara McDowell, Marie Todd, Arthur DeGrande, Freshmen.

Second row—Raphael Behrens, Josephine Johnson, Lillian Mallen, Gloria Hanley, Edward Cox, Seniors.

The WAG

II.

In our first class meeting the following officers were elected:
Class Advisor—Sister M. Wilfrid.
President—Virgilene Easley.
Vice-President—Joyce Rempe.
Treasurer—Jack O'Brien.

"Wait a minute!" "Who are those wild looking people in front of the school?" "Why, there's Mary Virginia Devlin from our class." "Why do they shout and wave their arms so desperately?" "Goodness, can't someone do something to put them out of their misery?" "Well, for heaven's sake, the whole school seems to have gotten a pain too." "Listen!" "They're yelling something awful." "What's that?" "Oh, they're the cheerleaders."

Weiners! Marshmallows! Buns! Fun! Games! 'Twas on a cool evening in October when we gathered in Nichols Park. Then out for wood, sticks, and paper to start that fire and then to sit back peacefully and watch it grow. Everyone overflowing with energy helped carry wood. "Here comes the eats!" "Where did they go?" We were plenty hungry but soon were too full. Games came next and laughter roared through the crowd. Soon the fire died down and we began climbing into the cars. A grand time in all. Ask any Sophomore.

We, the Sophomore class, extend our sympathy to Jack O'Brien in the death of his father.

III.

Well, the Juniors had their election and here are the results:

Class Advisor—Sister M. Kathleen.
President—Bernard Shanahan.
Vice Presdient—James Lonergan.
Sec'y and Treas.—Charles Pike.

We welcome Samuel Isaacs, Raymond Roth, Teresa Ring, Thomas Roach, Charles Pike and Edwin Zachow as new members of the Junior Class.

Congratulations, WAG staff of '34 and '35. You surely deserve praise for your success. We hope this year's staff can do as well.

We wish our new cheer leaders success—Virginia Day, Mary Virginia Devlin, James Tobin, and Carroll Ryan.

Five sentences are a long lesson in English sometimes; aren't they, Norbert?

Say, Juniors, try selling candy once in a while, or our finances will be low.

Poor Margaret, but doesn't she look happy for all those downs she's had in life?

A bit of Advice: Keep funny subjects from the Junior girls—they giggle too loudly; don't they, Lucille?

26

The WAG

Thomas, have you ever found out what "Inky-dinky" means? Some other Juniors are wondering also.

And why did the Juniors have a weiner roast? Just because we're not too big to eat "hot-dogs".

A Junior says "A Vocabulary is a dictionary of the human body", and "A Philologist is one who steals words or stories from another author." Hurry, run to the dictionary, Freshies.

Sister, we hope you don't collect too many English papers. You might get some I. O. U's. What about it, Catherine?

IV.

By this time, we, the class of '36, should all have a taste of the voyage on the good old vessel of Seniorship. We have elected as officers for this trip:

Captain—Sister M. Anaclete.
Pilot—Robert Lonergan.
Co-Pilot—Harry Buoy.
First Mate—Paul Bergschneider.

To Raphael Behrens of Hardin, to Leona Hermes and Luke Zeller of Alexander, new members of the crew, we extend a hearty welcome.

In football, our good ship is represented by Robert Lonergan, George Fritscher, Harry Buoy, Robert Ring, John Lair, Edward Cox, and Raphael Behrens.

And do we know our American History, especially that Paul Bergschneider! Paul even knows that the culture of the Mexican Indian was just plain old "culture and agriculture". Paul also is very sure that Canterbury Tales is the name of a city in England.

Are the Seniors ever smart? Rather than throw away the surplus marshmallows from our weiner roast, under the supervision of one very thrifty member (he must have been, or must hope to be president) those marshmallows were saved.

Robert Lonergan, so far as we know, has not as yet gotten that box of "Line Push" he sent one of our freshman managers for the other night.

Only One Change In Routt Faculty

There was but one change in the faculty this year. Sister Angelica who had been here for the past two years was transferred to Springfield, while Sister M. Anaclete, who taught at Routt previously has returned. Sister was WAG advisor while here.

The student body wishes the best of success to both teachers.

ROLL OF HONOR
First Six Weeks
1. Mary Frances Schneider.....II
1. Paul Mandeville I
1. Thelma LeBeau I
1. Albert DeSmet I
1. Arthur DeGrande I
1. Robert DeBarr I
2. Mary Rose Mollenbrok II
2. Robert Lavery I
2. James Tobin I
3. Irene Bergschneider III
3. Ann Devlin I
3. Sara McDowell I
4. Richard McGinnis II
4. Helen Schumm I
4. Jean Coonen I
4. Marie Todd I

Honorable Mention
1. Gloria Hanley IV
1. Howard Anderson IV
1. Catherine Maloney I
2. Lucille Schwabe III
3. Jean Hoecker IV
4. Lowell Gwinn III
4. Charles Pike III
4. Mardelle Thompson III
4. Mary Virginia Devlin II
4. Rose Mary Smith II
4. Mary Catherine Wacker I
4. Muriel Rodems I
4. Eileen O'Meara I
5. Charles Magner IV
5. Catherine Jordan III
6. Clara Ridder II
6. Margaret O'Donnell II
6. Joseph Tapscott I
6. Marjorie Yording I
6. Mildred Coleman I

During the last of August Right Reverend Monsignor Luke L. Mandeville, '08, received the title and rank of Domestic Prelate, which was conferred by Pope Pius XI. Monsignor Mandeville is now in York, Nebraska.

Miss Mary Mahoney was united in marriage to Frank Agnew of Chicago.

Edward Flynn, '23, of Chicago, has returned to the city to practice law with Robert Harmon.

Brother Eugene Kearney, S. V. C. has taken up his studies at the Catholic University, Washington, D. C.

Brother Aquinas, O. P. (Paul Duffner, '33) made his first profession in the Dominican Order at Ross, California, September 14. He is now at the Dominican House of Studies at Oakland, California.

Robert McCarthy was ordained to the priesthood in June and is assistant at Paris, Ill. He was very active on the WAG staff during his stay at Routt.

Miss Loyola Dowling, '18, was recently married to Mr. J. Sheenhan of St. Louis, Mo.

Howard Alyward, '30, is taking a course in medicine at the St. Louis U.

Tom Nelson, '28, is an interne at St. Mary's Hospital in St. Louis, Mo.

Catherine Schirz, '29, is director of Physical Education at St. Mary's of Wasatch, Salt Lake City, Utah.

Clarence Watts, '31, and Anita Schumm, '31, were united in marriage at Our Saviour's Church, October 10, 1935.

Dorothy Kumle, '31, is head bookkeeper of the Pasadena Community Playhouse in Pasadena, California. Wanda Kumle, '33, has returned to Junior College in Pasadena for a post graduate course.

Helen Hobbs, '31 is taking an advanced course in Nurse's Training in Detroit, Michigan.

Mary Louise Maloney, '35, past editor of The WAG, has a position in the office of Dr. H. N. Knight.

Mary Heffernan, Irene Hicks, John Proffitt, Gerald Hagen, Edna O'Connell, Cecilia and Elizabeth Pieper are enrolled at Brown's Business College.

Emma Bergschneider, '35 enrolled at MacMurray College.

Gertrude Hamilton holds the office of City Treasurer in Jacksonville.

Frank Berchtold, '23 is working at the Illinois School for the Deaf.

John J. Zeller, '32 is employed at the new Morgan-Scott Service Station in Jacksonville.

Cecil Doyle has taken the position of representative for the Uarco Cash Register Co. of Chicago.

Once more "THE WAG" welcomes all Exchanges old and new. We are convinced that the task of the Exchange Editors is going to be interesting as well as difficult. The difficulty comes not in reading, but in estimating and evaluating the periodicals.

The Campionette, Prairie du Chien, Wisconsin, deserves high praise on its first issue. News is real news to your reporters. The outstanding article is the editorial concerning the late Huey Long. The poems are delightful and carry a clear line of thought. The jokes, although we can't admit they're new, are cleverly treated. The **Campionette** is interesting throughout and we consider it a valuable Exchange.

Congratulations, **Victory,** De La Salle, Chicago, on your Honor Awards. We like your new type and larger paper. Your editorial, "The Unprepared Seldom Get the Breaks," is a thought provoking article. We are glad to welcome you back.

The Marywood College Bay Leaf, Scranton, Pennsylvania, carries many short stories, which in reality are splendid long stories. There are also several attractive poems. We wish to congratulate the editors on the number of their well written editorials. The review of new books is interesting, and your departments are as a whole well managed. We are glad to have the publication on our Exchange List.

J. Tapscott—"Sister, when we finish this freshman Algebra will we take Advanced Algebra next semester?"

Jack H. says, "I hit James," is a transitive verb, but "James hit me," would be war.

Fr. Formaz—"Miss Day, how can you tell Gothic architecture?"
V. Day—"Because it has a dome."
Fr. Formaz — "You've got a dome, too."

Bob L. (intelligently looking around library). S. M. G. "What do you want?"
Bob. "Basnet's Little History of America."

One freshman has discovered the ideal method of keeping students from copying his work—prepare work, then quickly rise and sit on it.

Luke Zeller might get his ears frost-bitten, but one thing sure he'll never get his feet frost-bitten as long as there are typewriter covers!

If Virginia D. stops you somewhere she'll probably want to tell you a rhyme something like this:
Dickory, Dickory, Dock,
The hands ran round the clock,
The clock struck 12,
And the mouse went out to dinner.

We wonder just how many times poor Geoffrey Chaucer turned over in his grave the day Gloria kept calling him Saucer.

Jean H. insists that all dogs are poodles. Why Jean!

Bud J.—"Hey, who made the touchdowns in the game yesterday?"
Pat McH.—"I did."
Bud J.—"No kiddin', who did make 'em?"
Pat McH.—"Yeah, I did. I made a ten yard gain through the line of reporters."

One of the reasons Ed Cox couldn't get his French—"Well, darn it, I couldn't find the ole dictionary." Could you say it in French, Ed?

Sr. W.—"You were late for class yesterday, William."
Wm. M.—"Yes, Sister, and I'm too late today to get a permit for yesterday."

THOS. C. CHUMLEY
GENERAL CONTRACTOR

All Kinds of Roofing   Diamond Weather Strip
1231 South Clay Ave.   Phone 1278

BE THRIFTY Buy Your
DRUGS, TOILETRIES AND TOBACCOS
—at—
MACE'S CUT RATE DRUG STORE
We Pay The Tax!

MILLER HAT SHOP
Rental Library - - - Harriet Smith

211 WEST STATE ST.   PHONE 1483W

MORGAN DAIRY CO.
... A SAFE MILK ...

PHONE 225   PHONE 225

Flexner's
"On The Square"

"Ladies' Wear"
"THE LATEST IN WEAR FOR LADIES WHO CARE"

Everything for the Graduate ...
CLASS RINGS - ANNOUNCEMENTS - CAPS AND GOWNS
R. L. JACOBS
PHONE 702-W   937 W. LAFAYETTE

Brady Bros.
Base Ball, Football, Basketball
Tennis
HARDWARE, PAINTS
TIN SHOP
Guns, Ammunition, Fishing Tackle
Largest and Most Complete Hardware
Store in Town

MAY BARBER SHOP
232 North Main Street

New   Modern
"WE TRY TO PLEASE"

ERNEST MAY
LEO MAY   R. G. HARMON

LUKEMAN CLOTHING COMPANY
Hart Schaffner & Marx Clothes
SPORT CLOTHES FOR COLLEGE MEN

DORWART'S MARKET
QUALITY MEATS
230 West State St.   Phone 196

HOPPER'S SHOE STORE
QUALITY FOOTWEAR
CAREFULLY
FITTED

South East Corner Square

ANDRE & ANDRE
The Home of
QUALITY
HOUSE FURNISHINGS AND
GIFTS SINCE 1898

TRADE HERE

WADDELL'S
THE STORE FOR WOMEN

Compliments of

Bahan's Cigar Store

32 NORTH SIDE SQ.

MATHEW'S
All Kinds of Good Things to
EAT
Chinese and American Foods
Luncheons   Dinners
Open 'till 2:00 a. m.

229 EAST STATE STREET

BAPTIST RADIO SHOP
Guaranteed Service on All Makes
AT ANDRE & ANDRE'S

PHONE 199   PHONE 199

LANE'S BOOK STORE
STUDENT HEADQUARTERS

CORN BELT CHEVROLET CO.
SALES AND SERVICE

Phone 278   307-15 South Main Street

Quality Footwear at Lowest Prices	Prescriptions Accurately Compounded
St. Louis Sample Shoe Store	Reliable Medicines and Toilet Articles Furnished with Guarantee of Purity and Stability at
231 EAST STATE STREET	**Shreve's Drug Store**
	15 West Side Square
"Keds" for the Gym	Make This YOUR Drug Store

F. J. ANDREWS LUMBER CO.
EVERYTHING IN THE BUILDING LINE

Phone 46   320 N. Main Street

USE
RED & WHITE   BLUE & WHITE   GREEN & WHITE
Brands of Canned Foods and Coffee
At All Red and White Stores
JENKINSON GROCER CO.

All Makes of Typewriters For Rent or Sale Including Portables
Student Special Rates for Period of 3 Months

EARL A. DAVIS
Phone 99W

317 W. STATE STREET   CITY   APPLEBEE BLDG.

Lucky Boy Orange Wrapped Bread		Wise Mothers Know Food Value Counts

There Is A Difference In Bread

Shadid's Shoe Store
206 E. STATE ST.

Quality Footwear For Men

SHOE REPAIRING   SUPPLIES

J. P. BROWN MUSIC HOUSE
Can Supply Your Musical Needs

No. 9 WEST SIDE SQUARE   PHONE 145

COMPLIMENTS OF

ILLINOIS TELEPHONE COMPANY

THE CITY GARDEN
"The Best That Nature Provides"
DUNLAP COURT AT COLLEGE AVENUE

Fruits and Produce

THE BOOK AND NOVELTY SHOP
GIFTS   FAVORS   SCHOOL SUPPLIES

59 East Side Square

EMPORIUM
STORE OF FASHION
EAST STATE STREET

Compliments of

Colonial Inn

Your Corner Pharmacy	**Hamilton's**
RING'S	Confectionery
	216 East State Street
DRUGS, CIGARS, CANDIES AND A COMPLETE LINE OF SUNDRIES	You're Always Welcome
	Fountain Candy
	Lunch Salted Nuts
Jacksonville's Largest and Finest Cleaners	SCHIRZ EAST SIDE DAIRY
J. W. LARSON & CO.	—FOR—
Exclusive Cleaners	Pure Milk and Cream
We Clean All Kinds of Rugs	
WE CALL FOR and DELIVER	
Phone 1800	Phone 1885-W
Fox Illinois Theatre	**SPIETH STUDIO** for **Quality Portraits**
Where All Jacksonville Is Entertained	

DR. J. J. SCHENZ, Optometrist

OPPOSITE POST OFFICE

Jacksonville, Illinois   Phone 473

Boosting for Routt...

J. C. PENNEY CO.

6 and 8 WEST SIDE SQUARE

Schram & Buhrman
JEWELERS

37 South Side the Square
On the Corner

EDWARD KEATING
Real Estate and
Insurance
(Over McGinnis Shoe Store...
62½ E. SIDE SQUARE
Call on him for Reliable Fire and
Tornado Insurance
Always Prompt Adjustment of Losses

HOFMANN FLORAL CO.
No. 9 West Side Sq.   Phone 182
"Flowers For All Occasions"

Two Stores to Serve You
S. S. KRESGE CO.

67 EAST SIDE SQUARE
45 SOUTH SIDE SQUARE

A Particular Laundry
For Particular People

FAMILY WASHINGS
A SPECIALTY.....
221-3-5 W. Court   Phone 447

LEONARD & SIX
QUALITY COAL

Sand, Gravel, Cement and Cement Products

Phone 621   509 NORTH EAST ST.

R. K. MATTHEWS
DeLuxe Shoe Repairing
New Location 215 West Morgan Street

We Print Anything...
BUNCE-BRANSTITER PRINTING CO.
...PRINTERS...

217 EAST MORGAN ST.   PHONE 533

PURITY CLEANERS

Phone 1000   216 S. Sandy St.
We Call For and Deliver

A. B. BAKERY

Fresh Bread, Rolls and Pastries

228 EAST STATE ST.

MOTHERS!   MOTHERS!
MOTHERS' BEST FLOUR at all Leading Grocers

J. H. CAIN SONS, Distributors

C. J. DEPPE & CO.
Known for SILKS and READY-TO-WEAR

Lukeman Motor Co.

SAFETY
SERVICE
FOR ALL CARS

Phone 331   West State St.

DRINK

Coca-Cola

IN BOTTLES
JACKSONVILLE
COCA-COLA BOTTLING CO.
311 Mauvaisterre Street
Phone 1074

JACKSONVILLE CREAMERY CO.
MANUFACTURERS OF
WILD ROSE BUTTER

COMPLIMENTS OF

SANER BROS.

Compliments of

GUSTINE'S

FURNITURE   RUGS   STOVES

THE MODERN SHOPPING CENTER

For Dry Goods
RABJOHN & REID

**SWEENEY
SUPPLY COMPANY**

BRICKLAYERS' AND
PLASTERERS' SUPPLIES

Best Grades of Coal

North Clay Avenue and Wabash R. R.
Phone 165

Home of . . . .

Crosley Radios
Estate Heatrolas
Hoosier Cabinets
Majestic Ranges
R. C. A. Radios

HOPPER & HAMM

LaCROSSE LUMBER CO.
for

QUALITY AND SERVICE AT A REASONABLE PRICE

SOUTH MAIN STREET   PHONE 192

SEVEN OPERATORS AND BARBERS
TEN YEARS EXPERIENCE AT

M. & P. BARBER AND BEAUTY SHOPPE
Phone 860

213 EAST STATE ST.   JACKSONVILLE, ILLINOIS

The New Royal Portable
with Touch Control Makes Typing
easier, faster, for everyone
. . . adapts Key Tension to You

W. B. ROGERS
Dealer

216 W. STATE ST.   PHONE 1098

No Job of Shoe Repairing Too
Large or Too Small

SHOE DYEING A SPECIALTY

Al's Shoe Hospital
218 SOUTH MAIN ST.

Phone 806X

FREE DELIVERY

COMPLIMENTS OF

H. N. KNIGHT, D. D. S.

213½ EAST STATE ST.

Stokely's Finest Fruits and Vegetables
at your
INDEPENDENT GROCERY
SAVE YOUR LABELS from Stokely and Cap Products for valuable premiums.
CAPITOL GROCERY CO.

MEET TO EAT AT
DAVISON'S
505 East State Street

The Man Who Knows Clothes...

WM. HUNTER
JACKSONVILLE'S LEADING CLEANER
We Call For and Deliver

PHONE 1674   207 EAST MORGAN ST.

MYERS BROTHERS.
Jacksonville's Largest Clothiers For Men and Boys

The Armstrong Drug Stores
...QUALITY STORES...
FILMS
Printing and Developing
24 Hour Service
S. W. Corner Square—235 E. State St.
Jacksonville, Illinois

GERMAN MOTOR COMPANY, Inc.
The House of Service Since 1918
Sales **BUICK AND PONTIAC** Service
Goodyear Tires and Tubes, Delco and Universal Batteries, Gas and Oil
Car Washing and Greasing

PHONE 1727   426-430 SOUTH MAIN ST.

MOLLENBROK

Photographer

234½ West State Street

Phone 808W

J. N. KENNEDY, General Agent

Penn Mutual
Life Insurance Company
Organized 1847

AGENTS WANTED

Students who have finished school or who have spare time will find soliciting insurance in this agency profitable

209 PROFESSIONAL BLDG.
314 West State Street

A Real Old Line Insurance Co.

Compliments of the  Letter Men's Club

---

Specify....
Kleen Maid Breads
BAKED FRESH DAILY
DELIVERED TWICE A DAY

IN THE BLUE WRAPPER

Peerless Bread Co.

PHONE 601

Jacksonville, Illinois

COMPLIMENTS OF

F. A. NORRIS, M. D.

AND

R. M. NORRIS, M. D.

Elliott State Bank

Capital, Surplus and Undivided Profits
$350,000.00

WE OFFER YOU THE SERVICES OF A SAFE, CONSERVATIVE BANK, AND THE BENEFITS OF SIXTY-FIVE YEARS BANKING EXPERIENCE

The Roach Press
Printers
310-312 South Main Street
Telephone 236

THE GEOGRAPHY OF WOMEN
A Romantic Comedy

A Novel
JACK FRITSCHER

The Geography of Women
Excerpt from the novel...
by Jack Fritscher

A fiction partially based on the memoirs, but not the autobiography, of Mary Pearl Lawler Day, specifically her story of the return of her jilted fiance, Francis Devine. The narrator is a fifty-year-old woman telling of her life as a teenager living in someone else's home as a housekeeper in the autumn of 1963. The voice speaking uses the combined South Midland Dialect of both Mary Lawler Day and Virginia Day Fritscher.

The autumn that year was a real late Indian Summer, right after Halloween an right before Jack Kennedy was shot. The afternoon was hot, so Mister Apple an Mizz Lulabelle [his wife] had a extra 7 & 7, which is 7-Up soda an Seagram's 7 whiskey, while the two little boys who, as I said, were all a four played out in the yard. I didn't mind, cuz a the heat an all, how late the supper was. I recall what we ate exactly: my beef stew with my Grandma's dumplins, which we sat down to eat aroun seven-thirty cuz the boys was gettin over-tired an over-hungry an cranky.

    Mister Apple said Protestant grace an Mizz Lulabelle helped one a the twins eat an I helped the other. We were about halfway through when we heard footsteps comin up the porch steps.

    "Are we expectin company?" Mister Apple said. He wiped his clipped black moustache with his white linen napkin.

    "Not anyone I know," Mizz Lulabelle said. Excitement reddened her cheeks. She adored company. Ask me. I cleaned an baked for em an washed up after em, then read in *The Canterberry Herald* that Mizz Smith an Mizz Jones paid a afternoon call on Mizz Lulabelle Apple an her twins, John an James, an angel food cake was served with ice cream an lemonade. Mizzy loved publicity. Certain kinds. She wasn't like my Grandma who read in *Cosmopolitan* that a lady's name appears in the papers only three times: when she's born, when she's married, an when she dies. Mizz Lulabelle was her own best-born press agent, cuz *The Herald* never mentioned the vodka in Mizz Lulabelle's sweatin glass in the summers or the rum in her tea in the winters, and I, acourse, with never a mention, was Mizz Invisible... but, oh, yeah, she did love company cuz it gave her a chance to be grand in her family's fine ol house with her arm through the arm a her prosperous pharmacist husband who might run for mayor.

"Who could that be?" Mister Apple said as the screen door on the porch creaked open an someone just walked onto an across the porch. You could hear their footsteps, big as you please.

"Just somebody needs a prescription filled," I said.

Then came a knock on the inner door to the house itself, kinda polite at first, then harder. Mister Apple pushed his chair back from the table an placed his napkin next to his plate. He pulled down his vest an walked directly toward the door. He paused, cleared his throat with that nervous tick he always had, an opened the door.

There stood Wilmer Fox in the flesh, red hair an all.

Mizz Lulabelle could see perfectly well down the hall. She placed her palm to her forehead an said, "The heat is makin me faint."

Wilmer Fox was makin her drool.

I wanted to howl an laugh like I did with Jessarose, but I was on my own an had to behave myself. "Mizzy, get a grip on yourself," I whispered.

"I'll be perfectly fine," Mizz Lulabelle said.

"Fancy this," I said. "It's *High Noon*. You're finally starrin in a real movie."

She shook her white cloth napkin at me the way you would shoo a fly.

"Hello, Fox," Mister Apple said down the hall in the deepest voice he could command.

"Hello, Mister Apple," Mister Fox said. He went straight to the point. "May I talk to Lulie?"

Mizz Lulabelle blanched like we was all hearin her called somethin more intimate n we were usta hearin.

"Really!" Mister Apple said. He blubbered an flustered an cleared his throat not like a man tryin to be mayor at all. "The nerve. Well! The cheek. Tch! The intrusion. Huff! Our supper. Puff! No appointment."

"I got to talk to Lulie," Mister Fox said. "I got to."

Mister Apple stood his ground like this was some tricks-or-treater he'd rather trick than treat.

"Please," Mister Fox said.

Somethin pitiful there was in his voice made Mizz Lulabelle stand straight up at the table.

The twins both stared at their mama.

It's alright," she said to everyone. She patted her hair with both hands, like she was exitin the *Titanic* with a concealed ice pick, an sailed real Princess Grace-ful down the hallway to the door takin her stand behind Mister Apple. "It's alright," she repeated near her husband's ear.

Mister an Missus Apple were actin like both a em thought Mister Fox had a loaded gun on his person an they didn't.

"It's alright, Henry," Mizz Lulabelle said to her husband. "Whyn't you go an finish supper an I'll have a word with Mister Fox to see what he wants. I won't take but a minute."

Mister Apple came back to the table where he an I both chewed away, like the world depended on our chewin, listenin to the voices risin an fallin in whispers on the porch.

Mister Henry sat through it all like somethin he had to endure.

Mizz Lulabelle was cool as a cucumber. When Mister Fox asked her about a baby that died, she called him impertinent. Then she denied there ever had been a red-hair baby boy, and wherever, Mister Fox, did you get a idea like that?

An then I heard her name.

Mister Fox said it first. "Jessie."

"Jessie who?"

"Jessarose Parchmouth."

I wanted to run to the door an ask Wilmer Fox where she was an was she alright.

Then Mizz Lulabelle repeated: "Jessarose? Where'd Jessarose ever come by such a notion? Nothin a the kind ever happened," Mizz Lulabelle said.

"I hope not, Lulie," Mister Wilmer Fox said. "It'd break my heart."

"You believe what you have to believe, Mister Fox. Excuse me," Mizz Lulabelle said, "but we're eatin supper. My family an I, my husband an our two children, his an mine, are eatin supper."

"Lulie?"

"Yes, Mister Fox?"

"I got to ask you just one question more."

"What's that, Mister Fox?"

"Lulie, are you happy?"

Silence landed thud on the house an nobody, not even the twins, made a noise for what seemed one a those moments that goes on forever waitin for the answer when the outcome for everybody's future depends on what a person says. Like in court under oath.

"Mister Fox," Mizz Lulabelle said, "I am happy. I am very, very happy."

"That's all I want to know, Lulie." Mister Fox looked straight into her eyes for what I figgered he knew was the last time an then without sayin anythin he turned an was gone down the porch steps an across the sidewalk into his waitin car.

"Mister Fox must be doin okay for hisself," Mizz Lulabelle said sittin back down at the table. "Baby blue, it was, his car. A baby blue Lincoln Continental."

"Are you?" Mister Apple asked.

"Am I what?" She knew full well what he meant, but she knew the game of women an men when they play wives an husbands.

"Are you happy?" he repeated.
She smiled, forkin her stew....

www.ingramcontent.com/pod-product-compliance
Lightning Source LLC
Chambersburg PA
CBHW021142080526
44588CB00008B/176